MAXIMIZE 365

A year of actionable tips
to transform your life

•••

Kristin A. Sherry

Black Rose Writing | Texas

First printing

ISBN: 978-1-68433-636-4
PUBLISHED BY BLACK ROSE WRITING
www.blackrosewriting.com

Printed in the United States of America
Suggested Retail Price (SRP) $22.95

Maximize 365 is printed in Sabon Next

*As a planet-friendly publisher, Black Rose Writing does its best to
eliminate unnecessary waste to reduce paper usage and energy costs,
while never compromising the reading experience. As a result, the final
word count vs. page count may not meet common expectations.
Cover: Crystal Davies
Editing: Beth Crosby

Praise for *Maximize 365*

"In a world of distraction, we often neglect doing the things we should. The opposite of distraction isn't focus, it's traction. Traction is any action that pulls you toward becoming the person we want to become. Kristin Sherry's book, *Maximize 365*, is a unique treasure map of daily tips that will guide you towards traction and give you insights for improving your health, wealth, relationships, and career."

– **Nir Eyal**, bestselling author of *Indistractable*

"Knowing yourself is essential for success. The more deeply you can know your strengths and weaknesses the better off you are in every area of your life. *Maximize 365* can help. Each daily entry provides you with actionable tips to transform your life in five areas: health and wellness, spirituality, relationships, career, and finances.

–**Vanessa Van Edwards**, bestselling author of *Captivate: The Science of Succeeding with People*

"If you want to change your life you must take action to make it happen. *Maximize 365* is your playbook to shift your mindset and creatively solve problems to improve your life in the most important areas. Give yourself permission to unlock your inner changemaker one daily tip at a time."

–**Beth Comstock**, Author, *Imagine It Forward* and former Vice Chair, GE

"Are you a life-long learner and high achiever seeking a holistic approach to continual improvement? Perhaps you're looking to own your mess and turn it into a masterpiece! No matter where you are on your journey, Maximize 365 offers one valuable insight after another, combined with relevant action steps to help you thrive in your personal and professional life."

–**Scott Jeffrey Miller**, Wall Street Journal best-selling author of *Management Mess to Leadership Success* and *Everyone Deserves A Great Manager*; EVP of thought leadership and chief marketing officer, FranklinCovey

"We all have blind spots that can block us from reaching our potential or achieving fulfillment. In *Maximize 365*, Kristin Sherry offers readers inspiration combined with information and application to deliver practical daily tips you can use to impact the most important areas of your life. If you're someone who wants to improve using a no-fluff, no BS approach, read this book."

– **Jordan Harbinger,** Creator, *The Jordan Harbinger Show*

"What I love about Maximize 365 is it helps you fulfill your potential in so many areas. Get out of your own way, get unstuck, or just get after your goals with daily bite-sized actions to love yourself, your relationships, your career, and your life!"

– **Susie Moore,** author of *STOP CHECKING YOUR LIKES*

"In a time of uncertainty, the world needs more inspirational voices to deliver messages of hope. Kristin has done just that with *Maximize 365*. Kristin has managed to create a book designed to help you transform your life in today's age. *Maximize 365* doesn't just offer you helpful tips, Kristin provides readers simple actionable steps anyone can take to empower themselves. There are 365 days in a year. 365 opportunities to manifest your dreams and fulfill your destiny. Kristin's actionable steps will help you get there.

– **CJ Johnson,** entrepreneur, speaker, and author of *The Maguire Method*

To my parents, Wayne and Judi Spear.
Most of what I know about living a life of gratitude
and improvement I learned from you.

Who This Book is For

- Learners and curious sorts
- Individuals interested in self-development
- Those who are unsatisfied in certain areas of life
- Bathroom readers
- Anyone seeking a holistic approach to growth
- Folks who like straight-to-the-point guidance
- People who want to increase their impact
- Anybody who likes learning but not reading at length

Acknowledgements

Maximize 365 is, by far, the most grueling book I've written. Many people helped make it happen. I'm especially grateful to my husband, Xander, for his unending support when I was writing seven days a week for months.

Thank you to those who contributed quotes, content, or inspiration to this book: Lila Smith, Char Aukland, Rob Morgan, Kellan Barfield, Kimberly Ficklin, Doug Thompson, Belinda Missen, Bob Sager, Lianne Hofer, Kris Macchiarola, Susan Britton, Alison Bucklin, Sharon Gill, and Jennifer Spor.

A big thank you to my beta readers Loreen Brown, Louise H. Reid, Virginie Lemay-Vriesde, Raha Sepehrara, Norma Kraft, Lianne Hofer, and Clark Finnical. So many great ideas from this group truly increased the book's quality and value.

Thank you to Jordan Harbinger, Nir Eyal, Vanessa Van Edwards, Susie Moore, Scott Miller, Beth Comstock, and CJ Johnson for your generous testimonials, and to Reena Friedman Watts for making the connections.

I'm thankful for my designer, Crystal Davies, and my editor, Beth Crosby, and the skills and fun they contribute to my writing projects.

Finally, thank you to Reagan Rothe and staff at Black Rose Writing. I am supported and appreciated.

CONTENTS

Acknowledgements
Who This Book is For
Introduction
HEALTH & WELLNESS 1
   Emotional Wellness 2
   Environmental Wellness 15
   Intellectual & Mental Wellness 25
   Physical Wellness 53
   Social Wellness 68
SPIRITUALITY 80
   Spiritual Growth 81
   Purpose 102
   Belief & Inspiration 116
   Service & Social 136
RELATIONSHIPS 158
   Communication 159
   Conflict 175
   Couples & Family 203
   Self-Development 214
CAREER 236
   Self-Discovery 237
   Career Management 250
   Entrepreneurship 270
   Job Search 282
   Professional Development 300
FINANCES 315
   Saving Money 316
   Managing Debt 332
   Building Wealth 352
   Financial Planning 365
   Family Money Matters 376
Reflect
Act
References
About the Author
Follow on Social Media
Other Books by Kristin Sherry
Index

MAXIMIZE 365

A year of actionable tips
to transform your life

"One can choose to go back toward safety or forward toward growth. Growth must be chosen again and again; fear must be overcome again and again."

Abraham Maslow

Introduction

"You're off to Great Places! Today is your day! Your mountain is waiting, So ... get on your way!"

Dr. Seuss

I'm truly excited you're reading this book. I started coaching people in 2007. I've walked alongside clients through victory and misfortune.

We all experience highs and lows in life, without exception. We can't compare ourselves to other people because we are each at different mile markers on life's highway. Whether you think you mostly have it together or believe things are mostly coming apart, you'll find something in *Maximize 365*. This book addresses topics common to humankind, despite our uniqueness as individuals.

In early 2019, I had a conversation with colleague and friend, Bob Sager. He is an innovation consultant and works with companies to increase revenue through innovation strategies.

During our conversation, Bob coached me on the topic of money. On that call, he explained finances are only one form of wealth and shared his Five Forms of Wealth model, which includes health, relationships, money, time, and satisfaction.

Our conversation influenced me to be more mindful to invest in each area of wealth.

If you're poor in health, what good is being rich in finances? If you're rich in finances but poor in time, how can you enjoy the fruits of your labor? If you're rich in time and wealth but poor in relationships, you'll have no one to enjoy life with.

Years ago, author and motivational speaker Zig Ziglar developed a model called the Wheel of Life. Ziglar's model has seven spokes representing seven areas of life: Mental, Spiritual, Physical, Family, Financial, Personal, and Career.

Inspired by Bob's concept of wealth and Ziglar's Wheel of Life, I settled on the idea to present the tips in this book within categories to allow you, the reader, to access content where you have greatest need or interest.

I've organized the book into five main chapters:

Health & Wellness, Spirituality, Relationships, Career, and **Finances.**

Each chapter has themed subcategories, and each daily entry includes three components:

1. An inspirational quote
2. A brief story or information on the topic
3. An idea for action

In the coming pages, I've compiled daily tips from my own work, as well as from others knowledgeable in each area. As a unique individual, you should prioritize taking action on the entries that will work best for you—watch out for limiting beliefs telling you something is impossible! "Impossible is an opinion," says my colleague, Bob.

At the back of the book, *Reflect* and *Act* sections encourage you to later recall your thoughts and intended action items as you read. List specific tips you want to act on as a running to do list. You can transfer action items with due dates to your personal weekly or daily to do lists to help you take action.

Take a week to work through a topic, if needed. Move to a new topic when you're ready. Though I've included 365 daily tips, it's unrealistic and would overwhelm you to try to implement a tip every day of the year.

You can tweak the "Idea(s) for Action" in each entry or come up with your own actions based on what you've read or need. You can read through the book from front to back or use the rating scale on the next page to prioritize your path. Choose your own adventure based on your needs and interests. For example, if you have money struggles, you might want to start with "Finances."

If you're committed to implementing the ideas for action in this book, you can expect to grow and expand your potential.

On the following page, rate your satisfaction in each of the five topics this book covers.

On a scale of 1-10 (1 being the lowest and 10 the highest), rate your satisfaction in these five areas of your life:

Health & Wellness

1	2	3	4	5	6	7	8	9	10
○	○	○	○	○	○	○	○	○	○

Spirituality

1	2	3	4	5	6	7	8	9	10
○	○	○	○	○	○	○	○	○	○

Relationships

1	2	3	4	5	6	7	8	9	10
○	○	○	○	○	○	○	○	○	○

Career

1	2	3	4	5	6	7	8	9	10
○	○	○	○	○	○	○	○	○	○

Finances

1	2	3	4	5	6	7	8	9	10
○	○	○	○	○	○	○	○	○	○

Based on your rankings or interests, choose where to start your journey through *Maximize 365*.

HEALTH & WELLNESS

"If you do not take time for your wellness, you'll be forced to take time for your illness."

Joyce Sunada

For years, I took my health for granted. Not until high blood pressure, headaches, back pain, and increased gastrointestinal problems became part of daily life did I decide to take control and make changes.

In November 2019, I changed my eating habits to release thirty-five pounds in sixteen weeks. A complete overhaul of my diet was hard. Many social situations revolve around food. I overcame cravings and withdrawals, but I also followed a process, which meant fewer decisions to make.

The benefits extended beyond physical into emotional well-being and have allowed me to engage in a more active lifestyle with increased energy and mobility.

Yet, health goes beyond physical. The "Health & Wellness" chapter takes a holistic approach to wellness with entries presented in Emotional, Environmental, Intellectual & Mental, Physical, and Social sections. Spiritual, Relationship, and Financial health are addressed in their own chapters.

Emotional Wellness

The following topics are covered in Emotional Wellness:

Loving Yourself
Affirmations
Self-Care
Monitoring Emotions
Anger
Disappointment
Self-Absorption
Emotional Insecurity
Emotional Temperature
Imposter Syndrome
Loneliness
Life Regrets

Loving Yourself

"To fall in love with yourself is the first secret to happiness." – Robert Morley

Somewhere along the line, we've lost the message of one of the most respected people to have walked the Earth. Jesus said, "Love your neighbor *as yourself*" (Mark 12:31 NIV). How many of us focus on the first three words of that statement but miss the last two?

Imagine treating your best friend the way you treat yourself each day. What if you said the things you say to yourself to others?

Your friend comes to you excited with an idea for a new business, and you say, "What a dumb idea. Who do you think you are to start a business? You'll just end up failing. You don't have what it takes."

What if your mother, sister, or daughter asked how you liked her new outfit, and you responded, "You look fat and terrible."

If we're honest, all of us, at some point in our lives have looped self-criticisms in our heads like a broken record, which probably made us feel needlessly inadequate.

Ideas for Action

The following link contains 30 ideas to practice self-love. Choose two or three ideas to implement right away: bit.ly/SelfLove30.

Speak self-affirmations when you wake up and when you go to bed. Set a reminder on your phone to do it!

Affirmations

"Believe in yourself. You are braver than you think, more talented than you know, and capable of more than you imagine." – Roy T. Bennett

Everything we repeat aloud or in our thoughts are affirmations. Repetition sews affirmation into our identity, positive or negative, by our brain's Reticular Activating System (RAS).

Since default thoughts are often negative (see *Mind and C.R.A.P. Boards* on page 50), positive affirmations are a way to influence our subconscious minds.

The subconscious doesn't know the difference between past and future; only here and now. The RAS reacts to affirmations as truths. We must speak positive affirmations and emphasize they're true *now*. Instead of, "I will be … ." say, "I am … ."

Affirmations don't need to be true. Shape your thoughts to affect your actions. It's not magic. Thoughts become reality because they influence behavior.

Idea for Action

1. Write an affirmation. An example, by Idil Ahmed is, "My life is great. I am great. Everything is happening for me. All of the things that I am currently experiencing are only taking me to the next level of my life. I am growing better. I choose to believe in sudden miracles and unexpected blessings."
2. Read your affirmation when you wake up and before you go to bed, as suggested previously in *Loving Yourself* on page 3.

Self-Care

"When I became chronically ill and left corporate, my husband encouraged me to start my month by filling my calendar with personal self-care and *then* fill in the rest. Too often we say we don't have time for self-care (which is why I got sick), but we actually do, we just don't make it a priority. So for me, all self-care goes in my calendar first, then the rest." – Kimberly Ficklin

Many people I know who faithfully practice self-care didn't do so until they had a physical, mental, or emotional crisis that forced them to pay attention.

Self-care is not something that comes naturally for many, as our tendency can be to focus on the external instead of the internal. We let immediate demands of our environment take precedent. We wouldn't drive our cars without oil and blow up our engines, would we?

When our basic needs, such as proper sleep, nutrition, hydration, intimacy, and relaxation are not met, it's just a matter of time until we end up in the shop. Only the shop is a hospital. The good news is self-care is something you can prioritize to greatly improve your health!

Idea for Action

Schedule blocks of time on your calendar for health and wellness activities such as stretching, walking, or meditating. Try a meditation app such as Headspace.

What is one thing you can schedule now, for today or this week, to increase your self-care?

Monitoring Emotions

"Your emotions are the slaves to your thoughts, and you are the slave to your emotions." – Elizabeth Gilbert

Have you felt yourself become anxious, depressed, or fearful without knowing why?

I remember standing in my garage about to enter my house. I was agitated and stressed but didn't know why. I wasn't tuned in to my body to intervene earlier.

This happens because 80 percent of our thoughts occur on autopilot. Our subconscious mind replays thoughts over and over, day after day. Thoughts, in turn, create emotions in response to those thoughts. If we don't actively monitor our thoughts, adrenaline and cortisol rush into our blood stream, placing us in fight/flight/freeze mode. Ideally, we can learn to arrest thoughts before they affect our mood. Until we master that level of control, we can start by training ourselves to react more quickly when thoughts negatively affect our mood.

Idea for Action

Monitor your body twice daily, morning and afternoon. Rate your mood on a scale of 1 to 10, with 10 being a great mood.

Observe your body. Are you anxious? Do you have tightness in your chest? Are your shoulders stiff?

If your body reveals signs of stress, stop and monitor your thoughts. What message are you telling yourself in that moment that is causing an emotional reaction? Replace the message with a more constructive one.

Anger

"Get mad, then get over it."– Colin Powell

Anger can rally us together to address injustice. It mobilizes us to act and initiate change. It protects our values.

Anger aids well-being by discharging stress after an upsetting event. Anger gets a bad rap, yet anger can be healthy. Your Life Counts International explains three kinds of anger:

Passive aggression – Unhealthy anger stemming from a need to be in control and includes the silent treatment, sulking, or procrastinating.

Open aggression – Unhealthy anger including sarcasm, accusations, criticism, shouting, quarreling, bullying, and verbal or physical attacks.

Assertive anger – Healthy anger which allows a person to communicate in a controlled, confident manner while listening and seeking to understand, such as calling out injustice with conviction.

Anger is triggered when our values misalign with a situation.

Idea for Action

If you're angry with someone, express it privately. Share feelings, not their flaws. Discuss current anger, not past, and avoid making the discussion a win/lose. Keep your cool, and let them speak without interrupting. Address positive qualities along with complaints to avoid defensiveness:

"I'm angry about your comments and need you to know their impact. I want to discuss how to go forward from here."

Disappointment

"If we will be quiet and ready enough, we shall find compensation in every disappointment." – Henry David Thoreau

Disappointment is sadness or displeasure caused by our unfulfilled hopes. When we experience disappointment, our hopes are out of alignment with reality.

We aren't disappointed only when we don't get what we want. Sometimes we're disappointed when we get exactly what we wanted. Think of people who pursue fame, and it crushes them. Our *hopes* are out of alignment with *reality*.

Some people turn their disappointment inward and blame themselves then experience shame. Others turn their disappointment outward and blame others, which creates bitterness. Unfortunately, both approaches keep you stuck.

Idea for Action

Consider using these three prompts to understand and manage disappointment:

1. Was the disappointment in or out of my control?
   Out of my control? Move on. Better days will come.
   In my control? Redirect thoughts to solutions, reframing failure mindset to a growth opportunity.
2. Are my expectations reasonable? Ask two or three objective people you trust.
3. How is choosing to remain disappointed helping me? Disappointment is inevitable, but remaining discouraged is a choice.

Self-Absorption

"Generally speaking, the most miserable people I know are those who are obsessed with themselves; the happiest people I know are those who lose themselves in the service of others ... By and large, I have come to see that if we complain about life, it is because we are thinking only of ourselves." – Gordon B. Hinckley

Excessive self-focus is "navel gazing." The most dissatisfied people I know spend a lot of time thinking of themselves and their problems.

What we focus on grows. When laser focused on ourselves, discontent increases. Self-absorption is not equivalent to selfishness. Selfishness is a lack of consideration for others, and concern for your own profit or pleasure.

Self-absorbed people can be generous, even if pre-occupied with themselves and their issues. Often, self-absorbed people complain and talk about themselves and their own lives.

Self-absorption can lead to depression or anxiety, if negative, and narcissism when fueled by self-importance.

Idea for Action

Journal answers to these questions to reveal consequences of self-focused thinking:

1. What is the purpose of my obsessive thinking?
2. Do I obsess over the past or worry about the future?
3. Was my thinking helpful? If not, how was it unhelpful?
4. What do I want to happen next?

Emotional Insecurity

"The reason we struggle with insecurity is because we compare our behind-the-scenes with everyone else's highlight reel." – Steven Furtick

Emotional insecurity is unease or nervousness often triggered by feeling vulnerable or inferior. Most people face insecurity from time to time. Dr. Melanie Greenburg cites three common causes of insecurity. Recent failure or rejection, low confidence due to social anxiety, and insecurity driven by perfectionism.[1]

To overcome insecurity, look inward. Are you insecure because of failure, a belief you're not good enough, social anxiety, or a combination of these?

Idea for Action

Examine signs of emotional insecurity. Do these describe you?
Social anxiety: Blushing, fast heartbeat, trembling, sweating, upset stomach, trouble catching your breath, drawing a blank, or muscle tension. *Embrace your awkward!*
Perfectionism: Struggling to celebrate success or get things done timely. Trouble accepting challenges where you could fail or not allowing yourself to make mistakes. *Challenge your thoughts!*
Failure/rejection: Low happiness due to job or relationship loss, seeking signs of rejection, or misreading or overreacting to what others say or do. *Reflect on your success. Talk yourself up!*
See *Perfectionism* on page 48, and *Failure … Or Temporary Defeat?* on page 301, and *Social Anxiety* on page 235 for more.

Emotional Temperature

"If you can't regulate your own emotional temperature, you'll regulate everyone around you to keep yourself comfortable." – David Schnarch

In April 2020, I attended a *Neuroscience of Resilience* webinar hosted by Pepperdine University. Dr. Izzy Justice, who holds a doctorate in Emotional Intelligence, led the session.

He used an analogy of a highway packed with cars to explain our overstimulated brains. He used a traffic light to explain three cognitive states:

Red – In this state, we release epinephrine, cortisol, and can experience increased blood pressure, ulcer formation, and muscle tension.

Yellow – In this state, our amygdala is agitated. We experience difficulty staying mindful and objective. Dr. Justice shared many of us are in this state much of our day!

Green – In this state, we're engaged, collaborative, perform better, and are willing to take risks. Our brain is focused and can respond mindfully.

Idea for Action

Take your emotional temperature twice daily. Set an alarm and ask, "How am I feeling now?" Red? Yellow? Green?

Examine your prior thoughts. Do they explain your result? This practice hones our ability to monitor our thoughts, which affect our emotions. With practice, you will learn to interrupt negative thought patterns more quickly. What gets measured gets managed!

Imposter Syndrome

"It's not what you are that holds you back. It's what you think you are not." – Denis Waitley

Impostor syndrome is a psychological pattern where a person doubts his or her accomplishments and fears being exposed as a "fraud."

Despite external evidence of competence, those experiencing this phenomenon remain convinced they're frauds and don't deserve all they've achieved. Individuals incorrectly attribute success to luck or interpret it as a result of deceiving others into thinking they're more intelligent than they perceive themselves to be.

Imposter syndrome affects men and women, typically high achievers. Even Albert Einstein experienced imposter syndrome![2] People generally recognize the psychological phenomenon in others but genuinely believe they, themselves, are imposters. Inadequacy and self-doubt are relentless and severe. Have you recently felt inadequate?

Idea for Action

Engage 5-steps when you experience imposter syndrome:

1. Acknowledge your emotions.
2. Discuss with others instead of hiding your thoughts.
3. Work on reducing perfectionism (see *Perfectionism* on page 48 in this chapter).
4. Connect your strengths to successes to show yourself you earned them.
5. Practice repeating a mantra such as, "I've earned my place here."

Loneliness

"Loneliness is not a lack of company; loneliness is a lack of purpose." – Guillermo Maldonaldo

Loneliness is a feeling of isolation. You can be surrounded by friends and be lonely. Loneliness is related to the quality and depth of intimacy of relationships rather than the quantity.

According to research, improving social skills, increasing social interaction, and enhancing social support are not the most effective strategies for loneliness. What is?

Changing maladaptive thinking.

"Lonely people pay more attention to negative social information like disagreement or criticism. They remember more negatives which happened during an encounter with another person and fewer positives.

"All this leads, as you might imagine, to more negative expectations about future interactions with others: Lonely people don't expect things to go well for them and, consequently, they often don't.

"The cure for persistent loneliness lies in breaking a negative cycle of thinking that created it in the first place."[3]

If you've experienced loneliness, try to trace the onset of loneliness to specific negative interactions.

Idea for Action

When lonely, engage the cognitive part of your brain to shift from an emotional to an adaptive state. Color, sing, complete a puzzle, or make a collage of places you want to visit. If you want to take a loneliness test go to bit.ly/lonelytest.

Life Regrets

"If only. Those must be the two saddest words in the world." – Mercedes Lackey

We can learn a lot from the wisdom of our elders. A unique area of insight they have is life regrets.

During my research for this book, I read a lot of articles and watched interviews of people who reached 100 years old and beyond. What I found most interesting was the common themes of regret, regardless of gender, race, or geographic location.

Our lives can benefit significantly from the lessons of others. We can even choose to change the course of our lives by making decisions today based on lessons we learned from experiencing regret or where we are likely to experience it.

Some common regrets people share are worrying too much, not spending more time with people they cared about, failing to pursue their dreams in favor of doing what others expected of them, not spending more time outside their comfort zone, neglecting their bodies, and working too much.

The good news? If you're reading this, it's not too late to avoid your regrets with changes starting today.

Idea for Action

Write your regret list. Imagine this is your last week on Earth, and create a list of regrets. Choose one thing you can start doing now to alter the course of your life to avoid this regret.

Watch this video for the full list and details of top 10 life regrets: bit.ly/top10liferegrets.

Environmental Wellness

The following topics are covered in Environmental Wellness:

Forest Bathing
Simplifying Your Life
Decluttering
Organization
Timing Matters
Managing Your Time
Delegating
Cell Phones
Seasonal Affective Disorder

Forest Bathing

"In every walk with nature one receives far more than he seeks."
– John Muir

A decades-old practice from Japan known as shinrin-yoku, which means "taking in the forest," is becoming popular for improved health.

Research on forest bathing, which is a leisurely forest walk, found 20 minutes of walking in the woods boosts mood.[4] Forest bathing also tends to lower the stress hormone, cortisol, over taking part in other activities, a review of 30 studies found.[5]

In addition, forest therapy appears to decrease depression levels in adults as well as boost the activity of antibodies, which help fight off infections and cancer.

The fragrant substances produced by plants and trees have been linked with lower inflammation and brain protection benefits.

Search online for forested areas within a reasonable distance.

Idea for Action

To engage in forest bathing, walk at a slow pace without jogging or running for at least 20 minutes a few times weekly. Take your time to look around as you walk on a wooded path. Engage your senses and observe your surroundings. Stop every so often and sit. Look up and around. Breathe in deeply and focus on the sounds you hear.

Simplifying Your Life

"Simplicity is an acquired taste. Mankind, left free, instinctively complicates life." – Katharine F. Gerould

Why do we brag about how busy we are?

"Blake, how have you been?"

"Busy! The kids are in football, and I'm spending half of my life in the car!"

"That's our life too. I'm driving my daughter all over for cheer competitions every weekend while my husband takes our son to Scouts."

Being busy has become a status symbol.

Do you know the reason we're so busy? We don't have the courage to make difficult choices. Every time we say we're busy, we're actually saying we can't prioritize our lives.

We don't tell our kids no. We don't set and defend boundaries. We are reactive instead of proactive. The outside world dictates our agenda and, therefore, our lives.

I like the quote from *Mansfield Park* by Jane Austen, "Life is just a quick succession of busy nothings."

Simplified living requires making tough choices. We chip away the unnecessary and are left with the important instead of a life filled with "busy nothings."

Idea for Action

Want to simplify your life? Say no more. Read *Saying No* on page 79 in this chapter, and put it into practice!

Decluttering

"Look around. All that clutter used to be money." – Unknown

If you struggle with clutter, you're not alone.

- Twenty-five percent of people with two-car garages have so much stuff in there they can't park a car.[6]
- One year of our lives is spent looking for lost items.[7]
- Twenty-three percent of adults say they pay bills late, earning late fees, because they lose them.[8]
- Forty percent of housework would be reduced by eliminating clutter in an average home.[9]
- $154 billion in revenue is made annually in the storage industry—more than the Hollywood film business.[10]

Clutter consultant Lianne Hofer says:

Make a commitment to give yourself space to own where you are in your clutter journey and move forward, aiming to get where you want to be. We all start somewhere! When you are ready to make changes, start with your space because the energy in your home effects the energy of your life. Clear the clutter in your physical space to make room in other areas of life. It is hard to accept blessings life has to offer if you are still holding on to things that do not fit the life you want to lead.

Idea for Action

Start a declutter project this week. Declutter by category, not room or location. For example, organize clothes or books to see quick progress. Visit Lianne at TheClutterConsultant.com.

Organization

"For every minute spent organizing, an hour is earned." – Unknown

Disorganization affects our physical and mental health. When our work and personal spaces are organized, we sleep better, eat better, improve our relationships, and are more productive.[11] Not sure if disorganization is affecting your quality of life? Ask yourself if you:

- Have piles growing in height and number
- Have pest problems related to clutter
- Are embarrassed to have people visit your home
- Struggle to find necessary items, manage finances, or stay on top of housework

Break tasks into bite-sized goals. Avoid dwelling on all your unorganized spaces at once, or you'll be overwhelmed.

Idea for Action

If you're organizing a pantry, closet, or set of drawers, pull everything out and into a space where you can see everything.

Clean the area and then sort items into five categories:

1. Trash or recycle.
2. Donate.
3. Sell. If you don't have time to sell, donate.
4. Keep. If you'll use it or you love it, put it on the shelf.
5. Undecided. Not sure? Put it in a box, date the box and look at it in six months. If you didn't need it in six months, you probably don't need it.

Timing Matters

"We are smarter, faster, dimmer, slower, more creative, and less creative in some parts of the day than others." – Daniel Pink

Researchers at Cornell University analyzed 500 million tweets on Twitter for a period of two years to explore the moods of people during a typical day.[12] They discovered a clear pattern. People often experience peak positivity in the morning. Moods rapidly drop in the afternoon and rise again in the evening.

This cycle occurs every day to everyone, regardless of race or nationality. Daniel Pink's book, *When*, describes this daily pattern as morning peak, afternoon trough, and evening rebound.

Understanding this pattern is crucial to accomplishing goals, getting what we want and avoiding troubles in the trough. Be mindful of the afternoon trough and how you spend time there. Set an intention to capitalize on the peak times that work best for you, whether that's morning or early evening.

Ideas for Action

1. Schedule meetings when you're trying to get a "yes" from someone midmorning (peak positivity).
2. Handle tasks that require more mental power in the evening if you're a night owl. If you're a morning person, handle complex mental tasks midmorning.
3. Schedule your mindless work in the afternoon during the mood drop period.

Managing Your Time

"Time equals life; therefore, waste your time and waste of your life, or master your time and master your life." – Alan Lakein

Five pressures derail people: Time, relationships, money, health issues, and expectations. Time is fixed to only 24 hours in a day. The only thing that can change is you and what's on your plate.

People who are skilled at managing time use it effectively and efficiently. They value their time, concentrate their efforts on more important priorities, get more done in less time than others, and can attend a wider range of activities.

People unskilled at managing time waste it. They flit from activity to activity with little rhyme or reason, don't set priorities, can't say no, are easily distracted, don't follow a plan or method, and don't control time wasters.

In general, are you productive most days, or does it seem like time often gets away from you?

Ideas for Action

Apply these tips to immediately begin to master your time and your life:

1. List points to make before a phone call to stay on task.
2. Use your most productive time of day for tough tasks.
3. List meetings/activities you participate in. Step aside where you aren't needed or if you don't enjoy it.
4. Practice saying: I have to get back to my next task. Can we pick this up another time?

Delegating

"If you want to do a few small things right, do them yourself. If you want to do great things and make a big impact, learn to delegate." – John C. Maxwell

"It's easier if I do it."

Have you said this when someone suggested you get help? My thoughts are, "Easier for whom?". Certainly not you if you have too much on your plate. Everything you take on that you shouldn't isn't easier. Second, easier isn't always better. Giving people responsibility is a gift, whether to children or coworkers.

Failure to delegate stems from control, fear of the ball being dropped or being too busy to explain what you need others to do. If you add up time spent on tasks because you don't have time to explain, delegation is an undeniable time saver.

When delegating, explain outcomes, constraints, or boundaries. Match responsibility with the authority needed. Let go of preferences for "how," and focus on outcomes. Provide support without managing too closely, and delegate to the lowest possible level. No data entry for skilled workers.

Delegating frees you up to add more value and grow your skills.

Idea for Action

Assess your delegation ability: bit.ly/assessdelegation. For a score below 20, practice low stakes delegation like folding laundry, making dinner, mowing the lawn, or tasks you tend do. Adjust as you go, and introduce more complex delegation.

Cell Phones

"A smartphone is an e-toy designed for the lonely inner child hidden in each and every one of us." – Dr. Saurabh Sharma

If you add up the hours we're projected to spend on social media apps in our lifetime, it's a solid five years, four months.[13] Imagine dedicating that many hours in a trance staring at a screen. That's alarming. To put that amount of time in perspective, it's 36 percent more time than any of us spend eating and drinking.

Five scary facts about your phone:[14]

1. Apps are intentionally designed to hook you, like slot machines.
2. Phones are altering our brain. The short attention required to scroll and swipe decrease our ability to concentrate.
3. Apps are free because we're not a customer, we are a product. The product being sold is our attention.
4. Digital tech innovators shield their kids from the devices they create.
5. Snubbing people during conversation has become so common it has a name: phubbing (phone-snubbing).

Idea for Action

Keep your phone in another room or the far side of your bedroom when going to sleep instead of at your bedside. This prevents late nights and early mornings on your phone. Also, check out Catherine Price's book, *How to Break up with Your Phone*: bit.ly/breakupwithyourphone.

Seasonal Affective Disorder

"Try to be a rainbow in someone's cloud." – Maya Angelou

Ten-to-twenty percent of Americans experience Seasonal Affective Disorder (SAD), a mental health condition that occurs several months of the year. Symptoms of SAD include sadness, fatigue, and a loss of motivation, and, sometimes, change in appetite and headaches.

Michelle Riba, a professor of psychiatry and the associate director of the University of Michigan Depression Center says, "For people who see a regular pattern every year of getting sad, anxious or a cycling of moods, the first thing they need to do is to see someone to get an overall diagnosis. They need to treat the underlying depression."

SAD should not be underestimated or brushed off as winter blues, as it is a complex mental health concern that can be aggravated by a lack of light, which is why it's more common in northern parts of the US where days are shorter during the winter.

Idea for Action

If you struggle with Seasonal Affective Disorder and haven't been diagnosed, consider seeing a doctor.

Natural remedies include using a light box, dawn simulators that slowly introduce light as you wake up, getting outside regularly for natural light, adding vitamin D to your diet, getting sufficient sleep, and exercising regularly.

Intellectual & Mental Wellness

The following topics are covered in Intellectual & Mental Wellness:

Daily Gratitude
Day Tight Compartments
Resilience
Growth Mindset
Control
Discipline
Embrace the Suck
Excuses
Good Habit Creation
Procrastination
Setting the Right Goals
It's JUST ...
Indecisiveness
Intellectual Wellness
Mental Sharpness
Realistic Thinking
Making Tough Decisions
A Problem a Day
Self-Reliance
Self-Control
Motivation
Optimism
Perfectionism
Perspective
Mind and C.R.A.P. Boards
Staying Stuck
Vision Boards

Daily Gratitude

"Developing an 'attitude of gratitude' is one of the simplest ways to improve your satisfaction with life." – Amy Morin

Each year, people say they can't wait for this awful year to end. Each year I wonder why I never look back and think my year was awful. Things I didn't like or thought were terrible surely happened.

I asked my husband, "Why do you think I never say the year was awful?"

He said, "You see the glass as half full. People who see the glass as half empty will focus on the bad things that happened instead of the good."

How we view each day, week, or year of our lives comes down to perspective. Gratitude is a powerful way to shape our perspective.

Research shows eight benefits of gratitude: Better sleep, more relationships, improved physical health, improved psychological health, increased empathy and lower aggression, higher self-esteem, and increased mental strength.[15]

Gratitude is a game changer for how we perceive our lives.

Idea for Action

In a notebook, daily write three things for which you're thankful. Be specific. For example, a compliment you received, or a goal reached. List reasons you're grateful as a daily habit. Over time it will reap big dividends. Review entries monthly to note trends and areas for future focus.

Day Tight Compartments

"Sometimes I succeed, sometimes I fail, but every day is a clean slate and a fresh opportunity." – Gretchen Rubin

I first read the concept of day tight compartments in Dale Carnegie's book, *How to Stop Worrying and Start Living*. The focus of the book is worry, but I believe the message of a fresh start to every day is imperative for a happy life.

The universe is created for fresh starts. Every day the sun sets on the day and rises on a new one. Have you ever thought about the mercy of that opportunity?

This concept is not new. The Bible discusses the concept of living in day tight compartments. "So don't worry about tomorrow, for tomorrow will bring its own worries. Today's trouble is enough for today" (Matthew 6:34 NLT).

We often associate fresh starts with moving to a new city, getting a divorce, and changing jobs—big events and major changes.

What if you looked at the eight-hour period of sleep as a reboot? Every day can be a new beginning.

Idea for Action

As a way to let go and start new, consider having a "funeral" at the end of the day. Write a note saying goodbye to a particular situation or problem. Burn the note (safely, please!) or crumple it up and throw it away. Say goodbye to the old and make way for the new. Wake up ready to receive a fresh start!

Resilience

"If your heart is broken, make art with the pieces." – Jodi Picoult

Psychologists define resilience as adapting well in the face of adversity, trauma, tragedy, or significant stress. Resilience doesn't mean absence of distress or difficulty. It is an ability to bounce back, often leading to personal growth.

The American Psychological Association recommends five ways to build resilience:

Build connections – Prioritize relationships and join groups.

Foster wellness – Take care of your body and mind; avoid negativity.

Find purpose – Help others, be proactive, set goals, and engage in self-discovery.

Embrace healthy thoughts – Keep things in perspective, accept change, learn from your past, and adopt a hopeful outlook.

Seek help – Get help when you need it! Ask someone you trust.

Idea for Action

Rate your effectiveness, 1 to 5, in the five areas of resilience introduced in this entry.

1 = Not at all effective, 2 = Slightly effective, 3 = Moderately effective, 4 = Effective, 5 = Highly Effective

For ratings below 4, find additional support to build resilience at bit.ly/resiliencetopics.

Growth Mindset

"It's not that I'm so smart. It's just that I stay with it longer." – Albert Einstein

Carol Dweck, Professor of Psychology at Stanford University, has published a body of research on what can be achieved by shifting from fixed thinking to a growth mindset—a building block of life-long learning.

She explains in her TED talk (bit.ly/dwecktedx) how retraining one's thinking in a simple, fundamental way changes how we manage life's challenges. This mindset shift caused Indigenous kids at the bottom of their school district to outperform kids in affluent areas of Seattle.

Dweck researched how children cope with challenge. She gave challenges to 10-year-olds slightly harder than they could solve.

Some kids responded positively, expressing enthusiasm for the problems and the love of a challenge. These kids believed abilities could be developed beyond present capabilities.

Other students reacted horribly. They felt their intelligence was being judged, and they failed. These students, in study after study, ran from difficulty.

Research shows growth mindset alters how people view setbacks or failure. Instead of a fatalistic view of failure, a growth mindset creates persistence.

Idea for Action

List areas where you have a fixed mindset. Add "yet" to shift to a growth mindset, "My business isn't profitable *yet*."

Control

"When you can't control what's happening, challenge yourself to control how you respond to what's happening. That's where your power is." – Unknown

One of my favorite pieces of advice is from the late Stephen Covey's book, *The 7 Habits of Highly Effective People*. He said, "Between stimulus and response there is space. In that space is our power to choose our response. In our response lies our growth and our freedom."

We can't control others, and we can't control everything that happens outside of us. We can control only what happens inside of us.

Surrendering control can seem threatening, but it's vital to recognize you were never in control anyway. Control is rooted in fear and being attached to a set outcome.

Einstein said, "The most important decision we make is whether we believe we live in a friendly or hostile universe."

If we believe in a friendly universe, we can loosen our grip and trust things will work out for our good.

Ideas for Action

Reflect on one or more times you didn't get what you wanted.

List outcomes that were good or better for you than your original plan. Some examples are a relationship ending against your will or a job offer that never came. What came into your life that was better than what you originally wanted?

Discipline

"Discipline is the bridge between goals and accomplishment."
–Jim Rohn

The Dalai Lama said, "A disciplined mind leads to happiness, and an undisciplined mind leads to suffering."

I've seen this in my life when I drifted from set routines, exercise, healthy eating, and a consistent bedtime. I replace focus, productivity, and energy with procrastination, lack of direction, and a general sense of malaise.

Increased discipline requires setting goals we believe in and a basic plan of execution. We achieve a mental shift when we perceive greater emotional benefits from *doing* a desired behavior than *not* doing it, which motivates us.

We must also drop the shame if we break from our plan.

An example is someone trying to lose weight. When they fall off the wagon and eat donuts, the shame of failure causes them to eat another. In a vicious cycle, they fall deeper into self-loathing. We shouldn't allow temporary defeat to lead us to believe we've failed.

Idea for Action

We are what we repeatedly do. Discipline is a skill we can build. To increase discipline, try a 30-day cold shower challenge. It sounds nuts, but discipline requires willingness to accept discomfort. Taking a cold shower for 30 days builds mental toughness. You will take a shower anyway, so you have no excuses. Do you think you could do it?

Embrace the Suck

"Nothing in the world is worth having or worth doing unless it means effort, pain, difficulty … I have never in my life envied a human being who led an easy life. I have envied a great many people who led difficult lives and led them well." – Theodore Roosevelt

When my friend Doug Thompson was participating in triathlons, he told me sometimes the workouts just "sucked."

Doug explained, "It could have been the weather, a really tough workout to push to the next level, not recovering from a previous workout, or any of a dozen other reasons. Usually those workouts that really sucked were the ones that did [me] the most good.

"Somewhere during one of my whining fits about a sucky workout, a coach or fellow athlete, I can't remember exactly who, told me to 'embrace the suck.' To this day, when I am trying something new or trying to push out of my comfort zone, I utter that phrase and push on."

Idea for Action

What area(s) of your health or wellness do you avoid embracing the suck? How can you reframe or take action?

When doing a task that isn't pleasant, use positive affirmations such as, "I've got this. I *will* do this." Or, as Doug suggested, say to yourself, "Embrace the suck!"

Excuses

"Never make excuses. Your friends don't need them, and your foes won't believe them." – John Wooden

We make excuses when we think circumstances fall outside our control. Some things are outside our control, but people who habitually make excuses routinely blame circumstances or people.

Excuses limit us. Of course, the "Just Do It" philosophy is oversimplified and misguided in some situations.

We must define a reason versus an excuse. Reasons are objective acknowledgement of our beliefs and emotions: I haven't looked for a job because my confidence is low.

Excuses are obstacles we erect to rationalize why we aren't pursing a goal, such as, "I can't find a new job. No one will hire me." Excuses are full of "can't" and "but."

The danger of excuses is we start to believe they are facts. Once we believe an excuse, we fail to set or pursue goals. Our excuses stop us from getting what we want.

Examine excuses you frequently tell yourself.

Idea for Action

1. Make a list of goals or issues you avoid.
2. Examine how you view your ability to control each.
3. Assess your belief in your abilities.
4. Identify small changes to build confidence and belief in your ability to make a change.
5. Add a follow up strategy, such as a weekly progress review.

Good Habit Creation

"We are what we repeatedly do. Excellence, then, is not an act, but a habit." – Aristotle

Behavioral scientist B.J. Fogg is the father of the tiny habit movement. He calls his three-step process to form new habits The Fogg Method.

The first step is to identify a clear goal or outcome, such as lose 10 pounds, run a marathon, or learn a new language.

Next, list out the easy-win behaviors, what he calls tiny habits, that you can do to achieve your goal.

Finally, identify a routine or habit you already have and graft the new habit onto the existing one.

Let's say you want to get in better shape and release 10 pounds as your goal. A tiny habit to achieve the goal might be to start incorporating daily squats.

I will assume you brush your teeth every day. Set a goal to complete 20 squats before you brush your teeth in the morning and again before you brush your teeth at night.

Before you know it, the tiny habits lead to goal attainment!

Idea for Action

Watch B.J. Fogg's TEDx talk on how to create tiny habits that lead to big change here: bit.ly/bjfoggtedx.

Next, select a goal you want to achieve, and choose a tiny habit to start implementing, attaching it to an existing habit.

Procrastination

"You can't just turn on creativity like a faucet. You have to be in the right mood. What mood is that? Last-minute panic." – Bill Watterson

People regret things they haven't done over things they have done.

Everyone procrastinates, but not everyone is a procrastinator. Chronic procrastinators have perpetual problems finishing tasks, while situational procrastinators delay *based on the task itself*. A perfect storm of procrastination occurs when an unpleasant task meets a person who's high in impulsivity and low in self-discipline.[16]

It's not effective to advise a procrastinator to buckle down and get it done, just as it's not effective to tell a depressed person to cheer up. Procrastination is not the same as laziness.

Sometimes people will say they work better under pressure to justify procrastination. Research shows most of us are less effective under pressure.[17]

Ideas for Action

If you struggle with procrastination:

- Set smaller tasks.
- Create a deadline.
- Try to find meaning in the task.
- Remind yourself time lost is lost forever.
- Develop new habits by linking to a task you do daily, like brushing your teeth.
- Forgive yourself when you procrastinate and refocus.

Setting the Right Goals

"Some goals are not going to fulfill you. Choose goals that you value and care about." – Henry Cloud

In *Weight Loss*, on page 57, I will share previous unsuccessful attempts to lose weight. Here, I discuss setting the right goals—for you.

When I wanted to lose weight, losing thirty-five pounds wasn't important to me. If I didn't care, it would never happen. Why did I want to lose weight? I started to have high blood pressure. I was afraid I would die before enjoying grandchildren.

I altered my goal from "lose 35 pounds" to "Imagine my youngest child crying, holding a newborn, wishing I were there to see her first child. Now, make daily decisions to prevent this scene from happening." Everything changed after I changed the goal.

When confronted with an all you can eat dessert bar, I could ask myself, "Will this help me live longer to hold my grandchild?" It made decisions easy as, well, pie. Connect your goal to something that matters to you.

Idea for Action

Why do you want to reach your goal? Dig two or three whys deep to get to what you value. I wanted to lose weight to live longer. Why live longer? To know my grandchildren. Why is that important? Because love and connection with my family is my top priority. Dig deeper to find your true motivation.

It's JUST ...

"There are all these 'just one' times throughout the entire year. Whenever we indulge, is it really just this one time? Pay attention to how many 'just this one' times you actually experience." – Char Aukland

Our "just" can be related to many areas, such as how we allow people to treat us by excusing behavior: "He's just stressed at work lately." Not holding our boundaries: "I'll give her money just one more time." Our relationship with food plays out through, "It's a special occasion, so I'll eat everything I want just this one time." Special occasions can be found all year long, from parties to holidays, birthdays, weddings, events, conferences, and vacations. Before you know it, every week becomes a "just this one time."

Often, our "just" serves a purpose by giving us security, comfort, control, or stemming some other fear.

Each "just" extends permission that might not serve us best.

Idea for Action

Observe your thoughts and behaviors for one week to become mindful of areas where you are making justifications.

Consider journaling everything you "just" about.

Related to your health, what have you been JUST-ifying?

Indecisiveness

"It is better to make a wrong decision than build up a habit of indecision. If you're wallowing in indecision, you certainly can't act, and action is the basis of success." – Marie Beynon Lyons Ray

Colin Powell follows a rule of thumb for making hard decisions. He says every time you face a tough decision you should have no less than 40 percent, and no more than 70 percent, of the information you need to make the decision.

If you make a decision with less than 40 percent of the information necessary, you are "shooting from the hip" and will make too many mistakes. If you wait to get over 70 percent of the information, opportunity will often have passed.

Powell's rule supports the fact that intuition separates great leaders from average ones. Intuition allows us to make tough decisions well, but many of us ignore our gut instincts.

Do you desire 100 percent certainty your decisions are right? Absolute certainty is unrealistic. Your intuition, combined with 70 percent of the information, constitutes an educated decision. Mathematically, a decision should not need to change course after acquiring 70 percent of the information.

Idea for Action

Write the consequences of indecisiveness the next time you're making a decision. Seeing the outcomes might help you move forward. If you're still stuck, flip a coin! Perhaps the choices aren't materially that different, which is why you can't choose.

Intellectual Wellness

"People with many interests live, not only longest, but happiest." – George Matthew Allen

Intellectual wellness refers to active participation in scholastic, cultural, and community activities.

We promote intellectual wellness when we commit to learn new things and possess an openness to new ideas and ways of doing things. We expand our knowledge and skills and foster creativity, curiosity, and lifelong learning.

The key to intellectual wellness is open-mindedness.

Reading, travel, and spending time with diverse groups of people who think different from you are great ways to expand intellectual wellness.

Ideas for Action

Enhance intellectual well-being by trying these ideas:

1. Ask a friend to debate and argue against your view.
2. Play board games such as Clue or chess.
3. Complete puzzles: sudoku, word search, or crossword.
4. Read fiction for fun.
5. Learn a foreign language.

Mental Sharpness

"Being fit will keep you mentally sharp, and people forget that." – Peter Shilton

Do you seem to always lose your wallet or purse, put things in odd places, or experience absent-mindedness?

You have options to sharpen your mind. The best method is a focus on overall health, rather than targeting specific areas. This includes exercise and eating "brain foods" like salmon, broccoli, walnuts, avocados, and blueberries. Through diet and light exercise, you can reduce the risk of developing health conditions that lead to memory loss.

Ideas for Action

Seven tips for brain fitness:
1. Give your brain a workout. The best activities teach you something new, build a skill, challenge you, and are rewarding. Try learning a language on Duolingo.
2. Oxygenate your brain with physical activity.
3. Get eight hours of nightly sleep; avoid caffeine in the evening and screen time an hour before bed.
4. Have fun with friends.
5. Keep stress under control.
6. Laugh daily.
7. Eat brain foods like wild tuna, sardines, fruit, vegetables, flaxseed, green tea, and red wine.

Keep a journal for a week of the actions you try. Assess where improvements can be made. If you are concerned about your memory, take the SAGE memory test: bit.ly/sagememorytest.

Realistic Thinking

"Believing in negative thoughts is the single greatest obstruction to success." – Charles F. Glassman

I've witnessed and heard stories from people who expressed opposing opinions and were silenced. They were written off as negative and given "constructive feedback" about their lack of positivity.

Excessive positivity discourages conflict. Conflict avoidance is one of the dysfunctions Patrick Lencioni discusses in his book, *The 5 Dysfunctions of a Team.*

Researchers Coyne and Tennen state the idea of adopting a "fighting spirit" against cancer as a solution to the disease is neither scientifically sound nor uplifting. It implies anyone who does not "beat cancer" did not have a sufficiently positive mindset.[18]

Oncologist Dr. O. Simonton says pure positive thinking ("I'm healed.") worked against cancer patients as much as grossly negative thinking ("I'm dying; there's no hope.") when he was asked who tends to survive. What seemed to make a difference was what he called realistic thinking. When a person could honestly say everything was being done to help, and they were doing everything they could to be better and healthier, they seemed to cross a threshold—from the fanciful into the possible—which is where real hope exists.[19]

Idea for Action

To combine an optimistic view with realistic thinking:

Combine your dream with realistic goals, then list possible challenges and ideas to overcome them.

Making Tough Decisions

"It doesn't matter which side of the fence you get off on sometimes. What matters most is getting off. You cannot make progress without making decisions." – Jim Rohn

Susan Britton, founder of TheAcademies.com, taught me an effective way to make hard decisions. When my oldest son was buying his first car, I was nervous. On one hand, he might buy a lemon that was mechanically unsound.

On the other hand, that was his first major purchase, and I wanted him to be independent. I kept going in circles on what to do or not do. It wasn't until I aligned the forces of my mind, heart, and gut that I was able to make the best decision.

Susan asked me to write what my *head* was telling me. Next, she had me write what my *heart* was telling me. Finally, she instructed me to write what my *gut* was telling me.

After capturing the voice of reason, my emotions, and my instinct, Susan asked me to come up with a decision that would honor all three. She described the method as making the most creative (head), compassionate (heart), and courageous (gut) decision possible.

I ended up offering my son a list of things I would look for in a car if he were interested in advice. I went with him to the dealer but stepped back and allowed him to manage the process. It worked out wonderfully!

Idea for Action

Try Susan's process for yourself!

A Problem a Day

"We cannot solve our problems with the same level of thinking that created them." – Albert Einstein

Problem solving skills improve with practice. If we let problems fester, we can spend more time worrying about the problem than finding a solution.

Perhaps a problem is overwhelming. We might think we have no control to solve it, or ability to influence a solution. My grandmother used to say, "A problem identified is a problem half solved." Life teaches us a problem ignored becomes a bigger problem, requiring more resources to solve.

A way to be proactive is to create a list of 1-3 problems you have. You can't solve all problems in a day, so the idea is to dedicate a day of constructive thought to a problem. Prioritize the problems, and tackle each using the *Idea for Action* below. Once a solution is found or in progress (or you conclude it's not in your control to solve) update your problem list with new challenges.

Idea for Action

Choose a daily time to brainstorm solutions like during your commute or lunch break. Work through these steps:

1. *Define the problem.* Dig to the root problem by asking, "Why is that a problem?" three times as you would ask why. See *Setting the Right Goals* on page 36.
2. *Write outcome(s) sought.* What do you want to happen?
3. *List all potential solutions.* Include help or resources needed and ways to obtain them.

Self-Reliance

"The best place to find a helping hand is at the end of your own arm." – Unknown

Self-reliance is not doing everything by yourself and shouldering your burdens independently. It's the capability to do things and make decisions by yourself.

Examples of self-reliance are the ability to think independently, embrace who you are as an individual, and boldly pursue your goals.

Self-reliance is important because help won't always be available. Also, it's important for making decisions, solving problems, and, most importantly, being able to be happy by— and with—yourself.

Moving from relationship to relationship and the inability to remain single is often a sign of low self-reliance.

Do you turn outward or inward as your first reaction to problems?

Ideas for Action

Three tips to increase self-reliance:

1. Accept responsibility to try to solve problems first before turning to others.
2. Practice making decisions before looking to others to help you make decisions. Start with small decisions, if needed.
3. Learn practical skills, such as how to cook, sew, do laundry, or fix basic things at home to increase self-reliance. Check out *Dad, how do I?* at bit.ly/dadhowdo.

Self-Control

"He who controls others may be powerful, but he who has mastered himself is mightier still." – Lao Tzu

Self-control is an ability to manage your actions and emotions.

Self-control is comprised of the ability to:

1. Control behaviors to avoid temptations and achieve goals.
2. Delay gratification and resist unwanted behaviors or urges.

Researchers found low self-control is detrimental to having and maintaining close interpersonal relationships, whereas high self-control brings relational success.[20]

Reflect on areas in which you struggle with self-control.

Idea for Action

Instead of struggling to resist temptation, try to reduce or remove it.

Name an area in your life where you lack self-control. Brainstorm ways to remove temptation. For example, if you find yourself getting into political debates online, limit social media time or scroll past topics that are pitfalls for you.

If you struggle to resist sweets, avoid tempting circumstances and carry healthy snacks, such as nuts, to help you pass the doughnuts.

Motivation

"Push yourself because no one else is going to do it for you." – Unknown

We all struggle with motivation. People ask how I find motivation to write books each year. The answer is, I don't always.

I write when I don't want to. Motivation follows action. Sometimes I get a dopamine hit after I get into it. Other times I dislike every minute and quit when I hit the daily goal.

I set bite-sized goals. When I write, I set the date I need to have the book to my editor. I calculate the number of words the book will have, how many days I plan to write weekly, and how many words I need to write daily. When I wrote this book, I set a goal of four entries seven days a week. Some days I wrote four, some days 10.

Lack of confidence can also cause loss of motivation. "Who am I to _____?" or "I'll never be able to do this."

If you're not motivated, maybe the goal isn't defined or set in achievable chunks. Goals that are large overwhelm us. A goal to write a book is vague. Write 5,000 words weekly is clear.

Idea for Action

Reflect to find the cause of stalled progress:
- What's blocking my path to achievement?
- Do I care and think about the goal?
- Is the goal aligned to a purpose?
- Is the goal bite-sized?
- Do I celebrate wins?

Optimism

"In my ninety-plus years, I have learned a secret. I have learned that when good men and good women face challenges with optimism, things will always work out! Truly, things always work out! Despite how difficult circumstances may look at the moment, those who have faith and move forward with a happy spirit will find that things always work out." – Gordon B. Hinckley

In his book, *Think and Grow Rich*, Napoleon Hill wrote:

"Optimism is a matter of mental habit. You can learn to practice the habit of optimism—and thereby greatly enhance your chances of achieving success. Or you can drive yourself into the pit of pessimism and failure."

Yikes!

The good news? If optimism is a mental habit, new habits can be formed by retraining and reframing your perspective.

Ideas for Action

1. Create an optimism jar. Write the best thing that happened each day and add it to the jar. Read the entries at the end of the month. Repeat each month.
2. Limit time spent with the "doom and gloom" crowd.
3. Look for silver linings in each day.
4. Practice speaking positive affirmations daily, for example, "I can accomplish anything I set my mind to."
5. Limit your consumption of negative news.

Perfectionism

"Research shows that perfectionism hampers success. In fact, it's often the path to depression, anxiety, addiction, and life paralysis." – Brené Brown

Studies say perfectionists aren't actually trying to be perfect. They're trying to avoid not being good enough.[21]

Whoa.

Even though the root of the word perfectionism—perfect— seems positive, perfectionists are shown to achieve less and experience more stress than other high achievers.[22]

The saying, "Done is better than perfect" doesn't always resonate with perfectionists. Try, "Is my constant tweaking creating significant new value that will benefit others?"

Idea for Action

Do you exhibit perfectionist tendencies?

bit.ly/PerfectionQuiz

If you are a perfectionist, do a cost analysis by making a list of the ways perfectionism hurts you. Ask friends, family, or trusted coworkers to add their perspective on the negative consequences of your perfectionism.

Perspective

"Not all storms come to disrupt your life. Some come to clear your path." – Paulo Coelho

Having perspective means being able to provide wise counsel to others and having ways of looking at the world that make sense to oneself and others. Plainly put, it's the way a person looks at things.

A wise perspective thinks things through, examines them from all sides, and doesn't jump to conclusions. A wise perspective enables us to change our minds in light of evidence weighed fairly.

People with perspective understand themselves better than most. They are aware of their strengths and weaknesses and have developed ways to work around their weaknesses so they don't become a barrier. These individuals have paid attention to how their minds work and are better able to understand the thought processes of others.

Ideas for Action

Try these six strategies to expand your perspective:

1. Listen more and speak less.
2. Ask more questions.
3. Spend time with new people.
4. Read more and more broadly.
5. Watch different programming, such as documentaries, biographies, or the news.
6. Be curious about things you don't understand or that surprise you.

Mind and C.R.A.P. Boards

"What consumes your mind, controls your life." – Ben Francia

Hans Berger, inventor of the electroencephalogram (EEG), first proposed the brain is constantly busy. We have conscious thoughts, but when our minds wander, or we perform repetitive tasks, we enter a Default Mode Network (DMN).[23]

In my Brain-Based Coach certification I learned we spend 60-70 percent of the day in the DMN. We reflect on ourselves, others, and think about our past and future in this space.

During my neuroscience studies, my coaching certification, and research for this book, I read several assessments on thoughts. General consensus is 80-95 percent of thoughts are repeated each day, and 80 percent are negative.

One study revealed 60-70 percent of students' spontaneous thoughts were negative, but students estimated 60-75 percent of their thoughts would be positive![24]

Implications of repeating negative narratives include misinterpreting facts, mood depression and anxiety, and releasing too much stress hormone, cortisol, into our bodies.

Idea for Action

Create a "C.R.A.P. Board" to record *Conflicts*, *Resistances*, *Anxieties*, and other *Problems*. Creating a space for these thoughts itemizes your brain's concerns. C.R.A.P. board creator, Mark Waldman, advises keeping the board. He says if discarded, the brain will remind you, taking up precious emotional energy.

Staying Stuck

"Fear is the glue that keeps you stuck. Faith is the solvent that sets you free." – Shannon L. Alder

A key mindset difference separates those who succeed and those who stay stuck. When I was coaching, I could tell within minutes of speaking with someone which team they were on: "Team Stuck" or "Team Possible."

People who stay stuck:

- Say, "I don't know how." Because they don't know exactly what to do, they do nothing.
- Fall back on habits standing in the way of their progress. These could be drugs and alcohol, poor eating habits, or unhealthy relationships.
- Make excuses. "The problems is … .", or "That won't work because … ."
- Fail to learn from mistakes and keep falling into the same bad decisions and behavior patterns, such as making impulsive decisions.
- Deny they, themselves, are the cause of being stuck. Reasons are almost always external and out of their control.

Review the five items above. Which of these challenges you?

Idea for Action

Review these three questions weekly and set tasks accordingly:

1. What outcome do I want?
2. How can I make it happen?
3. What help do I need, and who might help?

Vision Boards

"You are the author of your life. If you don't like your story, change it." – Jesse Lyn Stoner

A vision board is a board or poster with a collage of words and images to represent your goals and dreams. The idea for this book came from a vision board I created in Sharon Gill's G.O.R.G.E.O.U.S. Woman Bible study program.

When I created my board, I set goals in the areas of work, health, finances, relationships, and spirituality. I realized these are life's foundations and wanted to share them with others.

Visualization is one of the most powerful exercises to see your goal through. Olympic athletes have long used visualization to improve performance. Arnold Schwarzenegger swore by visualization to reach his bodybuilding goals.

As a child, Oprah Winfrey watched her grandmother toil endlessly. Winfrey says she'd tell herself over and over again: My life won't be like this. My life won't be like this, it will be better.

Vision boards work because they take unorganized thoughts from your head and organize them into something concrete you can set goals around. Your board should focus on how you want to feel, not just things you want.

Idea for Action

Start gathering words, images, and quotes aligned to your purpose and desired goals for your board. Watch this video for more guidance: bit.ly/howtocreatevisionboards.

Physical Wellness

The following topics are covered in Physical Wellness:

Power of Routine
Sedentary Lifestyle
Body Image
Weight Loss
Eating Mindfully
Gut Health
Food and Mood
Intermittent Fasting
Functional Medicine
Healthy Aging Secrets
Skin Health
Sleep
Stress Management
Burnout

Power of Routine

"Depending on what they are, our habits will either make us or break us. We become what we repeatedly do." – Sean Covey

Successful people swear by their routines and rituals. Routines create habits, and habits create consistent results. Warren Buffett reads 500 pages every day. He says knowledge builds like compound interest. Steve Jobs wore the same black turtleneck each day to create fewer decisions to maintain focus.

Our routine, or lack of one, determines how our day will go. If we aren't intentional, we succumb to interruptions, procrastination, and time wasting. Alternatively, people with a routine are more productive, focused, and motivated.

Ideas for Action

Start by adding a new routine in each of the following areas: personal care, relationships, career/work.

Personal care – Block off 20-30 minutes daily to do something you enjoy such as mediate, read with a cup of tea or coffee, or practice yoga or some other form of physical activity.

Relationships – Set up a weekly date night with a partner, add a family game night, or video chat weekly with friends and family who live far away.

Career – Make daily to do lists, blocking the time on your calendar. Start a learning habit to sharpen your skills such as reading a book each month related to your field. Join professional associations or take LinkedIn Learning courses.

Sedentary Lifestyle

"I encourage people to pick up small habits like taking a walk after meals ... we've become way too sedentary. Just move!" – Theo Rossi

You might have heard, "Sitting is the new smoking," which suggests a sedentary lifestyle has replaced smoking as a health hazard. The well-documented effects of smoking suggest they are not equally hazardous. The point is humans aren't meant to be sedentary, and inactivity yields consequences.

Some ramifications of a sedentary lifestyle include weight gain, anxiety, osteoporosis, type 2 diabetes, high blood pressure, stroke, inflammation, reduced immune function, and other ailments.[25]

As a full-time author, I make a point to spend half of my workday standing and practicing legs raises, squats, calf raises, and marching in place to keep my blood flowing. My husband also uses a standing desk and paces during phone calls to get in his 10,000 or more daily steps.

If you have a challenging schedule, adopt creative ways to keep moving without going to a gym.

Ideas for Action

Try implementing easy exercise-at-home ideas daily:

1. 12-minute walk at home YouTube videos: bit.ly/walkathomevideo
2. Side leg raises each time you wait for the microwave
3. 15 – 20 squats before getting in the shower each morning

Body Image

"Stop wishing for other people's bodies. Find peace in your own. Just eat food. Eat real food, be active and live your life. Forget all the diet and weight loss nonsense. It's really just that … Nonsense." – Gemma Collins

A study of 2,000 women commissioned by Lycra found women spend almost two hours each day, 12 hours and four minutes weekly, or an entire month of each year worrying about their looks.[26]

This isn't just a problem for women. Multiple studies found men worry about their appearance more than women and would exchange a year of their life for a perfect physique. Men worry about going bald and having a "beer belly." [27,28]

No universal ideal of beauty can be defined, because every culture differs. Remember people you view as ideal in appearance also struggle with body image. We are irrational beings.

We care about our appearance because we care what others think of us over what we think. Don't believe me? During the COVID-19 pandemic when people were holed up at home, people joked about not wearing make-up or showering and wearing pajamas all day since no one could see them!

Idea for Action

Create a plan to eat real food, avoid processed foods, and keep active according to your ability. Let go of everything outside your control. Set an intention to change what you can and practice telling your inner critic to stuff it. "Thanks for your concern, but I am in control here."

Weight Loss

"Weight loss doesn't begin in the gym with a dumb bell; it starts in your head with a decision." – Toni Sorenson

In my early 40s, I had two more children. I ate healthy during my pregnancies, but as is typical, I gained 30 pounds with each pregnancy. After my second daughter—and fourth child—I found myself 35 pounds above my ideal weight.

Determined to lose weight, I decided to try the Keto diet. After six months, I lost 22 pounds, yet every ounce found me again over the next year.

Trying Keto a second time, I lost five pounds in 30 long days, and my lips became intolerably chapped. Since Keto wasn't sustainable for me, I decided exercise was the way to go. After two weeks running on my treadmill without losing an ounce, I quit. I was convinced I was too old, my metabolism was too slow, and my genetics rebelled against my chances of losing weight.

I made a discovery. I had to shift my goal and connect it to a meaningful purpose. My "why" mattered if I intended to reach my goal. See *Setting the Right Goals* on page 36.

Idea for Action

Connect a goal which has eluded you to something you deeply value. Focus on what you value to guide behavior change instead of the goal itself.

What goal have you failed to reach? Rewrite your goal to align with something deeply important to you.

Eating Mindfully

"Mindful eating is eating with intention while paying attention." – Kati Konersman

In November 2019, I started mindful eating. Prior, I wasn't aware I was a mindless eater.

Many of us focus on what we eat but not *how* we eat.

I thought I was a healthy eater. I didn't eat processed foods or indulge in desserts. I ate my vegetables. When I continued to gain weight, I attributed it to my metabolism, age, and genetics.

I started paying attention to my eating habits and observed I ate more frequently than I realized because of mindless snacking. For example, when I made my daughter's lunch for school each morning, one slice of cheese went on her sandwich, and one went in my mouth.

Midmorning, I went to the kitchen for a snack and another slice of cheese. At lunchtime, I snacked on a cheese slice while I made lunch. By midafternoon, I indulged in a fourth slice, along with a fifth and final as I prepared dinner.

I mindlessly ate a whopping 525 calories in cheese. One-fourth the recommended daily calories for an average person! Luckily, a problem identified is half solved.

Idea for Action

Keep a daily food journal for a week to track your eating. Do you eat more than you realize? If so, read 13 science-backed tips to stop mindless eating at healthline.com/nutrition/13-tips-to-stop-mindless-eating.

Gut Health

"Your gut is not Las Vegas. What happens in the gut does not stay in the gut." – Dr. Alessio Fasano

In recent months I've become focused on gut health. I was experiencing a number of signs my gut health was poor.

Indicators of poor gut health include stomach disturbances, changes in weight, sleep issues or fatigue, skin irritation, autoimmune conditions, and food intolerances.[29]

I experienced most of the issues above, but since improving my gut health I released 35 pounds and improved my overall health by employing the following ideas for action.

Talk to your doctor before making drastic changes. Some advice is not compatible with certain medical conditions.

Ideas for Action

Research-backed ways to improve gut health: [30]

1. Take probiotics, and eat fermented foods like miso, kombucha, sauerkraut, kefir, or kimchi.
2. Add prebiotic fiber to your diet.
3. Eat less sugar, sweeteners, and processed foods.
4. Reduce stress.
5. Avoid taking antibiotics unnecessarily.
6. Exercise regularly.
7. Get adequate sleep.
8. Avoid smoking.
9. Increase intake of plant-based foods.

Food and Mood

"The food you eat can either be the safest and most powerful form of medicine or the slowest form of poison." – Ann Wigmore

Low serotonin, a neurotransmitter in our brains, can cause depressed mood, low energy, negative thoughts, irritability, and sweet cravings. Ninety percent of serotonin receptors are in our guts![31] Diet affects mental well-being.

In my own experience, my eating habits had a negative effect. My diet caused reduced energy levels and depressed my mood. This caused me to eat to cheer myself up. Negative self-talk went up, and so did my weight. I was stuck in a vicious cycle.

According to nutritional biochemist, Shawn Talbot:

"Weight loss is generally 75 percent diet and 25 percent exercise. An analysis of over 700 weight loss studies found people see the biggest short-term results when they eat smart. On average, people who dieted without exercising for 15 weeks lost 23 pounds; the exercisers lost only six over 21 weeks. It's easier to cut calories than burn them off. For example, if you eat a fast-food steak quesadilla, which can pack 500-plus calories, you need to run over four miles to 'undo' it!"

Exercise combined with clean eating is the healthy and natural way to improve our mood and overall well-being.

Idea for Action

Add 3-4 antidepressant foods to your daily diet. Examples are salmon, mussels, spinach, cauliflower, and strawberries.

Intermittent Fasting (IF)

"The best of all medicines are resting and fasting." – Benjamin Franklin

In history, fasting was part of life. Sourcing food was a challenge, and humans went without food for long periods.

Researchers from the University of Alabama conducted a study with prediabetic, obese men. They compared a form of IF called "early time-restricted feeding," where all meals are fit in an early eight-hour period of the day, compared with a group who spread meals over 12 hours (7 a.m. to 7 p.m.). Both groups maintained their weight, but after five weeks, the eight-hours group dramatically lowered insulin levels, significantly improved insulin sensitivity, and lowered blood pressure. The eight-hours group also experienced drastically decreased appetite.[32]

To fast, you should meet lifestyle guidelines of adequate sleep and water and eat quality food. Fasting is effective with a healthy lifestyle.

Individuals who are underweight, struggling to gain weight, under 18, pregnant, trying to become pregnant, breastfeeding, at risk for an eating disorder, or on multiple medications should not fast. Nor should you fast without consulting your doctor to make sure it's safe based on your medical history and current medications.

Idea for Action

Read Harvard Health Publishing's article on Intermittent Fasting at bit.ly/HarvardIFStudy. To learn about a 16:8 fasting lifestyle, visit bit.ly/16-8.

Functional Medicine

"Functional Medicine is medicine by course, not by symptom. Functional Medicine practitioners don't, in fact, treat disease, we treat your body's ecosystem. We get rid of bad stuff, put in good stuff, and because your body is an intelligent system, it does the rest." – Mark Hyman, MD

Functional medicine addresses underlying causes of health problems instead of treating symptoms. Traditional medicine does a good job tackling acute and emergency problems, while functional medicine is suited for chronic conditions. A good functional medicine practitioner will usually work with your traditional doctor to help you achieve the best health outcomes.

I admit, when my parents started seeing a functional medicine doctor, I assumed it was hocus-pocus or new age silliness. Until my parents looked like they were aging backward and eliminated chronic problems traditional medicine had been unable to solve.

My father used to have panic attacks and tried numerous medications which didn't work. The attacks became daily events. Through a series of adjustments to balance my father's "ecosystem," the panic attacks ceased.

If you have a chronic health problem, such as an autoimmune disorder or diabetes, consider exploring functional medicine.

Idea for Action

Read this article published by the Cleveland Clinic to see how functional medicine works and if you should consider it: cle.clinic/3bkOY0W.

Healthy Aging Secrets

"We don't stop playing because we grow old. We grow old because we stop playing." – George Bernard Shaw

Many cultures place a high value on youth. Fear of getting old is common. Interestingly, the second half of life is what many people consider more rewarding and fulfilling, not the first half. Increased confidence, patience, wisdom, less stress, better sex, more money, and stronger relationships are a handful of reasons cited in a Huffington Post article by Jack Anderson.[33]

On a scale of 1 to 10, as people age, their well-being quotient rises, climbing to its highest levels when people are in their 80s and 90s, according to Nielsen research.[34]

What are the secrets of healthy aging? According to WebMD, science-backed tips to healthy aging include:[35]

1. Eating whole, unprocessed plant foods
2. Walking
3. Connecting in meaningful relationships
4. Eating a fiber-rich diet
5. Practicing exercises to support balance, such as Tai Chi
6. Taking supplements (calcium, vitamins B6, B12, and D)
7. Choosing an optimistic attitude
8. Getting adequate sleep

Idea for Action

Review the eight tips above for healthy aging. Start by adding one or two to your routine then add more over time. See *Good Habit Creation* on page 34 in this chapter.

Skin Health

"The mirror of your health is your skin. If you drink, it shows in your face; if you eat the wrong foods, you have pimples. If you take care of your food and you lead a healthy life, your skin will look wonderful." – Sophia Loren

My friend, Alison Bucklin, is a skincare consultant. She says,

"What standard do you have for ingredients? Everything we put on our skin, including skin care, make up, lotions, and fragrances are absorbed through our skin in less than a minute.

"The products we choose contribute to what's absorbed into our bloodstream and our organs. Pay attention to the ingredients in the products you use."

I didn't pay attention to what I put on my body as in my body. I read the label on everything I eat.

I researched skin care ingredients and discovered ingredients widely considered harmful or toxic.

The best ways to maintain healthy skin is diet.[36] Moisturizers go skin deep, and aging develops at the cellular level. Some foods known to contribute to healthy skin are tomatoes, olive oil, kale, omega 3, and mangoes.

Have skin concerns? Review your diet and read ingredients.

Idea for Action

Avoid parabens, synthetic colors, triclosan, phthalates, fragrance, sodium lauryl sulfate (SLS)/sodium laureth sulfate, formaldehyde, toluene, propylene glycol, retinyl palmitate and retinol, lead (check lipstick), and hydroquinone.

Sleep

"A good laugh and a long sleep are the best cures in the doctor's book." – Irish Proverb

Sleep is often neglected but is vital to health. If it's no secret sleep is important, why do so many people neglect getting sufficient rest? In many cases, it's a trade-off to fit in other activities we need to get done or want to participate in.

As a society, we could do a more effective job helping people understand the effects of sleep deprivation, including weight gain, lack of concentration and productivity, depression, heart disease, inflammation, a weaker immune system, lower empathy, degraded athletic performance, and prolonged recovery from illness.[37]

You should be rested upon waking if you're getting quality sleep.

Idea for Action

Use a sleep tracker for 30 days to see how well you're sleeping.

Sleep recommendations: [38]

Newborns (0–3 months): 14–17 hours
Infants (4–12 months): 12–16 hours
Toddler (1–2 years): 11–14 hours
Preschool (3–5 years): 10–13 hours
School age (6–12 years): 9–12 hours
Teen (13–18 years): 8–10 hours
Adult (18–60 years): 7-plus hours
Adult (61–64 years): 7–9 hours
Adult (65+ years): 7–8 hours

Stress Management

"One of the best pieces of advice I ever got was from a horse master. He told me to go slow to go fast. I think that applies to everything in life. We live as though there aren't enough hours in the day, but if we do each thing calmly and carefully we will get it done quicker and with much less stress." – Viggo Mortensen

The best stress management is being proactive. If you wait to manage stress when you're already stressed, your ability to cope is diminished.

The number of people who are stressed out makes clear most of us aren't doing a good job of proactive stress management. Eighty-two percent of employees said their jobs fall on the more stressful end, and a workplace stress study found 60 percent of US workers are stressed all or most of the time at work.[39,40] Are you frequently overwhelmed in a typical week?

Idea for Action

Practice this daily mindfulness technique to manage stress. Close your eyes, take a deep breath to the count of five and slowly release. Repeat another deep breath and then:

Acknowledge *five* things you can see, then close your eyes.
Name *four* things you can feel.
Three things you can hear.
Two things you can smell.
One thing you can taste.

Practice mindfulness outdoors while walking. See *Mindfulness* on page 125 in the *Spirituality* chapter.

Burnout

"Burnout is when long-term exhaustion meets diminished interest." – Unknown

Burnout occurs when we are under excessive stress for a prolonged period. It can be emotional, physical, or mental. As burnout sets in, our drive and motivation wanes.

Signs you might be experiencing burnout[41]:

1. Believing every day is a bad day
2. Caring about work or life seems like a waste of energy
3. Continual exhaustion
4. Spending the majority of the day on tasks you find mind-numbingly dull or overwhelming
5. You don't believe you make a difference or are appreciated

Ideas for Action

Assess your priorities – Set boundaries, take social media and technology breaks, take up a creative hobby, prioritize sleep and relaxation time.

Exercise 30 minutes daily – Even if you need to break activities into 10-minute chunks, move your body daily.

Connect with your support system – Reach out to people you care about, build friendships at work, get involved with a group or cause you care about, limit time with negative people.

Eat a healthy diet – Limit alcohol, caffeine, refined sugar, and food with preservatives. All of these can alter your mood.

Social Wellness

The following topics are covered in Social Wellness:

Who Surrounds You
Choosing Friends Wisely
Belonging
Community
Social Media
Caring What Others Think
Fun
Laughter
Sense of Humor
Asking for Help
Saying No

Who Surrounds You

"A friend is someone who gives you total freedom to be yourself." – Jim Morrison

Are you familiar with the term "crabs in the bucket"?

Following is an excerpt from the novel, *The Great Escape,*

"Listen, he said, you ever seen a bunch of crabs in a bucket?"

"No, I told him."

"Well, what happens is that now and then one crab will climb up on top of the others and begin to climb toward the top of the bucket, then, just as he's about to escape another crab grabs him and pulls him back down."

Lids aren't necessary on a bucket of live crabs because they can be counted on to pull each other downward.

Discover what downward pull you're subjected to and think explicitly about whether or not to reject the pull.

Idea for Action

Reflect on behavior which is encouraged and discouraged in groups to which you belong. Every community enforces some level of conformity. For any given group, what are you required to believe? What are you forbidden to do? Are these conformities serving you well? If not, reconsider your presence and participation in these communities.

Choosing Friends Wisely

"As iron sharpens iron, so one person sharpens another." – Proverbs 27:17 NIV

The people you surround yourself with affect your future, for better or worse.

I participate in a group text with two friends, Char and Lila, and the productive ideas that have come from our daily texts are staggering. Both became authors because of my influence. I have written children's books, lost 35 pounds, and learned to communicate better because of our relationships.

Your circle of friends can act as a mastermind group which challenges and makes you better, or they can hold you back and keep you stuck. It might sound heartless to evaluate your friends, but your relationships can alter the course of your life.

Avoid these types of people in your circle:

Manipulators, criticizers, gossips, liars, people who never apologize, are envious of you, don't support you, are always negative, temperamental, or habitually self-absorbed.

Choose friends who offer empathy, support, honesty, generosity, trust, and reassurance, and be this kind of friend.

Idea for Action

Write a list of your friends. Do they inspire or drain you?

What changes can you make in the relationships which are not serving you, or them, well?

Belonging

"Those who have a strong sense of love and belonging have the courage to be imperfect." – Brené Brown

The importance of belonging cannot be underestimated. Much of our behavior stems from a need to belong. Sensing we belong is based on shared experiences, vulnerability, and feeling supported.

A large body of research exists on belonging. Our bond to others is a source of happiness. Social networks can cushion us from stress. Belonging affects our performance and motivation. Employees cite connections with coworkers as a greater reason for career satisfaction than salary.[42]

Neuroscientists have also found our brains react similarly to social injuries as physical ones. When connections are severed, we experience pain as if we've incurred physical trauma.[43]

The implications of this research are huge. During the COVID-19 pandemic, many reports surfaced about people suffering from the isolation. One heartbreaking example was a woman I follow on Twitter who shared her mother died alone (not from COVID-19) in a nursing home because visitation wasn't allowed. She felt anguished her mother died alone. She wanted to hold her mother's hand and tell her she was loved as an expression of belonging to each other.

Idea for Action

Do you hold the belief, "I don't belong"? If so, why? Feelings of not belonging occur when people feel different or not accepted. The path to belonging begins with self-acceptance. Join a group of like-minded people. You are not alone.

Community

"Alone, we can do so little; together, we can do so much." – Helen Keller

As a full-time writer, I spend a large amount of time alone. However, I've learned the importance of community, despite my personality tendencies.

At the time of this writing, I've certified coaches and consultants in the Middle East, Canada, the US, the UK, and Belgium. We meet monthly to build community among YouMap® practitioners. Our time together is high value because it creates a bond among us as we learn and grow from one another.

Communities create a sense of belonging, offer support, foster innovation, open up mentoring opportunities, turn a solo voice into a unified voice, challenge us to grow and see things differently, broaden our impact, provide resources, establish peace, and build humility.

A community can have many forms, including networking groups, the gym, professional associations, neighborhood groups, faith-based gatherings, clubs, and sports teams.

Do you belong to one or more communities? If so, what communities?

Idea for Action

Everyone benefits from community. Identify communities you currently belong to. List ways you contribute to the groups and how the groups contribute to you. What are the gaps and opportunities to enhance the relationships?

Social Media

"It takes discipline not to let social media steal your time." – Amy Jo Martin

Is social media really social?

Social media can connect and reconnect people. The average American internet user has seven social media accounts. Despite this level of access to connect with other people, two in five Americans report their social relationships aren't meaningful.[44]

A separate study had similar findings. Young adults who spend at least two hours daily on social media platforms were significantly less likely to report perceived emotional support in high numbers.[45]

Yet another study of adults between 19 and 32 found increased social media caused significant disturbances in sleep.[46]

One of the reasons we have trouble regulating our social media, despite its influence on mood and sleep, is social media is addictive. Do you need proof? Uninstall the app of your most used social media platform and count how many times in a day you reach to tap the icon.

Experts suggest 30 minutes or less per day on social media to experience better health outcomes.[47]

Ideas for Action

Remove apps from devices which don't bring you joy. Use an app timer to limit use. Commit to a weekly social media fast.

Caring What Others Think

"Enough about me, let's talk about you. What do you think of me?" – CC Bloom in *Beaches*

Research confirms no one is thinking about you because our brain defaults to think about ourselves. We talk about ourselves over any other topic, and we make assumptions based on our own experiences. When we believe we are judged, we're often judging ourselves.[48]

For example, we might assume people are glancing at us because of what we're wearing, our accent, or our weight. In reality, we often interpret behaviors to make them about us.

Yes, people will sometimes say negative things to you. Remember—and this is key—people use their own experiences and thoughts as an anchor to form assumptions about you. People are harshest with you in areas where they are the most insecure about themselves.[49]

Even when people appear to be focused on something related to you, it's *still* often about them. What a liberating thought. You're free to think whatever you want about yourself. Why not make it positive?

Idea for Action

Whenever someone judges or takes a jab at you, practice the following response until it becomes a habit.

Replace a hurt or negative response with curiosity by asking, "What negative thoughts do they have about themselves influencing their beliefs about me?"

Fun

Fun provides many benefits. Fun increases serotonin in our brains, which is believed to regulate our mood, sleep, appetite, and memory.

Fun can also increase our coping abilities and reduce stress levels. Not to mention fun is, well, fun! Why don't we intentionally have more fun if it's so good for us?

Maybe we're worried what others think. Or believe we need to spend money to have fun. Perhaps we don't think we have the time or shouldn't take the time. Maybe we believe fun needs to be planned, or struggle with mental health challenges causing us to be apathetic about having fun.

Fun doesn't have to be a grand production. Fun is found in the little moments: a spontaneous game of hide and seek, a family game night, a dance party for one in your living room to your favorite songs. If you have kids, create a fort with pillows. Maybe a fort would do your soul some good even if you don't have kids. Play with modeling clay, go to a museum, fly a paper airplane, take a bubble bath, put on a puppet show, learn some magic tricks, go for a hike, or tell a joke.

Idea for Action

Block time in your calendar for fun in the coming week. Don't worry if you're aren't sure what to do, just block the time! Use an idea from this tip or search online for "ideas to have fun." Be present and leave your mobile phone behind.

Laughter

"Always laugh when you can. It is cheap medicine." – Lord Byron

Laughter delivers a surprising number of benefits. Importantly, the positive emotions of humor and laughter decrease the risk for stress-related diseases.[50]

Laughter also creates positive social connections, promotes learning, reduces anxiety, increases optimism, and is even linked to the healthy function of blood vessels.[51]

Are you getting enough laughter in your life? I once read in a *Psychology Today* blog stating the average four-year-old laughs 300 times a day. The average 40-year-old, only four.[52] I think we can agree most adults don't laugh enough considering the positive benefits.

How many times would you guess you laugh in a day?

Ideas for Action

Need more laughter in your life? Here are six ideas:

1. Watch funny YouTube videos of animals, laughing babies, etc.
2. Listen to comedy tracks on an app such as Spotify.
3. See a live comedy show.
4. Laugh at yourself and your friends with some karaoke.
5. Journal for a week about times you laughed each day.
6. Listen to humorous podcasts. Check out this best comedy podcasts list: bit.ly/bestfunnypodcasts.

Sense of Humor

"A sense of humor is a major defense against minor troubles."
– Mignon McLaughlin

Developing a good sense of humor should be considered an essential life skill!

Ninety percent of men and 81 percent of women report a sense of humor is the most important quality in a partner and a crucial quality for leaders.[53]

Being funny is possibly one of the best things you can do for your health. Humor can help lower stress. It functions like an immune system for the mind. Reframing a negative event in a humorous light can serve as an emotional filter to help prevent negativity from initiating depressive emotions.

A wealth of evidence shows funny people are often smarter, healthier, and less stressed about their lives.[54]

Everyone is different, so your sense of humor should be authentic to you. When someone says you don't have a sense of humor, they're revealing your humor isn't the same as theirs. It doesn't have to be. Even if you're not confident to create humor, you can disperse humor others have created.

Ideas for Action

1. Practice laughing at yourself; see humor in situations.
2. Expose yourself to more humorous content.
3. Watch the TEDx talk, *The Skill of Humor*, by Andrew Tarvin, at bit.ly/skillofhumor.

Asking for Help

"Be strong enough to stand alone, smart enough to know when you need help, and brave enough to ask for it." – Ziad K. Abdelnour

If you've exhausted your options or you're in over your head, it's time to ask for help.

Maybe you don't ask for help because you don't want to be a burden to anyone. Perhaps you're independent and prefer to work alone. Maybe asking for help makes you look weak.

Dig into why you don't want to ask for help to understand your motivation for going it alone.

Asking for help makes others feel good. Think about a time you helped someone. Allow others the same fulfillment. If you're in a place which isn't sustainable without support, you will probably need help when it escalates to a crisis.

Asking for help can get you unstuck. Whether you're procrastinating or spinning your wheels, the help of someone you trust can take you farther than you'll go alone.

The good news? Asking for help gets easier every time.

Idea for Action

Make a list of current struggles. List the help you need and who might help you. Do you need help keeping up with household chores or cutting the grass? Are you struggling with administrative duties in your business? Can you delegate or barter services?

If you're not sure who can help you, ask friends, family, or colleagues for ideas or suggestions.

Saying No

"I refuse to please others at the expense of my own emotional well-being. Even if it means saying 'no' to people who are used to hearing 'yes.'" – Unknown

You have an obligation to create and protect your boundaries. Establishing boundaries prevents you being manipulated or used and allows you to filter what's acceptable—and what's not—in your life.

I struggled to say no for years because I felt guilty. It became easy when I reframed my thinking:

- Believing I'm the only one who can help is an ego trip.
- Saying yes could cause me to become resentful.
- Realizing the person wouldn't ask if they knew it would affect my emotional well-being. If they would, they don't care about me.
- Saying yes deprives someone else of an opportunity.
- Establishing boundaries builds confidence and respect.
- Saying no reduces stress and increases time, focus, energy, and satisfaction.

Ideas for Action

1. *Say no.* A reason is not needed, and the less said, the better. "I appreciate you asking; however, I'm currently stretched too thin."
2. *Say yes and no.* "I'm happy to but need to put a task on hold. Which project should I temporarily pause?"

SPIRITUALITY

"It's that strength of the human spirit, the strength of what's deep down in you, that's really going to get you anywhere and everywhere."

Christina Tosi

Never underestimate the power of the spirit.

When we fail to nurture our spirit, we erect barriers to joy. Much focus is given to cultivating mind and body while we neglect our spirit.

We can take inspired action to feed our spirit. The alternative is a barren soul yielding to irritability, depression, discouragement, bitterness, self-pity, hopelessness, jealousy, conflict, addiction, and self-centeredness.

While I follow the teachings of Jesus, entries focus on spirituality, not religion. As a former atheist, I realize people are at different points on a faith continuum. If you don't have faith in God, many entries, such as contentment and wisdom, apply.

The chapter is broken into sections of Growth, Purpose, Belief & Inspiration, and Service & Social. Focus on the entries relevant to you.

Spiritual Growth

The following topics are covered in Spiritual Growth:

Comfort Zone
Journaling
Spiritual Mentors
Alone Time
Contentment
Confidence
Character Traits
Patience
Wisdom
Attitude
Judging Yourself
Self-Actualization
Joy Killers
Complaining
Greed
Shame
Experience Bias
Temptation
Prudence
Materialism

Comfort Zone

"Everything you've ever wanted is one step outside your comfort zone." – Jennifer Aniston

What is a comfort zone? Why do we stay in it? Should we get out of it? If so, how? I'm glad you asked.

Your comfort zone is a space where your behaviors and tasks fit into a routine which reduces stress and risk. Reducing risk and stress are good, right? It depends.

Eustress is a "good" form of stress where we are excited versus "bad" stress where we sense a threat. Calculated risk can be good for us, whereas recklessness is not.

We stay inside our comfort zone because it's easy. Comfort zones aren't bad. They're neutral. However, they don't foster adaptability, creativity, heightened productivity, or growth.

If you aren't satisfied in areas of life, doing what you've always done won't yield different results. You must leave your comfort zone. But don't go too far. Psychologists Robert M. Yerkes and John D. Dodson explained to maximize performance, we need a state of relative anxiety—where stress levels are slightly higher than usual. This is "Optimal Anxiety," also known as the Yerkes-Dodson law, and it's just outside our comfort zone. Too much anxiety is unproductive.

How often do you leave your comfort zone in a typical week?

Idea for Action

Pick a skill to learn each year to leave your comfort zone. This book will get you out of your comfort zone. Entries ruffling your feathers most might be ones to pay attention to!

Journaling

"People who keep journals have life twice." – Jessamyn West

Journaling isn't for everyone; however, you can reap clear benefits should you decide to try it.

Journaling helps you organize your thoughts, sharpen your writing skills, set and track goals, log your ideas so you don't forget them, increase self-reflection, capture details and memories you might otherwise forget, relieve stress, and spark creativity.

You can journal the traditional way in a notebook, or electronically, which increases privacy, security, and the ability to search your entries for easy access.

What benefits of journaling appeal most to you?

Idea for Action

Start a daily journaling habit by setting a timer for 15 minutes.

Choose a topic to start, such as writing what happened that day, fleshing out ideas, future plans, or other topics of interest to help you avoid writer's block.

Don't edit or audit yourself as you write. You can clean up your entry when the timer goes off and you reread it—or not.

Spiritual Mentors

"In our faith we follow in someone's steps. In our faith we leave footprints to guide others. It's the principle of discipleship." – Max Lucado

Spiritual mentorship facilitates our spiritual growth. Spiritual maturity provides us greater wisdom, love, faith, joy, kindness, and self-control.

I've worked with spiritual mentors who were instrumental in answering my questions and helping me build faith, patience, and kindness. Mentors guided me toward clarity on the person I want to become. A practical example is how I govern and conduct my behavior online where it can be tempting to let loose on people we don't agree with.

Spiritual discipleship or mentoring builds our humility, equips us for life, and connects us to community.

Idea for Action

Make a list of what's important to you in a spiritual mentor. List the names of 2-3 people who fit your criteria.

Here is an example. I seek a spiritual mentor who ...

- Lives out the spiritual disciplines of my faith
- Creates a space of trust and intimacy
- Recognizes potential in people
- Leads a life worthy of emulating
- Is authentic, spiritually mature, and wise

Alone Time

"Alone time is when I distance myself from the voice of the world, so I can hear my own." – Oprah Winfrey

Spending time in solitude is powerful, yet some resist it. A study showed more people would rather experience mild electric shock than be left alone with their thoughts.[55]

What if you're an extrovert? After all, extroverts get their energy from other people! Even extroverts need alone time.

Without time alone, our souls aren't searched or evaluated. This can lead to decisions which aren't right for us. Also, when bombarded by interactions, we begin to compare ourselves to others, are pressured to impress people, and become overly dependent on others.

Here are six reasons solitude is beneficial:

1. Allows you to think more clearly
2. Helps increase concentration and productivity
3. Offers space for self-discovery
4. Facilitates deeper thinking
5. Gives you a chance to work through problems
6. Enhances the quality of your relationships

Do you avoid or embrace being alone? Why?

Ideas for Action

- Plan periods of solitude each week.
- Wake up earlier to have alone time.
- Schedule alone time on your calendar.
- Take a walk on your lunch break for time to think.
- Plan technology breaks to detach from the internet.

Contentment

"It isn't what you have or who you are or where you are or what you are doing that makes you happy or unhappy. It is what you think about it." – Dale Carnegie

Contentment is peace and satisfaction with your life. You might want to achieve more, yet you are content with what you have despite hoping for better.

Do you have ambition for things you want to achieve? You can choose contentment with where your life is and who you are. Contentment doesn't mean you stop improving.

The path to contentment begins with counting your blessings, such as people in your life, things you have, and who you are.

I've mentioned several months before writing this book, I was overweight and felt physically awful. Although, I was content. I'm thankful for my family, my work, and friends. Releasing weight was good for me, but I was content, overall.

Focusing on blessings keeps us in a posture of gratitude.

Ideas for Action

1. Create a daily habit of counting your blessings.
2. Find enjoyment in simple things: take walks with a friend, play board games, put together a puzzle.
3. Show one person each week you appreciate them.
4. Identify one thing in your life you wish to change. Create a plan and stay grateful as you implement change.

Confidence

"Because one believes in oneself, one doesn't try to convince others. Because one is content with oneself, one doesn't need others' approval. Because one accepts oneself, the whole world accepts him or her." – Lao Tzu

Did you know confidence is a skill? Research shows confidence can be learned and developed.

A Princeton study found confidence enhances our motivation to act.[56] When we're filled with self-doubt we hesitate and become indecisive.

If we're willing to attempt things we believe are daunting—not because we have blind faith, but because those things are worth doing—confidence compels us to act.

Confidence emerges when we realize two things:
- What we do best.
- Actions can influence results.

If you aren't sure what you do best, I've got you covered.

Idea for Action

Learn to tell T.I.M.E. to build confidence:

T – Talents. Uncover your abilities.
I – Important. Reveal what's important to you.
M – Motivating skills. Identify skills which motivate you.
E – Enthusiasm. Discover your passions. See *Finding Your Purpose* on page 103 and *Legacy* on page 115.

See *Discovering Your Strengths* on page 241, *Discovering Your Values* on page 244, and *Discovering Your Skills* on page 245.

Character Traits

"Character is the real foundation of all worthwhile success." – John Hays Hammond

People are often judged for their character. Our character traits are aspects of our behavior. Everyone has character traits, good and bad.

Building awareness of your character traits helps you become more intentional. This window into yourself also helps improve your relationships, strengthen your skills, and improve your overall well-being.

Only after we understand ourselves can we grow and improve by limiting our negative traits and expanding upon our positive ones. Our lives are a continuous process of discovery and improvement.

What feedback have others given regarding your character?

Idea for Action

Take the free VIA Character strengths survey: viacharacter.org/survey/account/register

I discovered my top result was perspective: Able to provide wise counsel to others; looking at the world in ways which make sense to oneself/others.

What's your top result? And your bottom? Both offer valuable insights!

If you'd like to take the YouMap® assessment to discover yourself, visit bit.ly/OrderYouMap.

Patience

"Patience is not the ability to wait, but the ability to keep a good attitude while waiting." – Unknown

Patience is a virtue. It's the ability to wait for things without becoming upset. Patience transcends frustration and ushers in peace.

Industries make money off of impatience. Disney sells a FastPass to avoid waiting in line. The LineAngel app allows you to hire people to wait in line for you! Despite these clever little bypasses, we will inevitably have to exercise patience in life. If not at Disney, then perhaps on the commute to work.

Why is it important to be patient? Aside from driving yourself crazy with impatience, patience makes you happier.[57]

Ideas for Action

Daily tips to build patience:

1. Slow down and deepen your breathing.
2. Ask, "Will this matter next year? In five years?"
3. Redirect your focus from end results; practice being in the present.
4. Scan your body for tension; loosen your jaw and shoulders.
5. Practice delayed gratification: Start with small things like waiting 15 minutes to eat something you want.

Wisdom

"Knowledge speaks, but wisdom listens." – Jimi Hendrix

Wisdom emerges from reflection on past experience. Wise people incorporate past observations into a nuanced style of thinking—considering multiple perspectives rather than black and white options.[58]

Wise people I know share common traits. They are open-minded, critical thinkers. They are humble, slow to speak, and choose words carefully. They are knowledgeable, insightful upholders of spiritual and moral truths. They accept people for who they are, are not judgmental, and are interested in the greater good.

Wise people are experienced, not all experienced people are wise.

Idea for Action

Check your wisdom with a test by neuropsychiatrist, Dilip Jeste. On a scale of 1 to 5, how much do you agree with each statement? (1 = completely disagree, 5 = completely agree)

1. I enjoy being exposed to diverse viewpoints.
2. I have a difficult time keeping friendships.
3. It is important I understand my actions.
4. I cannot filter my negative emotions.
5. I postpone making major decisions as long as I can.
6. Others look to me to help them make choices.

Tally your score for each question. Next, subtract scores for questions 2, 4, and 5. If you scored 10 or more, you are likely wise! Wisdompage.com offers help to grow in wisdom.

Attitude

"A great attitude becomes a great mood. A great mood becomes a great day. A great day becomes a great year. A great year becomes a great life." – Unknown

Attitude is, perhaps, the single, most important indicator of how a person will cope with the ups and downs of life. Our perspective—which forms our attitude—influences how we handle adversity, rejection, and disappointment. If we hold onto a certain attitude long enough, it becomes ingrained.

Trials are unavoidable in life. We also can't control every aspect of our lives; however, how we approach and respond to obstacles is completely within our control. Billionaire entrepreneur Richard Branson says, "Positive people don't just have a good day; they make it a good day."

When you control your attitude, it no longer controls you. Choosing your attitude requires intention and awareness. Every morning when you wake up, set your intention by asking, "Who do I want to be today?" Speak the answer to yourself as a daily affirmation.

Idea for Action

Imagine life not as something happening *to* you, but something happening *for* you. Choose to see challenging circumstances or people as a teacher brought into your life to impart a specific lesson. Ask, "What am I supposed to learn or gain from this?"

Judging Yourself

"Remember, you have been criticizing yourself for years, and it hasn't worked. Try approving of yourself and see what happens." – Louise L. Hay

In *Judging Others*, on page 144, I share how our judgments are based on arbitrary standards we set. We create rules for ourselves, too, not just others.

We cannot stop judging completely. Our goal should be to lessen the instances of beating ourselves up. We can shift from thoughts of guilt to becoming aware of when we're judging ourselves.

When we observe self-judgement, we can release it and change the mental channel without attaching guilt to our behavior.

Idea for Action

Practice pinpointing and observing your judgments about yourself. Redirect those judgmental thoughts with love, grace, and compassion.

When you have a judgmental thought:

1. Ask, "Does this thought come from a place of love?" No? Move from the thought.

2. Play with the thought and flip it around.
    Before: "I was so lazy today. I'm so undisciplined."
    After: "I wanted to accomplish more today. What got in the way? What can I change tomorrow to reach my goals?"

Self-Actualization

"If you plan on being anything less than you are capable of being, you will probably be unhappy all the days of your life."
– Abraham Maslow

Organismic theorist Kurt Goldstein coined the phrase "self-actualization." According to Maslow's hierarchy of needs, self-actualization is the highest level of psychological development. "Actualization" of personal potential is achieved only after basic and mental needs have been fulfilled.

Maslow's self-actualizing characteristics are:

- Efficient perceptions of reality
- Comfortable acceptance of self, others, and nature
- Reliant on own experiences and judgment
- True to oneself, rather than being how others want
- Task-centered; a mission to achieve in life beyond self
- Autonomy
- Continued freshness of appreciation
- Profound interpersonal relationships
- Comfort with solitude
- Nonhostile sense of humor
- Experiences marked by feelings of deep meaning
- Socially compassionate
- Few intimate friends over superficial relationships
- Gemeinschaftsgefühl: social interest, community

Idea for Action

Take a free test to see where you are most self-actualized and where you have growth opportunity: bit.ly/selfacttest.

Joy Killers

"A cheerful heart is good medicine, but a crushed spirit dries up the bones." – Proverbs 17:22 NLT

Joy transcends happiness. Happiness is often related to self-pleasure, whereas joy is emotional well-being deep down in your soul. These seven things threaten joy:

Disappointment – unmet expectations governing satisfaction with life

Negative self-talk – constant inner criticism provoking anxiety

Worry – living in fear rooted in future events which might never happen

Comparison – measuring areas of life against the lives of others

Isolation – separating from others, especially during difficulty

Unwillingness to forgive – harboring persistent bitterness toward another person

Living against your values – taking actions and making decisions which don't align with what is important to you

Which items in the list do you struggle with?

Idea for Action

Rate how often you engage in joy killers from 1 to 10: 1 is almost never, 10 almost always. Journal your observations. What could you do differently? What changes can you make? Implement, practice, and journal progress.

Watch Diana Nguyen's TEDx on joy, bit.ly/joyismycaffeine.

Complaining

"A thankful person is thankful under all circumstances. A complaining soul complains even in paradise." – Bahá'u'lláh

Complaining is expressing one's dissatisfaction and usually happens after a negative experience.

Psychologists have defined three types of complaining:[59]

Chronic – Habitually focused on setbacks

Venting – Expresses emotional dissatisfaction with the motive of receiving attention and affirmation. Venters aren't generally interested in solutions

Instrumental – Focuses on the impact of a problem and the importance of change

Instrumental complaining is the most constructive of the three types and is significantly less frequent than its negative counterparts. Complaining is not harmless. It rewires your brain toward negative thinking, which will affect your happiness. Happy people complain less.[60]

Idea for Action

Considering your complaining tendencies. When do you complain, and why? Wherever possible, shift to instrumental complaining to effect positive change. Finally, limit contact with chronic complainers.

Greed

"Greed is not a financial issue. It's a heart issue." – Andy Stanley

Constant tension exists between the spirits of selfishness and sacrifice. Mahatma Gandhi said, "The Earth provides enough to satisfy every man's need, but not every man's greed." The sentiment is the earth provides enough resources to take care of everyone but cannot support endless greed.

In general, greed lacks empathy. Greed doesn't always relate to money. Examples include taking credit for other people's work or hoarding supplies from work for personal use.

A sad characteristic of greed is it causes a futile quest. Greed is an endless pursuit and never brings happiness. The greedy will never be satisfied. This should come as no surprise, since most of us have an intellectual understanding material possessions don't lead to happiness.

Relationships, not things, are the building blocks of a fulfilled life. Data show lower-income individuals spend more time socializing with other people than their more well-to-do counterparts, who spend more time alone.[61]

The best way to guard against greed is to live a life of generosity. Generous people are shown to be happier, so there's also something in it for you![62]

Idea for Action

Try these 10 little ways to fight greed and become more generous: bit.ly/waystobegenerous. See *Generosity* on page 142 in this chapter.

Shame

"Unlike guilt, which is the feeling of doing something wrong shame is the feeling of being something wrong." – Marilyn J. Sorensen

Shame puts our spirit in shackles. People from all cultures and geographic regions experience shame.[63] Causes of shame include diverging from cultural norms, trauma and abuse, mental illness, and religious zealotry using shame as a tool to persuade followers to pursue moral behavior.

Shame is an affliction without boundaries. While guilt is a transient emotion tied to a particular wrongdoing, shame tells us we are a bad person.

One of the most damaging characteristics of shame is it silences the sufferer and creates isolation. This is especially true of abused children. Children who were shamed become adults who experience shame.

"When faced with shame, the brain reacts as if it were facing physical danger and activates the sympathetic nervous system generating the flight/fight/freeze response. The flight response triggers the need to disappear, and children who have this response will try to become invisible."[64]

Humility is the antidote for shame. Author Ken Blanchard said, "Don't think less of yourself, just think of yourself less." Become more accepting of flaws. All humans are imperfect.

Idea for Action

Do you experience shame because of your shortcomings? If so, watch *The Problem of Shame* at bit.ly/problemofshame.

Experience Bias

"If you accept a limiting belief, then it will become a truth for you." – Louise L. Hay

Experience bias, commonly referred to as limiting beliefs, can concern ourselves, others, or the world. These beliefs usually are not rooted in fact. Rather, they're opinions formed from negative experiences such as failure, abuse, or trauma that shaped our perspective. Most often, we accept our beliefs without challenging them. Holding onto a belief as truth affects our actions, which moves the belief into reality, a self-fulfilling prophecy.

An example of experience bias is telling yourself you aren't smart enough for a job you want or you'll never find love again.

Idea for Action

Complete this "One-Belief-at-a-Time" exercise by Byron Katie.

Write out a stressful belief and walk through these steps:

1. Is it true?
2. Can I absolutely know it's true?
3. How do I react when I believe the thought?
4. Who would I be without the thought?
5. Turn the thought around (flip it).

Example statement: He hurt me.

Possible opposites: I hurt me. I hurt him. He didn't hurt me. He helped me.

Consider how each flipped statement is truer than the original belief.

Temptation

"Free cheese is always available in mouse traps." – Baylor Barbee

Temptation is a desire to engage in short-term urges, which can threaten long-term goals.

I asked people on social media to share common temptations and received the following answers:

- Engaging in something wrong, like stealing
- Ditching work to sleep in
- Skipping a workout
- Impulse buying
- Overeating
- Gossiping
- Lying

Do you ever struggle to resist temptations? Giving in to temptation can lead to a plethora of problems.

Responding more thoughtfully to temptation can help avoid succumbing to cravings and urges.

Who you are in the future depends on choices you make today. Remembering this can help influence those choices.

Ideas for Action

1. Reflect, "Will what I'm going to do serve me well?"
2. Pledge to not give in for 15-minutes to allow a temptation to pass.
3. Reduce access to what tempts you.

Prudence

"Remember not only to say the right thing in the right place, but far more difficult still, to leave unsaid the wrong thing at the tempting moment." – Benjamin Franklin

What is the difference between wisdom and prudence? Wisdom is knowledge combined with practical experience used at the right time or the right situation. Prudence is careful judgment, such as ability to restrain oneself to align actions with knowledge and wisdom.

A remarkable eight-decade study showed a link between prudent living and increased longevity of life.[65] The results have been published in a book, *The Longevity Project: Surprising Discoveries for Health and Long Life from the Landmark Eight-Decade Study.*

Prudent, conscientious people often live longer than happy-go-lucky counterparts. The authors recommend pursuing meaningful, productive activities rather than treating life as a joy ride to enjoy a longer life.

One clear finding was prudent people have stable relationships. Strong social ties can add years to your life.[66]

Ideas for Action

Prudence is often demonstrated through our decisions. Following are two ways to increase prudent decision-making:

1. Practice calming techniques such as slowing your breathing when you sense yourself getting upset.
2. Identify options and pitfalls to improve your judgment.

Materialism

"If material things are what you're talking about when you say I'm blessed, you have no idea what a blessing is." – Unknown

Materialism is placing higher importance on material possessions and physical comfort than spiritual values.

When we're young, we measure success or worth by job titles and what we possess. Over time, we often learn money and possessions don't buy happiness. Research supports this wise old adage, concluding materialistic people are less happy than their peers who aren't materialistic.[67]

Money supplies happiness to the extent it supplies our needs. A person who doesn't have resources of enough food, safe and adequate shelter, and other necessities will experience a higher level of happiness once income rises to meet these needs. However, resources above and beyond needs do not contribute to happiness.[68]

In an attempt to learn why materialism undermines happiness, scientists have homed in on the fact more materialistic people report low levels of gratitude.[69]

One reason gratitude beats materialism is it strengthens relationships. Relationships are an ingredient of a happy life.

Have you witnessed examples of unhappy materialistic people? What about happy unmaterialistic people?

Idea for Action

Focus on experiences over things. At the end of each day, share three specific things you're grateful for with family, a friend, or in your gratitude journal.

Purpose

The following topics are covered in Purpose:

Finding Your Purpose
Belief by Design
Inner Harmony
Courage
Despair
Discontentment
Discouragement
Suffering
Thriving in Difficult Times
Hope
Happiness
Freedom
Legacy

Finding Your Purpose

"He who has a why to live for can bear almost any how." – Friedrich Nietzsche

People are wired with a deep need for purpose. This need is rooted in our deeply held values. Some common human values are meaningful work, making a difference, usefulness, belonging, and personal growth.

Purpose guides the direction of our lives and supplies our motivation. In short, purpose provides our reason to exist.

Finding reason to exist is an overwhelming thought, but it can be broken down to a few questions.

What fills your thoughts? What do you often talk about? Why?
What do people who know you say you're passionate about?
What do people say you do well?
What does a wonderful world look like in your eyes?

Idea for Action

Write a focused purpose statement based on your answers to the questions in this entry.

Mine is: I care most about helping people reach their potential to become the best possible version of themselves. It's why I write the books I do.

Another way to say it is, "My purpose is to maximize people to help them live out their greatest potential."

Work through the four questions above and be patient with yourself. Answers to big questions take time.

Belief by Design

"Are our brains wired for God? Not only does science support the idea, but it also shows us that belief in God and an active prayer life can make us healthier, happier people who do good in the world." – Mike McHargue

Scientists conducted research to look for an area in the brain linked to a higher power, similar to areas for language and vision. They found no single area of the brain devoted to belief, but scans showed brain changes in people who believe in God.[70]

Researchers at the University of Oxford ran a series of experiments across cultures and continents. Here are their findings:

People who focus on God's love through prayer and meditation experience less stress and reduced blood pressure. They also have more activity in the anterior cingulate cortex—the area associated with love, compassion, and empathy. Focusing on God's love makes us more loving and less angry.[71]

They also found people who view God as angry have a different response. When focused on God's anger the limbic system becomes more active, increasing stress levels. They have trouble forgiving themselves and others. Neuroscience shows God's love is better for us than God's wrath.[72]

Idea for Action

Science reveals the power of prayer. Transform your brain by praying or meditating 30 minutes per day, four days per week, focusing on God's love.[73]

Inner Harmony

"Do not let the behavior of others destroy your inner peace." – Dalai Lama

Inner harmony is a peace of mind involving self-acceptance, acceptance of the past, and acceptance of one's life in general.

Achieving inner harmony does not deliver a life void of conflict. Inner harmony or peace comes from knowing who you are, believing you are loved, changing negative thought patterns, practicing kindness to yourself and others, and accepting what is.

- When we know ourselves, we aren't derailed by criticism.
- When we know we're loved, we can overcome inadequacy.
- When we control negative thoughts, we view our lives with hope and optimism.
- When we accept what is, we don't strive to change things out of our control.

Daily habits largely influence how much peace we have in life. We can implement practices which promote inner harmony.

Idea for Action

To increase inner peace, review any habits working against you.

For example, use a social media timer to limit time online. Mute or unfollow people who regularly bring negativity. Identify boundaries you believe are violated. Set new boundaries and defend those boundaries from being crossed.

Courage

"Courage is the most important of all the virtues because without courage, you can't practice any other virtue consistently." – Maya Angelou

Cathy Lassiter outlines four kinds of courage in her book, *Everyday Courage for School Leaders*:

Moral Courage – Speaking up and acting when injustices occur

Intellectual Courage – Challenging assumptions and acting to change based on new learnings

Disciplined Courage – Remaining steadfast, strategic, and deliberate in the face of setbacks and failures for the greater good

Empathetic Courage – The courage to set aside biases and to be open and feel deeply for others

All four kinds of courage challenge the status quo and require making decisions which could cause fear, anxiety, or discomfort.

Do you consistently practice the four kinds of courage?

Idea for Action

Try filtering decisions through the four kinds of courage.

Ask, "Is this decision just, open-minded, purposeful, and compassionate?" Rephrased, "What is the most just, open-minded, decisive, and compassionate decision in this situation?" See *Making Tough Decisions* on page 42 in the *Health & Wellness* chapter.

Despair

"Despair is suffering without meaning." – Viktor Frankl

I debated including this topic, as I already included discouragement and disappointment.

But despair is not discouragement or disappointment. Despair is a loss of hope. That someone working through the book might be dealing with despair nagged at me. Then I realized even if only one person feels this way, I want to address it.

Hope gives you something to live for. You will generally lose hope when you succumb to victimhood. That is, you feel a complete loss of control. Despair can come from profound loss such as a death or abandonment. Others might have difficulty understanding your despair. "If you don't like something about your life, change it!" they say. However, if you're dealing with despair, you probably don't have the motivation or energy to change the situation.

You don't have to focus on changing the situation. Just focus on one step. Talk to someone who has gone through what you're facing. They can help you figure out your next step. Small steps can create a sense of purpose as you find your way.

Idea for Action

If you are experiencing despair, *Project Hope Exchange* shares messages from people who have experienced adversity. Others who have come through similar circumstances offer words of hope and healing at projecthopeexchange.com/messages-of-hope.

Discontentment

"Discovery comes as a result of positive discontent, a constructive dissatisfaction. In fact, one might quite truthfully say that there is no discovery when one is content." – Myron Allen

Discovering the distinction between negative and constructive discontentment was absolutely revelatory for me. We're socialized being discontent is ungrateful or thankless.

Is it? Motive matters.

Constructive discontentment looks for needed change or for opportunity. This mindset can help you succeed because it causes you to examine your life. You're sick of your debt situation or the abusive relationship. You're tired of your manager cutting you down. Productive discontentment comes along and says, "I will do something about this."

Negative discontent seeps into our lives like storm clouds. It's passive. Constructive discontent leads to progress because it's active.

Do you experience negative or positive discontent? Counter negative discontent by becoming an activator for change.

Idea for Action

Tap into your intuition. Let your gut guide you in areas of necessary change. What needs to change? List everything sabotaging your progress. A problem identified is half solved.

Discouragement

"Many of the great achievements of the world were accomplished by tired and discouraged men [and women] who kept on working." – Oscar Wilde

When writing this book, I lost a chunk of writing—twice. My first reaction was to shout an expletive when I realized what had happened. My second reaction was to sit on my bed in self-pity. I was steeped in discouragement, stepping through the stages of grief at warp speed. Finally, I decided to get back on the horse. I sat down at my computer to figure out a way forward.

Everyone experiences disappointment. There's no avoiding it, nor should we try to shield ourselves from the emotion. Discouragement is a result of a perceived setback. The key to overcoming discouragement is to employ an empowered mindset. My early reactions were not empowered. I allowed myself to be a victim of my circumstance.

What matters is flipping the switch to empower yourself. You can choose how to respond. To fight discouragement, stay focused on the big picture, not the setback. Cling to your vision. Do not compare yourself to others. You can get discouraged if you perceive others doing better, or doing things better, than you are. It's fine to be inspired by others but remember you're on a unique path.

Idea for Action

When you get discouraged, talk to a mentor, or find someone who can help. Others you respect and admire have a way of pulling you out of darkness.

Suffering

"Out of suffering have emerged the strongest souls; the most massive characters are seared with scars." – Kahlil Gibran

Pain is useful because it motivates us to recover, grow, release things which aren't good for us, or find meaningful ways to move toward recovery. Transformation happens when we move through suffering rather than remaining in it.

According to licensed therapist Matthew Jones, suffering must be difficult enough to motivate you to push beyond it. "It should push you to something larger and greater than yourself. Something transcending yourself."

One of the greatest sources of pain in life is the loss of a child. A young woman I attended church with lost one of her 11-month-old twins to Sudden Unexplained Death in Childhood (SUDC). Since his death, she created Smiles for Owen, an annual fundraiser to help families who've experienced the death of a child to SUDC.

She transformed her pain into purpose to move through her suffering. When we experience suffering, which we all do, we can try to numb it, ignore it, or deal with it head on. Only the latter leads to healing.

Idea for Action

Reflect on times your suffering, or the suffering of someone you know, generated purpose. Then watch Katie Mazurek's TEDx talk on finding meaning in suffering at bit.ly/meaninginsuffering.

Thriving in Difficult Times

"The habits you created to survive will no longer serve you when it's time to thrive. Get out of survival mode. New habits, new life." – Ebonee Davis

Many things are out of our control: economic crises, natural disasters, and hurt inflicted from others. Engage the following to influence better outcomes in difficult times.

Imagine worst-case scenarios. How would you respond to a job loss or unexpected illness? Plan your response. You'll be in a better position to execute the plan than reactively creating one under stress.

Diversify your interests. If you do nothing but work, you'll feel rootless if displaced from your job.

Diversify your finances. Devote effort to build passive income, a side hustle, investments, emergency funds, or other revenue streams. Diversifying helps you endure a tough economy.

Nurture your support system. Life is busy. We easily neglect relationships. Be intentional to invest in the people in your life.

Guard your mindset. Cling to hope and optimism for the future.

Remember this, too, shall pass.

Ideas for Action

Review the ideas above to assess where to make changes or plan better. Identify ways to simplify. Simplicity lowers stress. See *Simplifying Your Life* on page 17 in the *Health & Wellness* chapter.

Hope

"We must accept finite disappointment, but never lose infinite hope." – Martin Luther King Jr.

Hope is an expectation of a positive outcome. It's also one of the most important vehicles to success. Hope is not naïve, blind optimism. Blind optimism is false hope. Having no hope is distorted reality, and true hope is based in accurate reality.

Psychologist Charles Snyder, creator of The Hope Scale, studied the positive effects of hope on health, work, education, and personal meaning. He proposed three main elements of hope:

Goals – Approaching life in a goal-oriented way

Pathways – Finding different ways to achieve your goals

Agency – Believing you can instigate change and achieve these goals

Sometimes the best way to gain a better perspective on a situation is to ask for help. The big picture can be difficult to see because we're too close to it. Through the support of others, we can better navigate challenges. No matter what we're going through, others have gone through it ahead of us. We can benefit from their counsel and gain hope through their ability to overcome similar challenges.

Idea for Action

If you sense you are losing hope, ask someone you respect and consider wise to help reassess your position. A fresh point of view can help shift your perspective.

Happiness

"Happiness is a gift and the trick is not to expect it but to delight in it when it comes." – Charles Dickens

Happiness is a sensation when you know life is good, and you can't help but smile.

How is happiness different from joy? Joy is an attitude, whereas happiness is a destination. Happiness is linked to envisioning the life you desire. Joy doesn't need control.

You can't live a happy life without joy. But you can experience joy without being happy. Danielle LaPorte's quote drives this point home:

> *Happiness is like rising bubbles—delightful and inevitably fleeting. Joy is the oxygen—ever present.*

If you seek happiness, remember to also cultivate joy. How? Through gratitude! Happiness keeps you focused on your vision, desires, and goals for your life. Joy keeps you in a posture of gratitude for what you already have to avoid chasing butterflies. The more you try to catch butterflies, the more they evade you.

Idea for Action

Write a key goal for the year and the tasks, activities, or milestones to reach it. Practice gratitude each step of the way. See *Daily Gratitude* on page 26 in the *Health & Wellness* chapter.

Freedom

"The secret to happiness is freedom and the secret to freedom is courage." – Thucydides

Freedom is defined as the power or right to act, speak, or think as one wants without hindrance or restraint. To have freedom in life you need three things.

You must define what freedom means to you. Freedom is a value, so its definition is personal. Freedom hinges on being your true self. To become free, you must become your true self.

Next, figure out what you want in life. A tall order. At the end of your life, looking back, what would you want your life to look life? What did you accomplish? Look to your values to answer this question.

Finally, name barriers preventing the life you want. Do you have relationships marked with negativity, envy, or harsh criticism? Do you allow fear to keep you stuck somewhere you know isn't right? This is where courage enters. To make a change, you must be accountable for your life. It's tempting to blame others or the circumstances. As the saying goes, "Where there's a will, there's a way."

Idea for Action

Surround yourself with role models and people you admire. A mentor can help you discover your true self and inspire you to expand into your potential. See *Courage* on page 106 in this chapter.

Legacy

"Immortality is to live your life doing good things and leaving your mark behind." – Brandon Lee

Something every living person has in common is we will all return to dust. At the end of our lives, what matters most is the good we added to the lives of others.

People who leave a legacy also share something in common. They focus on something bigger than themselves. A life spent concerned primarily with one's own comfort, accomplishments and material gain does not produce genuine happiness. To be truly happy, we must invest in something greater than ourselves. Such investment plants the seeds which become our legacy.

Idea for Action

Begin to shape your legacy by reflecting on these questions:

What drives me? Desire and passion indicate purpose.

Who do I want to help? Do you desire to help people in your inner circle, such as your family? Do you want to make an impact beyond your circle? Identify a specific audience.

What kind of impact do I want to make? Consider your values, beliefs, and outcomes you want to influence. For example, perhaps your legacy is raising children who are kind and generous or starting a ministry to assist victims of domestic violence with rebuilding their lives.

What do you want people to say at your funeral?

Belief & Inspiration

The following topics are covered in Belief & Inspiration:

Awe
Beauty
Belief
Faith
Fruit of the Spirit
Poverty of Spirit
Intuition
Meditation
Mindfulness
Power of Music
Prayer
God's Character
Waiting on God
Blessings
Worship
Miracles
Mystery of Life
Creativity
Legalism

Awe

"The world is full of magic things, patiently waiting for our senses to grow sharper." – W.B. Yeats

Awe is an aura of reverential respect combined with wonder. It's the sensation we get when we witness the birth of a baby or standing on top of a mountain to view the expanse.

Research suggests a positive correlation between a tendency of experiencing sensations of awe and being happier, healthier, and humble.[74]

If you're caught on the hamster wheel of busy, chances are you aren't taking time to experience enough awe in life. Busy is the enemy of awe. Our constant pursuit of achievement, success, and productivity distracts us from the transformative power of awe.

How frequently do you experience a sensation of awe?

Idea for Action

Intentionally increase your exposure to awe-inspiring activities such as spending more time in nature, watching the sun rise or set, meditating, and listening in silence to beautiful classical music pieces. Some inspiring favorites of mine include:

Air by Johann Sebastian Bach
Nocturne in E Flat Major (Op. 9 No. 2) by Chopin
Four Seasons by Vivaldi
Moonlight Sonata by Beethoven
Canon in D by Pachelbel
O mio babbino caro by Puccini

Beauty

"I don't think of all the misery, but of the beauty that still remains." – Anne Frank

Beauty brings pleasure to the senses and lifts the mind and spirit. It's easy to see beauty in a fresh layer of snow on a mountain top or in the precious gift of a newborn baby.

Mountain top experiences and the birth of new babies are not things people experience regularly unless they are a mountain climber or midwife.

Artists see beauty where others don't, but this is a skill you can hone. Developing an artist's eye can help us see beauty even in the ordinary. When we fail to take the perspective of the artist, we look but don't see. Take time not to look, but to really see.

Ideas for Action

1. Use binoculars to view birds and animals.
2. Add wallpaper of inspiring scenes to your computer.
3. Keep fresh cut flowers in your home.
4. Plant a garden in your yard or flowers on a balcony.
5. Watch a documentary on the wonders of the world.
6. Eat dinner by candlelight on weekends.
7. Read poetry.

Belief

"Our only limitations are those we set up in our own mind." – Napoleon Hill

Napoleon Hill wrote in his bestselling book, *Think and Grow Rich*, "There is a difference between wishing for a thing and being ready to receive it. No one is ready for a thing until he believes he can acquire it. The state of mind must be belief, not mere hope or wish. Open-mindedness is essential for belief. Closed minds do not inspire faith, courage, and belief."

Do you believe with an expectant heart you will realize your plans and achieve your goals?

So often we operate out of routine and habit. Belief seeds hope, which leads to hopeful behaviors and actions that creates different outcomes. Have you considered how lack of belief can produce the opposite of what you want?

Idea for Action

Listen closely to the words you choose. Do you hear yourself speak words of doubt or certainty? Ask others for feedback too.

If I make…

If I achieve…

If I get…

Replace *if* with *when*.

Couple your belief with the daily visualization of your goal and take consistent action toward reaching it.

Faith

"Your faith can move mountains, and your doubt can create them." – Unknown

Faith is the expectation of good things to come. Everyone has faith in something. Just as oxygen fuels our lungs, faith fuels our souls. Without faith, life would have no purpose.

The Bible says, "Now faith is the assurance of things hoped for, the conviction of things not seen" (Hebrews 11:1 ESV).

Faith causes us to take the next step even when the path is dark and the next step is uncertain. We would be paralyzed with uncertainty moment by moment if we didn't step out in faith each day of our lives.

Ideas for Action

To build faith:

1. Read scripture, pray, or meditate daily.
2. Consider what can go right, not wrong.
3. Stretch out of your comfort zone.
4. Remove doubt by taking action. Write down what you want, learn what you need to know, create a plan and act!

Fruit of the Spirit

"But the fruit of the Spirit is love, joy, peace, patience, kindness, goodness, faithfulness, gentleness and self-control." – Galatians 5:22 ESV

Just as fruit takes time to fully ripen, so it is with Fruit of the Spirit. These character traits aren't developed overnight.

Regardless of your faith background, many of you would agree the following traits are vital for humanity:

Love – choosing to put others first

Joy – gladness not based on circumstances

Peace – embracing inner peace in the face of life's chaos

Patience – displaying endurance with situations and people

Kindness – being considerate and generous toward others

Goodness – displaying integrity inwardly and to others

Faithfulness – being reliable and trustworthy

Gentleness – exhibiting humility and extending grace to others

Self-control – keeping impulses under control

Idea for Action

Review the Fruit of the Spirit. Meditate on one trait each day for nine days.

Do you display the traits in your thoughts and actions? Is so, how? If not, why not?

Poverty of Spirit

"Blessed are the poor in spirit." – Matthew 5:3 NIV

Poverty of spirit, also known as poor in spirit, means we embrace daily reliance on God for everything we need. We don't believe we have sufficient resources in ourselves to face life's challenges. Poverty of spirit has little to do with being monetarily poor but whether we embrace daily dependence on God.

The idea is God will fill us when we empty ourselves.

This principle can be applied to every area of life. If we feel insufficient in our parenting, or in our relationships, poverty of spirit makes us humble enough to ask God for help through prayer.

We want to have it all together and be in control. This desire keeps us from relying on God and cuts us off from His power. Our ego resists the appearance of weakness. This is why we won't ask for help and don't like to admit when we're wrong. Willingness to ask for help takes courage. It is not a sign of weakness.

Idea for Action

Reflect on the following:

1. What are some blessings of being spiritually poor?
2. Where have I been living life solely in my strength and not relying on God's power?
3. Do I allow God, through daily prayer, to take the weight of the burdens I carry?

Intuition

"Intuition is the discriminate faculty that enables you to decide which of two lines of reasoning is right. Perfect intuition makes you master of all." – Paramahansa Yogananda

Jennifer Spor, coach and spiritual mentor, says, "We have two inner voices. One is our intuition, the other is mind chatter. Intuition never steers us wrong. It comes from a place of our highest good and guides us to growth and expansion. This guidance comes from our soul.

"Mind chatter is focused on keeping us 'safe.' This is where fear-based thoughts come from. Recognizing intuition as guidance and discerning between the two is life changing. It brings clarity and confidence in decision-making and the ability to take decisive action in every area of life.

"Everyone has intuition. What's different is the extent to which a person is tuned in."

Idea for Action

Be still. It's hard to hear when you're always doing.
Be present. Focus on where you are now, not the future or past.
Move. Make time for play and exercise. Movement creates space to receive and hear your inner guidance.
Trust. Pay attention and trust what you're receiving is right. You know what's best for you.
Choose differently. What's best isn't always logical. Your mind guides you based on past experience or what you believe is true, which might not be for your highest good.

For more on intuition follow Jennifer at jenniferspor.com.

Meditation

"Praying is the asking. Meditation is the receiving" – Unknown

Meditation helps controls anxiety, increases attention span, emotional control, self-awareness, and reduces stress. I decided to try meditation to increase my attention and learn to be present. I had no clue how to meditate, so my friend Jennifer Spor, an Olympian at meditation, gave me tips so I wouldn't fall asleep or ponder my to do list.

With her guidance I accomplished the following:

- Sat quietly, palms up, soles of my feet together
- Closed my eyes and took a deep, slow breath
- Set an intention to relax and have a clear mind

Breathing slowly and deeply, I viewed patterns on my eyelids and noticed the following:

- Gently pressed my tongue to the roof of my mouth
- Breathed more cleansing breaths
- Felt my hair touching my shoulders
- Noticed a slight stretch in the muscles of my spine
- Observed the silence of the room
- Took more deep cleansing breaths

When a thought came, I'd think, "Thank you." Then release.

Idea for Action

Download a mediation app such as Headspace, Calm, or Aura. Aura is the lowest cost option at the time of this writing. Add meditation time to your calendar with a reminder.

Mindfulness

"Our life is shaped by our mind, for we become what we think." – Buddha

Mindfulness is the state of being conscious and aware. It might seem strange to hear you should practice being conscious when you're awake an average of 15-17 hours each day.

However, if you read the entry *Mind and C.R.A.P. Boards* on page 50 in the *Health & Wellness* chapter, you know humans spend 60-70 percent of the day in a mind-wandering state.

Mindfulness practices help us regulate emotions and decrease stress, anxiety, and mood depression. We can increase our focus and observe our thoughts without judgment instead of our thoughts arising from our subconscious and negatively affecting our mood and well-being.

The benefits of mindfulness cannot be overstated, as it is shown to improve emotional and physical well-being.[75]

Idea for Action

Set an alarm on your phone to stand and stretch every hour. Yawn to increase oxygen to your brain and take several deep, cleansing breaths. Note how you feel at the end of the day compared to a day where you refrained from this exercise.

Experiment with over 2,000 free mindfulness exercises to find what works best for you at mindfulnessexercises.com.

Power of Music

"Where words fail, music speaks." – Hans Christian Andersen

Scientists and researchers have spent a great deal of time studying the importance of music. While *The Mozart Effect*—listening to classical music to make you smarter—has been proven a myth, music offers many benefits.

Music releases immune-boosting hormones and improves mood. Daniel Levitin, a researcher at McGill University, found people who listened to music were calmer before surgery than subjects who were given sedatives to help calm them.[76]

Who has not experienced the unparalleled sensation of nostalgia and excitement when a favorite song from your past comes on the radio?

I wrote a post on LinkedIn asking people to share a song which never fails to lift their mood. It generated a lot of engagement with some great song ideas! Check out the post at bit.ly/feelgoodsongpost.

Idea for Action

Write a list of a dozen or more songs which make you feel happy or inspired. Then create a playlist to listen to the next time you need a mood boost.

Prayer

"Our prayers may be awkward. Our attempts may be feeble. But since the power of prayer is in the one who hears it and not in the one who says it, our prayers do make a difference." – Max Lucado

An atheist until the age of 30, I didn't know how to pray. If you'd like to try prayer as a daily spiritual discipline, I hope this helps you. Following are four types of prayers:

- Prayers offering *praise* to God as an act of worship
- Prayers of *regret* or seeking forgiveness
- Prayers giving *thanks*
- Prayers of *supplication*: requests for ourselves or others

The primary purpose of prayer is to connect with God. Additional benefits include a stronger mindset and more positive outlook on life. Search online for "benefits of prayer" to discover more. Some might surprise you!

Idea for Action

Practice daily prayer time. The words you use matters less than having an open heart.

- Start with five minutes.
- Ask God to draw near you.
- Express things you're grateful for such as a person, sunshine, health, or a meal you enjoyed.
- Ask forgiveness for wrongdoings and regrets.
- Pray for people in need or who are suffering.
- Pray for yourself by requesting help you need.
- Ask for God's grace to help you through the next day.
- The Lord's Prayer is a great example.

God's Character

"We reflect God's character the most when we give freely of ourselves with no strings attached, no secret motives, no hidden agenda." – Craig Groeschel

Our view of God is often influenced by authority figures from our childhood. These are some common views of God:

Judge – A cold disciplinarian who punishes us if we screw up

Buddy – A permissive friend we don't take seriously

Genie – A giver of gifts or grantor of wishes

Distant Entity – A distant power. We understand God as Creator but have no relationship.

In reality, God is wise, faithful, loving, perfect, merciful, gracious, and great. These descriptions can be hard to accept if caregivers or parental figures did not emulate them.

Nonetheless, our behavior or experiences do not change God's character. God is unchanging and offers unconditional love.

Idea for Action

Reflect on your view of God, shaped by your family, experiences, and culture.

What are some ways you could accept God's unconditional love for you, trust His judgment, understand His timing is not your timing, respect His power, or enjoy His presence?

Waiting on God

"We want God's blessings now, not tomorrow. God isn't a microwave. God is a slow cooker!" – Bill Hood

I love making crockpot meals. My husband's favorites are pot roast and stew. I always know he's enjoying a meal because he makes funny little "Mmm" sounds as he eats.

To make his favorite crockpot meals, I need to plan ahead—usually seven hours beforehand.

Now, I *could* microwave the pot roast. Dinner would be ready faster, but I guarantee my husband wouldn't make joyful sounds.

Timing is part of learning to trust God. If we got everything we wanted when we wanted it, we wouldn't grow. A blessing given at the wrong time can be a curse. Our blessings should never get ahead of our character.

Do you struggle with waiting?

Idea for Action

Implement a daily practice of waiting on God:

1. Pray for the situation, then release it.
2. Spend time in scripture reading God's promises.
3. Surrender to God's timing instead of fighting Him.
4. Ask, "What lessons do I need to learn in this waiting?"
5. Keep your eyes on blessings not on what you lack.

Blessings

"Things you take for granted someone else is praying for." –
Marlan Rico Lee

You won't be blessed with everything, but you can choose to
be blessed by anything.

Family: blessing

A warm hug: blessing

A cozy blanket: blessing

A hot cup of tea: blessing

Quiet time alone: blessing

Laughs with friends: blessing

Clean drinking water: blessing

Reading a good book: blessing

The sun rising this morning: blessing

Going to bed without hunger: blessing

A challenge which brings growth or change: blessing

We don't need more blessings. We are already blessed. "Blessed
are they who see beautiful things in humble places where other
people see nothing." – Camille Pissarro

Ideas for Action

Write 3-5 blessings daily and listen to the song *Blessings* by
Laura Story for encouragement: bit.ly/blessingssong.

Worship

"Turn your worry into worship and watch God turn your battles into blessings." – Unknown

Worship is an expression of reverence and adoration. God does not want us to worship Him because he's an egomanic. He knows worship transforms us. It accentuates our joy, repels depression, strengthens our faith, brings us closer to God, and keeps us from obsessing over ourselves.

Worry and worship cannot coexist in the same moment. Since worry is a worthless time waster, worship throughout our day is a constructive use of our minds.

We worship in prayer through praise and giving thanks. We worship through song and dance. We worship by enjoying the beauty of the world and quietly spending time in God's presence. We worship by serving others and by reading scripture. Meditating on blessings with a posture of thanksgiving is one way I worship. How do you worship?

Ideas for Action

Choose a creative way to worship this week:

1. Lay in the grass, look at the sky, and talk to God.
2. Meditate on God's awesomeness on a hike.
3. Do a prayer walk in your neighborhood and pray for each home.
4. Read scripture aloud.
5. Pray for your city as you run errands or travel to work.

Miracles

"We live on a blue planet that circles around a ball of fire next to a moon that moves the sea, and you don't believe in miracles?" – Anonymous

Seventy-four percent of physicians believe miracles occurred in the past, and 73 percent hold the belief miracles occur today.[77]

It doesn't surprise me so many physicians believe in miracles. Miraculous recoveries, mysterious illnesses healed, and patients with a 1 percent chance of survival who recover are not as rare as they should be. Are those miracles? I'd like to think so.

The belief in miracles is fairly common, with similar numbers in the general population. Seventy-eight percent of people under the age of 30 believe in miracles versus 79 percent among those older than 30.[78]

If we change how we think of miracles, they become easy to believe. Life is a series of thousands of tiny miracles. In fact, you, yourself, are a miracle!

Ideas for Action

Would you like to live a more wonderous life? Actively look for miracles in everyday situations!

Try letting go of set outcomes. Leave room for miracles. The more attached you are to the way you think things should be, the more disappointed you'll be if things don't work out the way you expect. I like to say, "Everything will work out for my good in this situation."

Mystery of Life

"The great beauty of life is its mystery, the inability to know what course our life will take, and diligently work to transmute into our final form based upon a lifetime of constant discovery and enterprising effort. Accepting the unknown and unknowable eliminates regret." – Kilroy J. Oldster

A few years ago I met an unemployed man at a workshop. We spoke of his situation and what he might do next. He told me, "I like to leave room for the mystery of life."

His was a magnificent comment.

Ambiguity is often scary. Accepting the unknown requires letting go. Have you pondered the beauty of mystery?

I wonder why we enjoy some mysteries and don't enjoy others. I suppose it's control or how big the stakes are. Imagine if you knew what was in every present you opened for the rest of your life. No mystery, no anticipation. Wouldn't that stink?

Why do we look at unknowns and assume they are threatening, bad, or scary? Why not look at life's unknowns like unwrapped presents?

Idea for Action

Leave room to embrace the mystery of life. Mystery offers an opportunity to create an exciting future based on new information. Embrace the fun of not knowing and arrest fearful, "What if … ." thoughts. What if things are turning out exactly as they should?

Creativity

"Creativity involves breaking out of established patterns in order to look at things in a different way." – Edward de Bono

Creativity drives us not only to create but to innovate. Many things important to humans are the result of creativity.

Children commonly ask questions and explore, which means the curiosity behind creativity is in all of us. As we age, we sometimes leave creative thinking behind and become routinely set in our ways.

Land & Jarman conducted a famous study in 1968. At age five, 98 percent of participants scored at a genius level of creativity. By age 10, the number decreased to 30 percent. By age 15, only 12 percent of the children tested received a genius level score in creativity.[79]

Creativity is not a nice-to-have skill, it enhances our problem-solving ability by helping us generate ideas and solutions, making it an essential life skill.

Idea for Action

Implement a weekly creativity walk dedicated to entertaining your creative thoughts while taking a stroll. Stanford research shows walking improves creative thinking.[80]

Combine *Problem a Day* on page 43 with this creativity tip to take your walks to the next level.

Legalism

"Legalism lacks the supreme sense of worship. It obeys but it does not adore." – Geerhardus Vos

Legalism is dependence on moral law over personal faith. A person becomes more preoccupied with obeying religious laws than loving God. Criticism and judgment can sometimes follow. R.C. Sproul put it this way, "There's no love, joy, life, or passion. It's a rote, mechanical form of law-keeping."

A core characteristic of legalism is an attempt to assume complete control instead of recognizing, and yielding to, the power of God in our lives. What is our need for God if we can strive for moral perfection in our own strength?

Ideas for Action

Without criticizing or judging yourself, reflect on your personal faith. Do you walk your talk? Do your actions speak louder than your words?

As an example, let's take the world's two largest religions.

The essence of the Christian faith is grace, and the essence of Christian ethics is gratitude. If you are a Christian, does your life display grace and gratitude?

Islam teaches God is merciful. Does your life reflect mercy toward others in your thoughts and actions?

Create a personal faith statement expressing your beliefs and values. You don't need to be affiliated with a religion to create a statement of personal faith. Periodically assess your thoughts and actions against your faith statement.

Service & Social

The following topics are covered in Service & Social:

Love
Kindness
Mercy
Forgiveness
Grace
Generosity
Justice
Judging Others
Second Chances
Unity
Marriage: Keys to Success
Sex and Sexuality
Divorce
Reconciliation
Bitterness
Guilt
Death
Service
Stewardship
Spiritual Fatigue
Spirituality in Crisis

Love

"Love is patient, love is kind. It does not envy, it does not boast, it is not proud. It is not rude, it is not self-seeking, it is not easily angered, it keeps no record of wrongs." – 1 Corinthians 13:4-5 NIV

The word love is used often and casually by many: "I love that movie!" True love is selfless, which is not natural for most people.

Eight ancient Greek words describe the kinds of love:

Agape – unconditional love, love of mankind

Eros – romantic love

Philia – affectionate love, such as for friends

Philautia – self-love

Storge – love of parents for children

Pragma – enduring, lasting love

Ludus – playful love, infatuation

Mania – obsessive love; not a healthy kind of love

Which kinds of love have you experienced or offered?

Idea for Action

What kinds of love do you want in your life? To attract more love into your life, think of ways you can intentionally spread love to others this week. One solution is to vocalize your appreciation for others.

Kindness

"Do your little bit of good where you are; it's those little bits of good put together that overwhelm the world." – Desmond Tutu

Kindness is important for others but also for you, with correlations to happiness and health.

Professor David Orr said, "The plain fact is the planet does not need more successful people. But it does desperately need more peacemakers, healers, restorers, storytellers, and lovers of every kind. It needs people who live well in their places. It needs people of moral courage willing to join the fight to make the world habitable and humane. And these qualities have little to do with success as we have defined it."

Kindness is a key predictor of satisfaction and stability in marriage.[81]

Whom do you know who is consistently kind?

Ideas for Action

Seven daily tips to make kindness a habit:

1. Start a kindness journal. Track kind deeds from others and how their kindness impacted you.
2. Start small. Ask a cashier or barista, "How is your day?"
3. Set a kindness goal, a specific action, for the day.
4. Look for opportunities to express sincere appreciation.
5. Support a cause you believe in with time or resources.
6. Smile more.
7. Remember to be kind to yourself!

Mercy

"Blessed are the merciful, for they will be shown mercy." – Matthew 5:7 NIV

Mercy is compassion toward others, especially when we are in a position to treat them harshly.

Mercy chooses not to take offense. To see a situation through a lens of empathy. When we choose mercy, love and peace flow from us into the world.

Why mercy? Living a merciful life leads to a happier life. Plus, someday we will need mercy. We aren't perfect and will hurt others. If we have a reputation of showing mercy, we reap what we sow.

The story of the Good Samaritan is a wonderful example of mercy. A helpless Jewish man fell victim to thieves who beat him, robbed him, and left him to die. Samaritans and Jews despised each other, but the Samaritan helped the man. This is a tall order for many of us to fill. It's okay to start smaller!

Every act of mercy is a win against evil.

Ideas for Action

Choose one of the following six ideas to put into practice:

1. Resist sarcasm.
2. Write a letter of forgiveness to someone.
3. Offer a kind act to a person you don't get along with.
4. Carry $5 fast food gift cards for the homeless.
5. Hear someone's fear or hurt instead of losing patience.
6. Make a list of those who oppose you and pray for them.

Forgiveness

"Forgiveness is the fragrance that the violet sheds on the heel that has crushed it." – Mark Twain

You've heard countless times advice to forgive. Maybe you've even heard research shows unforgiveness shortens your life and degrades health. You've been told you've hurt people too. You've been advised forgiveness is for your benefit, not the person who hurt you.

Unforgiveness prevents you from living in the present because it enslaves you in the past. You can tell if you've forgiven someone by the way you react when his or her name is mentioned or when they walk into a room.

Are you wondering *how*, exactly, one forgives?

Ideas for Action

Dr. Wayne Dyer created 15-steps to forgiveness accessible at drwaynedyer.com/blog/how-to-forgive-someone-in-15-steps.

Choose someone you want to forgive and apply one of these methods:

Journal about the offense and thoughts you're experiencing.

Unforgiveness could stem from a termination, an unfaithful spouse, a friend who betrayed a confidence, or someone who stole from you.

List people you blame, including yourself.

Imagine unchaining yourself from a person or past situation.

Release each person as you state forgiveness for each.

Repeat the last two steps as often as needed.

Grace

"Grace is the love that gives, that loves the unlovely and the unlovable." – Oswald C. Hoffmann

Do you give people grace? Grace is a temporary exemption. An act of clemency. Lenience.

Grace isn't a free pass. A free pass says, "I will ignore what you did and not recognize it for what it was.

With grace, we can address difficult subjects and say, "What you said was hurtful. I want to be open with you instead of trying to cover it up and bury it. I forgive you. Let's figure out a way forward, so we can avoid this in the future."

Grace can help people change. By extending grace, we acknowledge we are a work in progress. After a person has received grace from another, she can be motivated to grow in humility.

If you extend grace to someone, and they don't care to invest in the relationship, you have a choice in the role they hold in your life. You can restructure your relationship with them. Relationships are a two-way street.

Has someone offered you grace? If so, what did it mean to you?

Ideas for Action

To extend grace to someone:

- Be honest, but kind.
- Seek to understand what they're going through.
- Share the impact they had on you with compassion.
- Tell them you are choosing to forgive them.

Generosity

"For it is in giving that we receive." – Francis of Assisi

Despite evil in the world, the human spirit bends toward generosity. During the coronavirus pandemic, actor John Krazinski created a YouTube channel called *Some Good News*. Each week showcased the creativity, kindness, resourcefulness and, yes, generosity of people around the world.

The inspiring stories, from people raising money to help furloughed workers to restaurants preparing meals for the unemployed, spurred others to join the generosity in their community.

The benefits of generosity are plentiful, but perhaps some don't believe they have the resources to be generous. Even if we don't have a lot to give financially, we can start small by donating one dollar at the grocery store when they collect money for nonprofit organizations.

Generosity doesn't require money. Be generous with your time by investing in a young person you believe in. Share what you know in online articles to help people in your area of expertise. You can find many ways to be generous.

Ideas for Action

1. Plan quarterly giving weeks during the year.
2. Collect unused clothes or items to donate.
3. Donate blood, or volunteer at a food pantry or shelter.
4. Ask your employer to participate in a financial match or a giving program.

Justice

"True peace is not merely the absence of tension: It is the presence of justice." – Martin Luther King Jr.

Justice is an ethical concept that people behave in a way which is fair, equal, and balanced for everyone. Justice is vital to create a safer society. The book, *The American Courts*, by Jeffrey A. Jenkins outlines four forms of justice:

Distributive – Economic justice: the fairness of what people receive

Procedural – Fair play, or believing a fair process was used

Restorative – Restitution or corrective justice. The simplest form is an apology but could include monetary payment.

Retributive – Punishment, such as incarceration

What form of justice do you see lacking in your community?

Idea for Action

Five ways to respond to injustice are:

1. Take a stand – Make changes where you contribute to injustice, such as people you hire or don't hire.

2. Speak up – Call out injustice. If you see bullying, speak up for others or help them exit the situation.

3. Share with others – Tell others when you become aware of injustice. Others might not agree, so don't keep pressing if they're unwilling to listen.

4. Vote – Use your right to vote to promote a just government.

5. Contact people with power – Call elected officials or the media.

Judging Others

"Hesitancy in judgment is the only true mark of a thinker." –
Dagobert D. Runes

We judge others by our own standards. We think our standards
are right and true. In reality they are arbitrary. In other words,
how we measure our life is how we judge others, and the
measurement is based on what we think is important.

For example, if a person values success, they will likely judge
others as winners or losers. If a person values intellect, others
might be judged as smart or dimwitted. If one consults a moral
standard of measurement, such as good deeds, they might
judge people according to perceived moral character.

If this same person is criticized, she might conclude the other
person is jealous of her success, intellect, or character. On the
flipside, if others are nice to a person, judgment might induce
suspicion of motive. Perhaps the person is trying to curry favor
to get close to them.

Do we want to be judged? People who live in glass houses
should not throw stones.

Idea for Action

Use mindfulness to observe when you judge others. Be curious
why you're judging and ask yourself these questions.

- What bias or preconceived notions do I have?
- Do I judge based on a past experience?
- Do I judge based on my values?
- Am I judging due to my limited view of the world?
- Am I jealous?
- Am I projecting? Is the judgment true of me?

Second Chances

"I did then what I knew how to do. Now that I know better, I do better." – Maya Angelou

There are no do-overs, but there are second chances. Do you give others second chances? Forgiving others increases your well-being and happiness. Second chances, however, do open you up to the possibility the person will disappoint you again. How do you know whether to give someone a second chance?

Decisions like this are largely made with emotions and are not cut and dry. However, you can evaluate a few questions to determine if a second chance makes sense:

1. Does the person accept blame and demonstrate insight or lessons learned from the mistake?
2. Does the person display empathy to those they hurt? Or is the remorse shown more for themselves?
3. Does the person have a pattern of this behavior or was it a one-off situation?
4. Does the person regret their mistake?

If a second chance doesn't seem right after answering these questions, you can confidently say yes to forgiveness and no to a second chance.

Idea for Action

If you decide to offer a second chance, first do some soul searching on what went wrong and your role in it. Take a cooling off period, if needed. Openly share your opinion and discuss realistic expectations going forward.

Unity

"Make every effort to keep the unity of the spirit through the bond of peace." – Ephesians 4:3 NIV

Unity opposes staunch individuality. When society is comprised of people who are primarily concerned for their desires and needs, suffering results. Life without unity equals life with division.

On an individual level, if our body acted independently of the other parts, it could not function. Our body is wonderfully designed and offers a beautiful illustration of interdependence.

Just as we have individual cells in our body, individual human beings collectively contribute to the total human experience. I resisted this concept for a long time. As a Western Generation Xer living in Canada, I was raised in individualism.

The only way to truly achieve unity with others is to release the false need to win, to be separate, to be right, and to have things your way. Preoccupation with our ego is a barrier to unity. Unity is part of community.

Idea for Action

Examine key relationships where unity is absent. Consider where you have common goals and work toward them without selfishness and with open communication, giving each other the benefit of the doubt. To be unified in our relationships, families, and even work teams, these factors must be present.

Marriage: Keys to Success

"The more you invest in your marriage, the more valuable it becomes." – Unknown

While no one has determined a right or wrong way to be married, some behaviors lead to the demise of a marriage, and others lead to a healthy marriage.

Dr. John Gottman conducted a study of couples and predicted with 94 percent accuracy which ones would divorce.[82] He found couples with six characteristics often divorce:

1. Harsh start to discussions, such as sarcasm or criticism
2. Criticism, contempt, defensiveness, and stonewalling
3. Overwhelming and sudden negativity
4. Body language reveals increased heart rate
5. Failed repair attempts – Couples cease to extend an olive branch.
6. Bad memories – Failure to look back on struggles and draw strength from them.

To build a strong marriage, Dr. Gottman suggests three areas of focus: create friendship, resolve conflict, and create shared meaning and goals.

Idea for Action

Want to further strengthen a healthy relationship? Visit healthymarriageandfamilies.org for resources and ideas.

Need help? Relentlessmarriage.com and reallifecounseling.us offer interventions with higher success rates than traditional counseling. Relentless Marriage offers free downloadable resources like "12 Rules for Fighting Fair."

Sex and Sexuality

"Your soul is your connection to the Divine. Sacred sex is an activity of joining souls in holy, celestial creation, expressing your appreciation for the gift of life, of sharing your body's vitality with another." – Brownell Landrum

Sex is a spiritual act. It is vital, expressive, bonding, and joyful. Sex can often be regarded as dirty because of selfish, exploitative, and abusive behaviors which have perverted what is meant to be a pure and beautiful expression of love.

In the most satisfying sexual relationships, partners put the other first—achieving pleasure through generosity, giving, sensitivity, and affection.

This is a difficult topic for people who've experienced trauma, abuse, or had a sexual partner who was hurtful. Reclaiming sex as a positive and enriching aspect of a relationship is emotionally and mentally difficult work, yet it is possible.

Idea for Action

Practice using your voice. Gently tell your partner what you enjoy and what you don't enjoy, in a supportive way. Ask her/him what they enjoy and don't enjoy. Write your sexual preferences as a safe way to start if you're not ready to talk. If the idea is uncomfortable for you, try speaking up. Sharing your preferences becomes comfortable with practice. A research study found couples who communicate about sex have better sex.[83]

The following resource offers guidance for talking about sex problems, including timing do's and don'ts: bit.ly/discusssexproblems.

Divorce

"And so rock bottom became the solid foundation on which I rebuilt my life." – J.K. Rowling

Psychologists suggest it takes a year for every five to seven years of marriage to get over a divorce, depending on the circumstances. Men take longer, even though they remarry faster than women.[84]

Divorce is difficult. I've read going through a divorce is experienced similarly to the steps of grief. I went through a divorce myself. In the moment, it seemed life would never get better. It sounds cliché to say, but this, too, shall pass.

My first husband and I have a cordial relationship now, and we're both happily remarried. At the time, I felt like a failure. I heaped guilt on myself and convinced myself the divorce would ruin our children's lives. Thankfully, they're happily adjusted young adults.

My youngest son told me when he was 13 he was so used to me being with my current husband, the thought of me married to his dad was weird.

Idea for Action

To cope with divorce, give yourself a break. Avoid power struggles and arguments with your ex. Allow people to support you. Take time to explore interests, and take care of your emotional and physical health.

Read this solid advice for coping with a divorce: www.mentalhelp.net/divorce/emotional-coping

Reconciliation

"Reconciliation heals the soul. The joy of rebuilding broken relationships and hearts. If it's healthy for your growth, forgive and love." – Unknown

Reconciliation ends estrangement. Not all relationships should reconcile. If the estrangement is for your safety or well-being, reconciliation is optional. Only forgiveness is needed.

Reconciliation is not a fast process and requires working through a series of steps, none of which can be skipped.

Take Responsibility – Without accountability for actions or wrongdoing, reconciliation is not possible. Excuses and blame must be released.

Admission and Remorse – This step is not required to forgive someone, but if reconciliation is a goal, admitting wrongdoing and sincerely expressing regret for one's actions is a prerequisite.

Forgiveness – If the transgressor takes ownership and remorse is sincerely expressed, the path clears to extend forgiveness.

Make Amends – For reconciliation to occur, restitution must be given for a loss or wrongdoing. Often restitution is financial but can also be made through acts of service.

Reconciliation – People agree to be friendly again or come to an agreement.

Idea for Action

If you are estranged and wish to reconcile, work through the first four steps. Read more on reconciliation at psychcentral.com/blog/reconciling-relationship-conflicts.

Bitterness

"Bitterness is how we punish ourselves for other people's sins."
– Matshona Dhliwayo

Bitterness is one of the most toxic human emotions.

The root of bitterness is hurt. Over time, hurt can fester into bitterness. Our anger becomes corrupt and transforms into self-righteousness, a kind of moral superiority over our wrongdoer.

However, bitterness comes with a hefty cost, including prolonged emotional pain, increased depression and stress, and undermined relationships as others turn away from our hostility, and an eroded sense of well-being.[85]

The keys to overcome bitterness are acceptance and forgiveness. Bitterness and forgiveness cannot simultaneously coexist inside you.

Ideas for Action

1. Make a list of people who hurt you. Write what you expected from each person.
2. Write how you felt when your needs or expectations were unmet next to each name.
3. Write down if you think the person will ever meet your needs. Be honest and realistic.
4. Think of times you haven't met the needs or expectations of others and try to have compassion for those who haven't met your needs and expectations.
5. Ask God to help you forgive others who have hurt you.

Guilt

"Guilt is to the spirit as pain is to the body." – David A. Bednar

Unlike shame, which is not constructive, guilt can be a useful tool. It upholds the standard of right and wrong in society.

Like anything, guilt can be used positively or negatively. If guilt causes you to ruminate and beat yourself up, that's not a productive use of the emotion.

However, if it prompts you to apologize and make amends for wrongdoing, that's a useful outcome. For guilt to be productive, it should prompt action. If you promised someone you would do something but have procrastinated, guilt could move you to deliver on your promise.

The key to productive guilt is harnessing the emotion and channeling it into something good. A common source of guilt is not calling or spending time with loved ones. Guilt can bring relationships back together.

Guilt can also cause the hurt person to forgive the offender since guilt is an indication of remorse.

Does guilt generally prompt you to action?

Idea for Action

Do you periodically experience guilt pangs? Why? Get to the bottom of why you feel guilty. What are your options to productively channel your guilt into action?

Death

"The song is ended but the melody lingers on." – Irving Berlin

When I was a young child, any time the phone rang at a late hour, I had a pang of fear someone was calling to say my grandma died. I have no idea why, but I know the fear of her death hung over my head like a cloud for decades. I'm grateful my grandmother died peacefully in her sleep shortly before her 99th birthday after 40 years of my misplaced worry.

Many, if not most, people fear either being dead, or the act of dying. Perhaps you no longer fear death, though you certainly don't invite it. I'm sure you know people you want to love, support, and enjoy life with for as long as possible.

When we fully embrace and knowingly accept we will die, our perception can shape the way we live our lives. We can become more accountable for the life we live and avoid the regrets of petty disagreements and grudges.

Realizing our life on earth is temporary can help us avoid sweating the small stuff, which frees our spirit to be kinder, more generous, and take the high road. Living life in view of our mortality offers us a valuable perspective encouraging us to be more grateful.

Idea for Action

Learn to accept mortality by getting comfortable discussing death. Consider completing the necessary administrative details of your death such as your will, funeral decision, and what you would like done with your remains. These plans can bring peace, if not remove fear.

Service

"Your job is to fill your own cup, so it overflows. Then, you can serve others, joyfully, from your saucer." – Lisa Nichols

In a world dominated by social media, it's easy to get caught up in our goals and dreams as we are reminded of the good life others appear to live. We see the highlight reels of our colleagues, friends, and families scrolling before our eyes day after day.

In *Volunteer Work* on page 314, I share positive benefits of volunteer work. Service is good for your soul.

Giving back to others can increase well-being, from lowering stress, depression, and loneliness, to expanding your social network.[86]

Organizations help people in your areas of interest, and you can get involved. For example, if you're interested in the environment, serve in an organization focused on conservation.

If you're concerned for a certain demographic, such as children, the elderly, or the unemployed, contact nonprofit organizations which serve those individuals.

Idea for Action

Google "local volunteer opportunities (your town/city)" to discover targeted opportunities to serve others in meaningful ways or visit volunteermatch.org. Adding meaning, purpose, and a greater sense of well-being to your life through service is a win/win.

Stewardship

"The one principle that surrounds everything else is that of stewardship; that we are the managers of everything God has given us." – Larry Burkett

Stewardship is supervising or taking care of something. An example is taking care of the earth and using its resources wisely. Stewardship is both a responsibility and an ethic.

The term originates from the tasks of domestic servants. The concept does not only apply to natural resources but also to our finances, health, property, and even information.

To be a good steward of our resources, we must love people and use things, rather than love things and use people. Being a good steward involves being faithful even when we have a little. We can still be generous no matter how much we've been given.

Another way to be a good steward is to avoid debt. We are unable to properly steward what we have been given when debt is strangling us. Debt causes us to pay interest instead of paying it forward and can also cause us to be less generous with what we have.

Finally, to be a good steward, we must not be wasteful. Some ways to avoid waste are to eat leftovers instead of throwing food away, repurpose items, and turn off the water when brushing our teeth.

Idea for Action

Want to be blessed? Bless someone else. Seek tangible ways to meet needs such as serving meals at your local food pantry.

Spiritual Fatigue

"Your body knows more about your spiritual well-being than your mind does. Teach your mind to listen to it." – Necole Stephens

Spiritual fatigue comes from serving others beyond your capacity. When you give of yourself to others to the point of exhaustion, you wind up spiritually fatigued.

Spiritual fatigue is not a "good" tired. Good tired is how you feel after a productive or satisfying day. Perhaps you planted a vegetable garden and feel satisfied, though physically depleted.

The dangerous form of tired comes after a prolonged, hectic stretch of weeks, months, or years. Our spirit tries to warn us something is wrong, but we keep going and ignore it. We might believe we need to rescue others, and our persistent hard work is honorable. More likely, those around us become concerned and disturbed by what they are witnessing. They might plead with us to take a break.

Sit quietly and listen to what your spirit tells you. If you have a sense something is wrong, it's a warning to listen before fatigue becomes a crisis.

Ideas for Action

1. Examine the *why* behind your fatigue. Are you serving outside your area of gifting or passion?

2. Examine your reasons for service. Do you set boundaries and observe them? Have you learned to say no to respect yourself and others?

Spirituality in Crisis

"Sometimes the chapter ends and you can keep re-reading it but it's over and to keep insisting on reading the same chapter prevents us from being free and actually living the rest of our days on earth." – Mimi Novic

Does spirituality make a difference in times of crisis? According to Gallup data, yes.

Frank Newport, a senior research scientist at Gallup, shares:

"A great deal of research, including analyses of Gallup data conducted by myself and my colleagues, has established the positive correlation between personal religiosity and well-being. Research using Gallup data conducted by researchers at MIT, Baylor, and Duke Universities shows religious Americans were better able than those who were less religious to weather the economic storm of the 2008 recession, at least in terms of well-being."[87]

Gallup found similar findings during the 9/11 terrorist attacks, and the COVID-19 global pandemic.[88]

Is your spirituality your first line of defense in crisis?

Idea for Action

Promote your spiritual well-being by intentionally engaging in self-transcendent emotions. When we focus on God and creation above ourselves, our observations become fixed on compassion, awe, gratitude, appreciation, inspiration, admiration, and love rather than our emotions of shame or embarrassment.

RELATIONSHIPS

"When dealing with people, remember you are not dealing with creatures of logic, but creatures of emotion."

Dale Carnegie

Life revolves around relationships.

I wrote this book during the 2020 COVID-19 global pandemic. People were largely expected to stay home except for necessities or working in jobs essential to the public.

Social media posts detailing the struggles of staying home, except for introverts, filled the feeds. Even celebrities expressed emotional strain from isolation despite their posh surroundings. These reactions underscore material possessions cannot fill our human need for love and connection with others.

Most of what I've learned concerning relationships came the hard way. I'm a better wife because my first marriage ended in divorce. I hope the following tips spare you bumps and bruises in your relationships. Entries are in Communication, Conflict, Couples & Family, and Self-Development.

Communication

The following topics are covered in Communication:

Listening
Assumptions
Acknowledging Feelings
Giving Feedback
Taking Feedback
Admitting Mistakes
Vulnerability
Agreement Building
Reassurance
Showing Appreciation
Respect
Giving Time and Space
Sparking Conversation
Little White Lies
Relationship Needs

Listening

"The word 'listen' contains the same letters as the word 'silent'." – Alfred Brendel

It's safe to say the goal of communication is to be understood. Yet many of us listen to others to respond, not to deeply understand. Our goal should be to exercise the three levels of listening:

Level 1: Listen for information. Most people don't move beyond Level 1. We listen long enough to grasp the basics then shift our attention to problem solving, defending, or responding.

Level 2: Listen for impact. If you listen only for information, you're likely to miss the true message. Move beyond what's said, and consider the impact on people involved.

Level 3: Listen for what's not being said. I refer to this as listening between the lines.

Idea for Action

Practice listening between the lines:

- Listen carefully to the words a person uses.
- Ask questions to get to the truth.
- Ask for clarification when hearing mixed messages.

Assumptions

"Assumptions are the termites of relationships." – Henry Winkler

Human beings make assumptions regularly, often without realizing it. We treat our assumptions as fact, and our emotions soon follow.

"She's dismissing my ideas because she's threatened by me."
"He's not promoting me because he doesn't like me."
"She doesn't include me in decisions because she's a control freak."

In any situation many explanations are possible. Some circumstances might be the result of our own blind spots. Instead of assuming, ask. Open, honest communication works best.

"During the past few weeks, I've observed _____. Would you help me understand what led to the decision?"

I've presented three ideas this quarter, all rejected. I'd be interested in feedback to present ideas differently to increase acceptance."

The gap between love and hate is created by misunderstandings.

Idea for Action

Monitor your reactions for assumptions.

1. Challenge yourself to consider possible alternatives.
2. Give people the benefit of the doubt.
3. Ask!

Acknowledging Feelings

"When a person tells you that you hurt them, you don't get to decide that you didn't." – Louis C. K.

Acknowledging a person's feelings doesn't mean you agree with his or her feelings. It gives a person's emotions space to exist instead of shutting them down. Invalidation resembles this:

"Well, I'm sorry you feel that way."
"You're being too sensitive."
"I'm not having this discussion."

It says, "I don't care about you," which is highly destructive in relationships.

Instead, to acknowledge a person's feelings:

1. Remember, validation doesn't require agreement.
2. Avoid being defensive.
3. Listen with intent to understand.
4. Reflect by saying, "I can see (hear) you're upset."
5. Summarize: I understand you're upset I haven't returned your calls.

Idea for Action

Assess and indicate difficulty level of acknowledging feelings on the continuum below. Ask a close friend or partner to rate his/her perception of you. If moderate or difficult, keep practicing the five steps.

|--|

Easy   Moderate   Difficult

Giving Feedback

"Criticism, like rain, should be gentle enough to nourish a man's growth without destroying his roots." – Frank A. Clark

Feedback, given poorly, has the power to cause destruction and despair. Feedback delivered well uplifts, encourages, and appreciates. My mother taught me a simple, yet effective, process to give feedback she calls a Plus/Delta.

Plus (What's going well?)

Ask the person what they think is going well with whatever you're evaluating. After they finish listing what's going well, add something you think the person is doing well.

Delta (What needs to change?)

Next, ask the person to list what they think could be done better or what needs to change. After the person is finished, if they mentioned your concern, state your agreement on the item and expand the conversation to offer your observation. If they haven't mentioned what you think needs to change, add it to the list after they've finished.

Idea for Action

Practice giving feedback using the Plus/Delta model with a trusted friend before giving feedback to someone else. Ask your friend to give input on how well you delivered your message in a direct and respectful manner.

Taking Feedback

"Feedback is the breakfast of champions." – Ken Blanchard

Everyone's a critic. Lila Smith, founder of Say Things Better, shares some unsolicited feedback is constructive, and some seems like an attack.

She says it's our job to learn and be open. We should gratefully receive anything we can use to be better. Why?

She explains it helps us to have better relationships and increase our potential for upward mobility.

The alternative is to go through life resentful and negative, carrying the weight of thinking you are being judged.

She adds, "You miss out on your potential for impact, in your relationships, and to grow in your personal life."

Idea for Action

Lila's tip for taking feedback comes from a dramaturgical research technique from her work in theater.

When receiving seemingly negative feedback, black out with a mental marker any words that are offensive. Do this until you have the main message of what can be actioned out.

What would it look like if you saw only the words?
Which words would you remove to find useable information?

Cross out negative tone and words to find what you need to understand and act on.

For more communication tips, follow Lila Smith on LinkedIn at linkedin.com/in/lilasmith.

Admitting Mistakes

"Mistakes are always forgivable, if one has the courage to admit them." – Bruce Lee

What makes it so hard for people to admit mistakes? Cognitive dissonance.

According to Carol Tavris, coauthor of *Mistakes Were Made (But Not by Me)*, "Cognitive dissonance is what we feel when the self-concept—I'm smart, I'm kind, I'm convinced this belief is true—is threatened by evidence we did something that wasn't smart, that we did something that hurt another person, that the belief isn't true."

To ease the discomfort of cognitive dissonance, we either dismiss the evidence or change our concept of ourselves—the former being the easier path. Failing to admit mistakes creates more problems, damages our credibility, and causes others to lose respect for us.

Idea for Action

Consider these five steps to immediately admit a mistake:

1. Apologize sincerely.
2. Take ownership of the mistake.
3. Create a plan to clean up the mess.
4. Accept the consequences of your mistake.
5. Put yourself in other people's shoes, showing compassion, if your mistake hurt others.

Vulnerability

"Vulnerability is our most accurate measurement of courage."
– Brené Brown

Brené Brown's TEDx talk, *The Power of Vulnerability*, is one of the top 10 most viewed TED talks in the world.

Vulnerability is hard. It exposes us, which could lead to the possibility of attack or harm.

Why should we be willing to be vulnerable? When we reject vulnerability, we deny people who care for us the opportunity to truly know us. We restrict intimacy and, therefore, the quality and depth of our relationships.

Brown says, "The difficult thing is that vulnerability is the first thing I look for in you and the last thing I'm willing to show you. In you, it's courage and daring. In me, it's weakness."

Interpreting vulnerability in others as courageous makes sense. Most of us instinctively don't trust people who always project perfection.

Do you struggle with vulnerability? Do you consider letting people see the real you as weakness?

Ideas for Action

Reflect:
1. What is my fear?
2. How and why do I want to be braver?
3. How am I protecting myself from being seen?

Watch Brené Brown's talk on vulnerability: bit.ly/bbrowntedx

Agreement Building

"It's hard to be on the same page when you're reading different books." – Unknown

Have you ever been in a meeting where no agreement was reached, or the action items were outlined but lacked clarity on who was doing what?

Meetings without decisions or accountability agreed upon wastes everyone's time.

Before leaving a discussion, participants must know everyone supports the decisions made, and are clear on next steps. Agreement building gives all parties the information needed for accountability and follow through.

Agreement building also ensures decisions are communicated to people impacted, even if they weren't in the meeting. It also helps make sure appropriate actions are taken.

At the end of a meeting or discussion, engage in agreement building to confirm everyone understands what is expected.

Idea for Action

Document conversations to create a record of decisions made and next steps. Use the following questions for agreement building:

1. What decisions did we make?
2. Who is completing each action item? By what date?
3. Who isn't here who should know what we decided?

Reassurance

"We can only reach the highest height, if we encourage each other." – Lailah Gifty Akita

In relationships, different personality types have different priorities, needs, and preferences. In general, relationship-oriented individuals want to be on good terms with people and to be liked.

Because of these relationship needs these individuals are likely to need reassurance the relationship is okay during conflict.

You might notice they make repair attempts to smooth things over with you during and after a conflict. This is because providing and receiving reassurance is important to them.

While others might move past disagreements quickly, relationship-oriented people hang on to hurt feelings and might worry the relationship has been damaged.

Idea for Action

Ask for reassurance when you need it:

"Look, I need some reassurance, because I'm feeling ... ."

Offer reassurance if the person you've had a disagreement with needs it. Be present, listen, and tell the other person you're there for them.

Show Appreciation

"If you don't show appreciation to those that deserve it, they'll learn to stop doing the things you appreciate." – Unknown

I once read a story of two rooms in the book, *The Love Dare*, by screen writers Stephen and Alex Kendrick. Though the illustration applied to marriage, it's relevant to all relationships.

The first room is the Appreciation room. This is where we spend time pondering a person's positive qualities. As we spend time in this room, our good opinion, affection, and positive regard for a person increases.

Conversely, as we spend time in the Depreciation room, we dwell on our irritations and amplify the weaknesses and failures of the person. People fall out of love and create enemies in this room.

Ideas for Action

Observe your daily thoughts regarding key people in your life for one week. Are you appreciating or depreciating the people in your life?

Intentionally look for what you can appreciate about others rather than depreciating them.

Respect

"One of the most sincere forms of respect is actually listening to what another has to say." – Bryant H. McGill

Similar to trust, respect isn't something you pursue directly. Respect is formed from a series of consistently lived out traits and behaviors.

Six ways to demonstrate respect:
Listen to others.
Affirm others.
Serve others.
Be kind to others.
Be polite to others.
Be thankful for others.

Six ways to earn respect:
Conduct yourself with integrity (be honest, reliable, fair).
Manage your emotions (respond versus react).
Speak up for others—and yourself.
Have an open mind.
Practice humility.
Learn to say no.

Idea for Action

Write the name of someone you respect. List behaviors or attributes he or she exhibits which you admire.

List ideas to consistently incorporate the behaviors or attributes you listed into your own life.

Giving Time and Space

"Sometimes the best thing you can do for someone you love is to give them time and space to think." – Unknown

Each individual in any adult relationship should be a fully functioning and independent person. Together, people in relationships become interdependent, or two self-reliant people who are mutually reliant on each other.

Sometimes, in a relationship, people need time or space to themselves. This is healthy and shouldn't hurt your feelings. Give both yourself and other people space when they need it to process information, discharge emotions from a tough day, recharge the body battery, and just "be."

Allowing people room to breathe gives them respect and shows them you care. If you resist, you place your needs first, and they will never forget it.

Idea for Action

Tips to handle a request for space:

1. Resist taking it personally. It's about them.
2. Thank him/her for being open and honest.
3. Ask him/her to define what giving space looks like.
4. Respect the request by giving him/her what they need.
5. Use the time to enjoy hobbies, family, and friendships.

Spark Conversation

"Good conversation is just as stimulating as black coffee and just as hard to sleep after." – Anne Morrow Lindbergh

Conversation is a cornerstone of any satisfying relationship. When one or both people lose interest in each other, they can get stuck in a rut of small talk or no talk. Once they get caught up on what happened that day ... crickets.

The good news is you can stimulate good conversation. To build an enduring friendship, continue to ask questions to get to know each other better.

Affirming conversations explore what you appreciate about a friend or partner. Share what you value and admire about the other person.

For romantic relationships, couples who talk about sex have better sex. Sensual conversations can add playfulness to your relationship. Discuss boundaries so the conversation feels safe.

Ideas for Action

Incorporate relationship-building discussions as a weekly or monthly practice. Search "relationship building conversations" online for ideas or check out these resources:

The six types of relationship-strengthening conversations are explained, along with ideas, at mantelligence.com/relationship-questions.

Want to add sizzle to your marriage? Try the book, *Let's Talk About ... Sexual Fantasies and Desires: Questions and Conversation Starters for Couples Exploring Their Sexual Interests*, by J.R. James.

Little White Lies

"A single lie discovered is enough to create doubt in every truth expressed." – Farrah Gray

People have various motives to lie. They lie for a reason. Do motives matter? Your values govern how you view white lies.

Someone lies to us every day. And we lie too. According to research, the average person lies 1-2 times per day.[89] Not so sure? Do you ever give insincere compliments? Have you told someone you were well when you felt awful? Do you tell people you're busy to avoid going somewhere? Have you told a child Santa is real?

Some lies we tell are "prosocial" lies—falsehoods told for someone else's benefit, as opposed to "antisocial" lies told for your gain.[90] A silver lining is prosocial lies require compassion. You tell a friend his bad singing isn't bad to avoid inflicting pain. However, if he plans to audition for a singing competition, the lie benefits you over your friend.

Empathic connection drives white lies, but are they acceptable? You can say nothing, deflect with humor, or tell the truth from a loving place. A question to consider is, "Are you first being truthful to yourself?"

Ideas for Action

Consider who a white lie benefits before telling one. If a friend asks if an outfit looks nice for an interview (which doesn't) you can tell the truth by suggesting outfits flattering to their body type. Offer to help find something to make them feel confident. Also, watch Jeff Hancock's TEDx talk on the science of lying, bit.ly/scienceoflying.

Relationship Needs

"You don't need someone to complete you. You only need someone to accept you completely." – Rapunzel, Tangled (2010)

All relationships need basic ingredients to grow and thrive. According to therapist Dr. Barton Goldsmith, we have 10 basic relationship needs:[91]

1. Regular kind and honest communication
2. Willingness to work through disagreements
3. Humor and fun to deal with life's challenges
4. Sharing life lessons to better the relationship
5. Support, affirmation, or compliments
6. Love and intimacy (Add romance and sex for partners.)
7. Sharing goals and dreams
8. Compassion, acceptance, forgiveness
9. Shared interest to try new things and experiences
10. Admitting and discussing mistakes

Idea for Action

On a scale of 1 to 10 (1 being the lowest and 10 the highest) rate the 10 relationship needs with a key person in your life.

Ask the other person to also rate the 10 needs and discuss your answers.

What needs did you rate similarly? What needs did you rate with greater than a two-point difference? Discuss reasons for the differences and ideas to improve areas with a score below eight.

Conflict

The following topics are covered in Conflict:

Healthy Conflict
Personality Conflict
Root Cause of Problems
Games People Play
Picking Your Battles
Apologies
Seek Resolution
Compromise
Fight Fair
Arguing
Belittling
Caving In
Defensiveness
Dismissing Opinions
Drama
Exaggerating
Exclusion
Finger Pointing
Gossip
Hypercriticism
Overpowering
Passive Aggression
Revenge
Sabotage
Sarcasm
Stonewalling
Withdrawing

Healthy Conflict

"Peace is not absence of conflict. It is the ability to handle conflict by peaceful means." – Ronald Reagan

Healthy conflict is good for your relationships! It might sound counterintuitive, but healthy conflict builds intimacy.

Conflict can tear relationships apart when destructive behaviors are employed. The key to healthy conflict is even though you disagree, you retain and display respect for each other.

Some benefits of healthy conflict include surfacing pent-up issues so they can be resolved, increased trust and confidence in the relationship, and making better decisions because topics are fully and openly discussed.

The best relationships aren't absent of conflict. They are able to successfully resolve conflict.

Idea for Action

Eight steps to practice healthy conflict:

1. Be direct with respect.
2. Be clear and to the point to avoid confusing the issue.
3. Observe the person's reactions and adjust.
4. Use "I" language, not "you" language.
5. Focus on the issue, not the person.
6. Listen carefully and paraphrase back if needed.
7. Seek to understand rather than convince.
8. Agree to disagree.

Personality Conflict

"Wherever you have people, you have factions and disagreements and personality conflicts." – Jerry B. Jenkins

Personality conflicts arise because people have different needs and priorities. When priorities differ, we find ourselves in disagreement. How we respond determines if the relationship succeeds.

Dominant people are *direct* and *strong-willed* and prioritize getting *results*.

Influential people are *outgoing* and *enthusiastic* and prioritize *collaboration*.

Steady people are *accommodating* and *patient* and prioritize *supporting others*.

Conscientious people are *analytical* and *reserved* and prioritize *accuracy*.

People who adapt to the needs of others have the most effective relationships.

Idea for Action

Think of a person with whom you have conflict. Identify their style and try these strategies:

Dominant: Be brief and focus on the bottom line.

Influential: Acknowledge feelings; include them.

Steady: Encourage them to speak up; express concern for them.

Conscientious: Avoid emotional displays, be objective and factual.

Root Cause of Problems

"There are a thousand hacking at the branches of evil to one who is striking at the root." – Henry David Thoreau

When we don't eliminate the root of a problem, the challenge will keep resurfacing. While true with all problems, this is especially relevant for relationships and conflict.

Do you find yourself continually having a particular issue crop up with a person in your life? If you don't seem to be making progress, it's possible you haven't gotten to the root of the issue. Until you do, nothing will change. You'll keep going around, doing the same dance, staying stuck in a rut.

Critical thinking techniques can help surface the cause of a recurring problem.

Idea for Action

Use the *5 Whys* technique to find the root of a problem.

- Identify a problem you're having.
- Ask "why" the problem is occurring. Base your answer on facts. You should be able to offer evidence.
- Ask "why" again to dig deeper into the problem.
- Continue the process until you reach the root cause. You should identify the root cause after asking "why" 3-5 times.
- Generate solutions once you've identified the cause to prevent a reoccurrence.

Games People Play

"Oh the games people play now, every night and every day now, never meaning what they say now, never saying what they mean." – Joe South

Why do people play games in relationships? The illusion of control. Games include expecting the other person to read his or her mind, power trips, and not saying what you mean.

Games frustrate everyone because they lack a key ingredient of successful relationships: clear communication.

Expecting people to read your mind – Unspoken expectations and assumptions cause everyone to become frustrated when one person doesn't correctly guess the other person's expectations

Power trips – Exerting one's influence or authority over another

Not saying what you mean – Only 18 percent of people are assertive enough to say what they think or feel.[92] The rest never learn how or shrink from conflict. Alternatives to saying what you mean are the silent treatment or passive aggressive communication.

Relying on subtle or passive aggressive communication sets you up for unhealthy relationships.

Idea for Action

When someone is playing games, constructively call it out. Ask them to communicate using a "direct with respect" approach. If it's you, stop. Discuss reasons why open communication is not present and hold each other accountable.

Picking Your Battles

"Don't let something that doesn't matter cause you to lose something that does." – Steve Jobs

People will disappoint us, and we will disappoint them. When addressing a frustration with someone in your life, choose to be calm and direct rather than argumentative or passive aggressive (See *Passive Aggression* on page 197.) Ask yourself, "In what scenario will everyone win?"

Not all frustrations must be aired. Sometimes a perceived problem is rooted in our own insecurities, past hurts, personal preferences, and arbitrary expectations. While it's important to be honest regarding our struggles, it's not another person's job to manage our healing or live up to our expectations.

We have to do the inside work ourselves.

Idea for Action

Evaluate your battles:

1. Is this problem *truly* important?

    a. No? Let it go.
    b. Yes? See #2.

2. Do the benefits of going to battle outweigh the costs?

    a. No? Let it go.
    b. Yes? Address calmly, seeking a win/win.

Apologies

"The best apology is changed behavior." – Unknown

Is it hard for you to sincerely apologize? It is for many people.

Renee Garfinkel, PhD, author, psychologist, and radio host shares why in one of the best explanations I've read. The following quote is from her article, "What's so Tough About Apologizing?" published in *Psychology Today*.

"Apologizing is difficult because it requires humility. Apologizing temporarily reduces one's self-esteem. The offender who apologizes yields some power, some control. Having announced their imperfection and error, the offender is now vulnerable. It takes humility to make a sincere apology, and for some people humility is just too uncomfortably close to humiliation. True narcissists never apologize."[93]

Idea for Action

Assess your difficulty apologizing. Mark it on the continuum. Ask a close friend or partner to rate their perception.

|--|

Easy   Moderate   Difficult

If you scored moderate-to-difficult, practice these steps:

1. Say, "I'm sorry."
2. Admit responsibility without excuse.
3. Find a way, or ask how, to make amends.
4. Express a commitment to not repeat the offense.

Seeking Resolution

"Sometimes, God doesn't send you into a battle to win it; he sends you to end it."– Shannon L. Alder

We've all witnessed disagreements ending in hostility. Perhaps we've been involved in such conflicts. Disputes aren't necessarily bad. Gary Smalley reveals in his book, *The DNA of Relationships,* resolved conflict builds greater intimacy. Deep intimacy is achieved by getting to the other side of a conflict.

Rather than dig our heels in with a focus on being right, we must focus on the goal of our relationships being *effective*.

Ideas for Action

How hard is seeking resolution? Mark it on the continuum. Ask a close friend or partner to rate their perception of you.

|--|

Easy   Moderate   Difficult

In the book, *Getting to Yes*, Roger Fisher and William Ury developed the Interest-Based Relational (IBR) approach to conflict resolution. The six steps are:

1. Make sure good relationships are a priority.
2. Separate people from problems.
3. Listen carefully to different points of view.
4. Listen first, talk second.
5. Set out the "facts."
6. Explore options together.

For more on the IBR method of conflict resolution visit bit.ly/mindtoolsibr.

Compromise

"It's time to recognize what compromise means: No side wins or loses all." – Madeleine M. Kunin

Compromise is a willingness to discuss a resolution rather than insisting on a win/lose outcome. In relationships, win/lose is lose/lose.

When I was a young adult, I called my mother and complained about a disagreement with someone. My mother asked, "How does being right serve you? Do you want to be right, or do you want to be happy?"

Our relationships suffer if we always insist on our way. And, truly, who do we think we are, anyway? Refusing to compromise in our relationships is selfish.

Idea for Action

Practice these behaviors when seeking a compromise:

1. Be honest about your feelings.
2. Let go of the goal to be right.
3. Release your expectations of others.
4. Keep an open mind. Put all options on the table.
5. Start with small changes to find middle ground:
    a. "If you do this for me, I'll do this for you."
    b. "Let's try your way this week and mine next."
6. Show appreciation: Acknowledge someone who was willing to compromise. Behavior rewarded gets repeated.

Fighting Fair

"Explain your anger, don't express it, and you will immediately open the door to solutions instead of arguments." – Unknown

Do you set ground rules for disagreements in relationships? Guidelines remind us to step back when boundaries are crossed.

Recognize the kind of fighter you and your partner are. Do you:

- Avoid conflict?
- Believe criticism or disagreement is an attack?
- Hit "below the belt"?
- Raise your voice?
- Feel out of control when conflict arises?
- Withdraw and become silent?
- Store up complaints from the past?

Know your pitfalls to customize ground rules for your relationship. Some basic guidelines are no name calling and no put downs. Stay on topic, and be respectful. What ground rules should you add based on your fighting tendencies?

If ground rules aren't helping, and your disputes seem insurmountable, consider seeking help from a professional.

Idea for Action

Throw a flag as part of your ground rules. "We agreed in our ground rules we will never _____. Let's take a break, calm down, and pick a time to resume the conversation."

Arguing

"Arguing isn't communication, it's noise." – Tony Gaskins

Sometimes we have so much confidence in our opinions it's frustrating when others can't see what's obvious to us. As frustration grows, we might defend our position aggressively. The other person not backing down could intensify our need to assert ourselves. Unhealthy exchange centers on winning, not finding a solution.

We protect our ego, put others in their place, or give up as little ground as possible. We don't evaluate another person's position objectively when we're upset.

Thoughts leading to arguing include:

"There's no way I'm backing down."
"I don't get you. I'm obviously right!"

Idea for Action

Overcome arguing: Reflect and reframe.

Reflect. Step back from your emotions.

Is my thought actually true?
Am I overreacting or exaggerating the problem?
Is there another way I could look at the situation?

Reframe. Instead of: "He has no idea what he is talking about,"

Try: "He is coming at this from a different perspective than I am."

Belittling

"He called her dreams stupid. It was then she realized she was here to serve a greater purpose. Not to be defeated, she carried on." – Toni Payne

Belittling is making someone feel unimportant. There's no one-size-fits-all reason why people belittle others. Some people are unaware of their behavior and might say a person is too sensitive or dismiss it as joking.

People might belittle because they have unresolved anger. Other times the behavior is rooted in insecurity, and they put others down to lift their perception of themselves. Regardless, realize belittling behavior destroys relationships.

Thoughts leading to belittling include:

"I will make you look like a fool."
"I will show you your opinion doesn't matter."

Idea for Action

Overcome belittling: Reflect and reframe.

Reflect.

Has someone accused me of putting a person down?
Did I justify or defend my behavior?
Do I have unresolved resentment toward the person?
Am I struggling with insecurities another person triggers?

Reframe. Instead of, "She is being so sensitive,"

Try: "Maybe I'm not coming across as I intend."

Caving In

"You gotta know when to hold 'em, know when to fold 'em, know when to walk away, know when to run." – Kenny Rogers, "The Gambler"

Caving in is giving in to something after first opposing it.

Caving in can be tempting; it seems the quickest path to end a disagreement. You might actually be sacrificing legitimate rights. The pain of conflict can cause us to take shelter. The short-term gain of this option, however, comes at the expense of long-term resolution and can create unbalanced and unhealthy power dynamics in your relationships.

Thoughts leading to caving in include:

"I don't want to upset anyone."
"Putting up a fight just isn't worth it."

Healthy conflict increases commitment and accountability.[94]

Idea for Action

Overcome caving in: Reflect and reframe.

Reflect.

Do I often let others have their way to avoid personal discomfort?

Will I be satisfied with the outcome if I give in, or will I be resentful?

Reframe. Instead of: "If I speak up, things could get messy,"

Try: "It's important I share my viewpoint. I will share my concerns openly."

Defensiveness

"You can't see clearly through defensiveness." – Bryant McGill

Defensiveness is being protective in the face of criticism. When we trust things will be okay when faced with criticism, we have no reason to be defensive. We can be open to different opinions.

At the heart of defensiveness is insecurity. We don't want to admit failure, shortcomings, or be wrong. Did you know our brains treat an intellectual threat the same a physical one?

Thoughts leading to defensiveness include:

"Her opinion is off base."
"This isn't my fault."

Do you view criticism as a win/lose?
Is there a reason you won't face your shortcomings?
Is it possible the person is giving feedback because he cares?

Idea for Action

Practice these four steps the next time you receive critical feedback:

1. Choose to be open, receptive, and curious about other perspectives.
2. Take a slow, deep breath before you respond.
3. Look for opportunities in the feedback to grow.
4. Ask the person for suggestions to improve.

Dismissing Opinions

"When people can't cope with who you've become, they will try to remind you who you once were." – Wayne Gerard Trotman

When we dismiss opinions, we treat others as unimportant.

Dismissing is a blocking strategy to win an argument and an ego protection mechanism. We dismiss opinions when someone paints a picture we don't like. If we are insecure, fearful, or challenged, we override the other person. The "backfire effect" causes us to reject anything that doesn't align with our worldview.

Thoughts leading to dismissing opinions sound like:

"Nothing anyone says will change my mind."
"There's no other way to think about this."

We can choose to attempt to understand the opinions of others whether or not we agree.

Idea for Action

Overcome dismissing opinions: Reflect and reframe.

Reflect.

How do I react when faced with different opinions? Am I curious and interested in learning other views?

Reframe. Instead of: "If this person can't see the obvious truth they are stupid, evil, or both,"

Try: "I'm curious to understand why their opinion is so different. I'll ask questions and listen to their point of view. I still might disagree, but I will hear them out."

Drama

"Drama does not walk into your life. Either you create it, invite it, or associate with it." – Brandi L. Bates

When we display over-the-top reactions to situations, we create drama.

In essence, when we create drama, we are drawing attention to a troubling situation. The attention we draw to ourselves validates our dilemma and the severity of the injustice done to us. Creating drama can also produce a sense of control where we feel powerless. Ultimately, we undermine ourselves and cause people to dismiss us or not take us seriously.

Thoughts leading to drama include:

"Everyone is against me!"
"This situation is unfair and hopeless!"

Idea for Action

Reflect.

Do I react dramatically before attempting to problem-solve?

Reframe. Instead of: "This situation is so unfair!"

Try: "This wasn't what I wanted to happen, but I'll take slow, deep breaths and try to think of some solutions."

Skip drama and move to problem-solving, asking for the help you need.

Exaggerating

"Man is inclined to exaggerate almost everything – except his own mistakes." – Unknown

Exaggeration is representing something as being worse than it is. Sometimes a minor offense can make us extremely upset.

Thoughts, sometimes unconscious, leading to exaggerating sound like:

"I need to get your attention."
"This needs to sound as bad as it feels."

Exaggeration can damage relationships because people might take you at your word and believe you lied. Also, when you do have something extreme to say, people are less likely to listen.

Idea for Action

Reflect.

Would two reasonable people justify the intensity of my emotions in this situation?

Am I trying to make a person's behavior seem more terrible?

Reframe. Instead of: "People need to know what an awful thing she did,"

Try: "I feel upset and offended. I will share the impact of what she said [did], and ask her to explain her side."

Choose to constructively express your opinions. Offer feedback and ask the other person to share their point of view. For example, "I need your help with what just happened. Do you have a few minutes to talk? I want to hear your perspective and share mine, as well."

Exclusion

"Exclusion is never the path forward on our shared paths to freedom and justice." – Desmond Tutu

Exclusion is deliberatively leaving someone out. During conflict, it's common to exclude someone because we don't want to spend time with them.

However, exclusion goes beyond just avoiding someone. It can damage their connection to the other people in the group, whether on a team or in a family.

Thoughts leading to exclusion sound like:

"Maybe you'll get the message if I don't invite you."
"Leaving you out will show everyone's on my side."

Idea for Action

Reflect.

Do I exclude people as a way to shape how people perceive a conflict and gain support?

Do I use exclusion to increase my own status?

Reframe.

Instead of: "If I don't invite them, things will go much easier for me,"

Try: "Working with him is a challenge, but learning to manage the relationship will demonstrate I am a leader."

Choose to include others, even if they challenge or disagree with you. Growth comes from struggle.

Finger-Pointing

"Wherever you find a problem, you will usually find the finger-pointing of blame. Society is addicted to playing the victim." – Stephen R. Covey

Finger-pointing appears as an aggressive behavior, but it usually stems from defensiveness. We divert attention away from our own shortcomings and failures by pointing them out in someone else.

By shifting blame, we might save our reputation in the short term, but we risk damaging our integrity in the long term.

Thoughts leading to finger-pointing include:

"I shouldn't get in trouble for this ... It's all their fault."
"This is because of you, not me."

Choose a productive attitude, rising above who is right or wrong. Being right serves only to stroke our ego and is insufficient for being effective in relationships.

Idea for Action

Reflect.

Do I minimize or ignore how I might have contributed to the situation?

When reviewing past conflicts, do I ever accept blame, or do I more often shift blame?

Reframe.

Instead of: "You're wrong, and I'm right,"

Try: "Let's focus on getting to the truth and what to do instead of who is right or wrong."

Gossip

"Great minds discuss ideas. Average minds discuss events. Small minds discuss people." – Eleanor Roosevelt

Gossip can feel good. We gossip with people we trust, and they affirm our opinion. Tearing down someone who hurt us can be satisfying.

Gossip can relate to power. It rallies people to our side by getting our perspective out first and most convincingly. Gossip can create a perceived sense of authority as people turn to us for inside knowledge. People who gossip might be insecure about their status or position.

Thoughts leading to gossip include:

"I will tell everyone what so-and-so did to me."
"I probably shouldn't say anything, but they deserve it."

Show respect to everyone, not as a reflection of their character, but a reflection of yours. The truth always comes out.

Idea for Action

Reflect. When sharing information about someone, do I have noble motives for my actions? Will sharing this reflect well on my character?

Reframe. Instead of: "Everyone needs to know what so-and-so did,"

Try: "I'm tempted to damage this person's reputation, but my reputation as someone who takes the high road will serve me better in the long run."

Hypercriticism

"We can improve our relationships with others by leaps and bounds if we become encouragers instead of critics." – Joyce Meyer

Hypercriticism is an attempt to undermine someone by objecting to as much as possible: shooting down suggestions, finding holes in their logic, and scrutinizing their output for mistakes. In short, becoming overly judgmental of someone's work or actions.

The strategy is sometimes used as an attack fueled by competitiveness, resentment, or insecurity.

Thoughts leading to hypercriticism sound like:

"I need to knock you down a peg or two."
"I need to look like the smartest one here."

Idea for Action

Reflect.

Am I threatened by the intellect, skills, or talents of this person?

Is my criticism to help them improve or to make them look bad?

Reframe.

Instead of: "I need to stay on the offensive to remain on top,"

Try: "I will choose to admire the talent and skill of so-and-so. I will focus on my strengths to stand out in the ways I am unique."

Overpowering

"Man is not, by nature, deserving of all that he wants. When we think that we are automatically entitled to something, that is when we start walking all over others to get it." – Criss Jami

Overpowering involves drawing on all sources of power available to us to defeat someone in conflict with us. Sometimes power is our social status or authority. Sometimes, it's using the force of a strong, vocal personality or physical stature.

Overpowering keeps the other person off balance and attempts to eliminate a fair, even-handed discussion.

Thoughts leading to overpowering echo these:

"I won't quit until I win."
"I'll use intimidation to get my way."

Choose to exercise patience and empathy with others.

Idea for Action

Reflect.

Do I view differing opinions as a challenge to my status or authority?

Do I use an overpowering strategy to retain or gain control?

Reframe.

Instead of: "I'm just doing what it takes to get results,"

Try: "What's the worst outcome if I listen and hear this person out?"

Passive Aggression

"Some people are like Slinkies. They aren't really good for anything, but they still bring a smile to my face when I push them down a flight of stairs." – Patricia Briggs

Passive aggression is indirect expression of negative emotion.

Most of us can think of a time we wanted to express anger but avoided being direct. Passive-aggression seems like a perfect solution. We subtly punish someone enough to be noticed but not so much they call us out. Passive-aggression takes many forms: eye rolling, ignoring, nitpicking, pouting, and sarcasm.

Sometimes the goal is to bother someone enough it initiates conflict, giving us permission to unleash.

Thoughts leading to passive-aggression include:

"I will make my point without being the bad guy."
"I don't want to discuss this but won't pretend nothing is wrong."

Idea for Action

Reflect.

Do I try to lead others to conflict indirectly to assert myself?
Do I use indirect methods to communicate my concerns?

Reframe.

Instead of: "You irritated me, so I will make sure you're irritated too,"

Try: "I will speak up and share the impact she had on me and give her a chance to explain."

Revenge

"Weak people revenge. Strong people forgive. Intelligent people ignore." – Albert Einstein

Revenge seeks to even the score for injustice. Nothing sets the human spirit ablaze quite like injustice. Approximately one in five murders in the United States is motivated by revenge.[95]

We stew over being hurt or mistreated and fantasize about getting even. It can feel good, even if we don't want to admit it.

Most of us realize overt revenge won't be tolerated, but it doesn't stop us from employing creative, backhanded, and petty ways to inflict damage.

Thoughts leading to revenge sound like:

"I need to get even."
"You will regret what you did to me."

Accept some people will break your trust. That reflects on them, but your response reflects on you. Confucius said, "Before you embark on a journey of revenge, dig two graves."

Idea for Action

Reflect.

Am I fixated on evening the score?
Do I find myself scheming ways to bring someone down?

Reframe.

Instead of: "You stick it to me. I'll stick it to you. An eye for an eye,"

Try: "A child chooses revenge. I'll move on and let fate do the dirty work."

Sabotage

"Some people aren't satisfied until they sabotage someone else's happiness. Be careful who you trust. Not everyone who smiles at you is your friend." – Unknown

Sabotage is deliberately obstructing or destroying someone's work to make sure he or she fails. Sabotage can be social—lying, spreading rumors—or physical tampering. Some choose this path because they lack the power to address the person directly. Or they want to express anger without a direct clash.

Sabotage requires us to suspend our normal view of right and wrong to rationalize our behavior.

Thoughts leading to sabotage include:

"You should be punished for the problem you caused me."
"I have to regain the upper hand."

Idea for Action

Reflect.

Do I find satisfaction in seeing others fail?
Would I find this behavior reprehensible if it were done to me?

Reframe.

Instead of: "If I bring her down, I'll be on top again,"

Try: "When one of us fails, we all fail to reach our goals."

Sarcasm

"From the Greek word sarkazein, which means 'tear flesh.'
Somehow, in simple words [sarcasm] means to speak bitterly."
– Literarydevices.net

In conflict, sarcasm is a close cousin to passive-aggression. It allows us to take a shot at someone or express hostility without being as direct with our real motivations. We're not quite committed enough to yell at someone but want to take them down a notch or two.

Sarcasm is a tempting method because in the thick of conflict we can claim, "I'm just joking. Seriously, lighten up." We might think "just kidding" offers immunity after subtly attacking or demeaning someone.

Thoughts leading to sarcasm include:

"That [idea/thought/position] is obviously ridiculous."
"Why would [he/she] say something so stupid?"

Idea for Action

Reflect.

Do I use sarcasm to subtly put people in their place?
Do I pretend I'm joking when my message is my true intent?

Reframe.

Instead of: "What an idiot. I'd better let him know it with some sarcastic wit,"

Try: "I think he's being an idiot, but it's probably best not to employ a petty response."

Stonewalling

"The four horsemen: defensiveness, stonewalling, criticism, and contempt." – Malcolm Gladwell, *Blink*

Stonewalling is refusing to answer, show emotion, or respond to someone.

When we stonewall, we make clear to the other person that communication is completely shut down. Although we don't want to admit it, stonewalling can be gratifying because we punish the other person while acting as if our behavior is strong and dignified. In reality, it's more of a preservation strategy when we're in uncomfortable situations.

Thoughts leading to stonewalling sound like:

"You don't get to know what I'm feeling."
"I'm not responding to this."

Choose to engage in discussion, even if hearing the emotions of others is uncomfortable. Ignored problems become bigger problems harder to solve.

Idea for Action

Reflect.

Am I unwilling to compromise?
Do I shut down and refuse to discuss situations which make me uncomfortable?

Reframe.

Instead of: "I'm not discussing this with you. Time for me to check out,"

Try: "If I don't address this, it won't improve."

Withdrawing

"Avoidance is the best short-term strategy to escape conflict, and the best long-term strategy to ensure suffering." – Brendon Burchard

Withdrawing is to remove oneself from a situation.

If a situation is hostile or dangerous, removing yourself is wise. Healthy conflict is key to producing better outcomes. Avoiding conflict is destructive because nothing is resolved, and you leave a trail of damaged relationships behind.

Withdrawing stems from a desire to return to stability and safety. Emotions can be chaotic and messy, and conflict can be tiring. Dawn Metcalfe, author of *The HardTalk Handbook*, says 70 percent of people faced with conflict will avoid it.[96]

Thoughts that lead to withdrawing sound like:

"This needs to end as soon as possible."
"I will stay quiet until this is over."

Idea for Action

Reflect.

Do I run or hide from conflict?
Do conflict situations cause me to experience anxiety, anger, insecurity, or threat?

Reframe.

Instead of: "If I just keep quiet, this will blow over,"

Try: "Can I talk to you about something? I want to hear your perspective and share mine as well."

Couples & Family

The following topics are covered in Couples and Family:

Love Languages
Opposites Attract
Intimacy
Long-Distance Relationships
Avoiding an Affair
Surviving an Affair
Betrayal
Commitment
Kids Come ... Second!
Parent/Teen Conflict

Love Languages

"Love is something you do for someone else. Not something you do for yourself." – Gary Smalley

Have you been in a relationship where you showed love, but the other person didn't see it? Maybe you've received complaints of unmet relational needs.

Relationship dances sometimes go like this:

Partner 1: "I don't feel you pay attention to me. You rarely tell me you love me or I'm attractive."

Partner 2: "I show you I love you all the time. Yesterday I washed your car and fixed the sticky drawer that bugs you."

Partner 1: "How is fixing drawers related to what I said? If anything, when you're fixing things I feel ignored."

The 5 Love Languages by Gary Chapman reveals what's meaningful to us in relationships. We value our top love language most because it's what *we* want most. Yet, our friend, family member, or partner may have a different way to express love and care.

In the example, Partner 1 values Words of Affirmation. Partner 2 values Acts of Service. Therefore, one partner thinks they're demonstrating love, while the other fails to receive it. The 5 Love Languages are: Acts of Service, Quality Time, Physical Touch, Receiving Gifts, and Words of Affirmation.

Idea for Action

Take one of the free *5 Love Languages* quizzes. Compare and discuss relationship needs with a loved one. 5lovelanguages.com/quizzes

Opposites Attract

"At first opposites attract. Then opposites attack." – Rick Warren

It's common for partners to have opposite personalities. At first, we admire positive traits we lack. Over time, differences can begin to grate on our nerves and cause conflict.

One prefers to make decisions carefully, the other is spontaneous. One is collaborative, the other makes decisions independently. One prefers laundry folded neatly, the other leaves it in a pile in the basket. One likes to spend money, the other is a saver. One likes security and stability, the other takes risks.

The career team I volunteer with conducts an exercise with job seekers. We create "Day in the Life" posters to describe a typical day with our personality. The groups laugh and joke how different they are from those with the opposite personality. One person commented the other poster gave him anxiety just looking at it!

Couples with opposite personalities can have well-functioning relationships with the right perspective. Capitalize on the strength of differences! Have you considered how, at work and home, people who are opposite can help you by filling in your gaps? Your different perspectives create a diverse vault of knowledge and ability to draw from.

Idea for Action

Reduce conflict by seeking common ground. Respectfully compare and contrast your opinions. Express your top concern and what it would take to alleviate it.

Intimacy

"Intimacy is not purely physical. It's the act of connecting with someone so deeply, you feel like you can see into their soul." – Reshall Varsos

Psychologists identified four types of intimacy: emotional, physical, spiritual, and mental. Five levels comprise each type.[97]

Level 1: Safe communication – No emotions involved, just sharing facts or information.

Level 2: Shares others' opinions – An example is, "My father always says ... ." Level 2 tests the waters and is safer since we're not stating our opinion.

Level 3: Shares personal beliefs and opinions – We start taking small risks.

Level 4: Shares feelings and personal experiences – Opens the speaker to a higher level of vulnerability and risk.

Level 5: Shares needs, desires, and emotions – In this level, we reveal the core of ourselves to another.

Intimacy takes time to build. We must move through the levels together. If I share on level four, but you share on level two, we have false intimacy. Relational intimacy is gauged by the person functioning at the lowest level of vulnerability.

Idea for Action

Do you have a romantic relationship or friendships at mismatched levels of intimacy? Reflect on your closest relationships. Plot where you and each person fall on the intimacy levels.

Long-Distance Relationships

"Long-distance relationships are hard, but they're also incredible. If you can love, trust, respect and support each other from a distance, then you'll be unstoppable once you're physically together." – Unknown

My husband and I had a long-distance relationship for several years before he relocated to my city. I learned many lessons from the experience. First, I learned the heightened importance of communication in this arrangement. Relationships can rely on crutches instead of communicating, such as watching television or physical intimacy.

I also learned consistency matters. When physically distant, know when you will connect. Consistent contact lessens anxiety about the distance and replaces it with stability. My future husband made a habit to speak with me on the commute to work and before bedtime.

Early on, phone calls were inconsistent, which created some stress. Once we discussed it, finding a solution was easy.

Last, I learned to be creative in how we spent time together. I wore ear buds so we could chat on the phone while I cleaned. Cleaning toilets went by much more quickly!

Idea for Action

My husband and I enjoyed watching movies together or reading the same book to discuss. Implement the following activities if you're in a long-distance relationship: modernlovelongdistance.com/long-distance-relationship-activities.

Avoiding an Affair

"Cheating isn't always kissing, touching, or flirting. If you gotta delete text messages so your partner won't see them, you're already there." – Moses Gazman Mukhansi

Affairs stem from a need for external affirmation. A few simple rules can guard you from tearing your life apart with an affair. Gretchen Rubin, author of *The Happiness Project*, offers these seven rules:

1. Never take a first step in flirtation, even in jest.

2. Never have more than one drink with coworkers. If that.

3. Never confide in people from work about your personal life, and don't allow them to confide in you.

4. Never allow yourself to have a "special friend," or "work spouse," to turn to for particular support.

5. Unless it's an unmistakably professional context, don't meet alone with colleagues or clients.

6. If you end up with a platonic "work spouse," make an effort to know his or her family.

7. Ask what your spouse would think if he or she were to walk into the situation or read your email.

Idea for Action

List things you want to be different or better in your life. Affairs are almost always discovered. What changes can you make to meet your inner longing in healthy ways that won't devastate you and those you care for?

Surviving an Affair

"Affairs don't start in bedrooms. They start with conversations." – Dave Willis

Discovering a spouse has been unfaithful is devasting. It threatens our future and security and often our self-worth. Everything we've built is suddenly on sinking sand.

Marci Payne, a licensed professional counselor, offers sound advice for dealing with infidelity. First, guard your mind from questioning your self-worth. Your value is not defined by other people's behavior or choices.

Second, don't obsess over the affair. Keep your attention on what's important, which is your marriage and family.

Set clear boundaries. Be clear on what you will and won't tolerate. Defend your boundaries instead of trying to put boundaries on your spouse. Take the empowered position.

Recognize if your spouse is in denial. If they are minimizing or denying the affair, even when you have evidence, they aren't ready to take responsibility for their actions.

Idea for Action

It's tempting to try to control or dictate the behavior of a spouse when they've betrayed us. Focus on what you can control. Practice self-care such as getting sleep, exercising, eating healthy, meditating, or find other ways to manage stress. Set boundaries of what you will and won't accept and stick to your boundaries. Read more at marcipayne.com/dos-donts-surviving-spouses-infidelity.

Betrayal

"The saddest thing about betrayal is that it never comes from an enemy." – Anonymous

Betrayal is devastating because it comes from someone we care about and sideswipes us. Examples of betrayal include abuse from a family member or friend, an unfaithful partner, or someone lying to us or abandoning the relationship.

If betrayed, we must decide if we want to rebuild or release the relationship. To rebuild, the offender must be sincerely apologetic, and the best apology is changed behavior. If the perpetrator isn't sorry, trust cannot be rebuilt.

To overcome betrayal, actively plan for emotional recovery. Lean on friends and family whom you trust, seek professional help, and/or consult a spiritual mentor or confidante who has been in your shoes. Work through your pain, and give purpose to it. Avoid confiding in people who keep you stuck in anger. Seek those who propel you forward. We can lessen self-pity and regret by serving others in meaningful ways.

Idea for Action

Should you keep a person in your life? Reflect to decide.

- Do we both have good intentions without using each other?
- Are we there for each other in good times and bad?
- Do we have a connection beyond the superficial?
- Does he/she help me become a better person?
- Do we want what's best for each other?
- Does he/she accept me for who am I?
- Can I be vulnerable with him/her?

Commitment

"When you make a commitment to a relationship, you invest your attention and energy in it more profoundly because you now experience ownership of that relationship." – Barbara De Angelis

We live in a time when marriage rates are trending down, co-habitation is rising, and the majority of first-born children are born to unmarried parents.

Because of this, knowing the status of your relationship can be more confusing. Even when a relationship is committed through the legal contract of marriage, one partner can have an uncommitted attitude toward the marriage.

What are the criteria for a committed relationship?

1. Promises are made to each other about the permanent nature of the relationship, and those promises are kept.
2. Explicit, formal, or public declarations of commitment have been made.
3. Commitment is clear to both partners and to others.

Both people need to be in agreement and have similar expectations. If one partner has expectations of permanence and the other doesn't, trust and deeper intimacy cannot form.

Idea for Action

Actions speak for themselves. Show your partner commitment by keeping your word, showing respect, and being honest how you feel. If they don't reciprocate, discuss your concerns with them openly.

Kids Come ... Second!

"Once you're parents, your marriage matters more, not less, because now other people are counting on you." – The Gottman Institute

I remember a conversation with my mother from childhood. "Kristin, I love you and your brother very much. But your father is number one. Someday, you and your brother will have your own lives, but it will always be your father and me."

Her words gave me security. I didn't feel unloved or unimportant. It was the best thing she ever told me.

Still, I got it wrong in my first marriage. My parents placing their marriage as priority was the best gift they gave me; yet I fell into the trap many couples do. My first husband and I worked opposite shifts to avoid paying daycare. Guess how it worked out?

Now, I have young children in my forever marriage, and I learned from my mistakes. Our relationship is number one. We don't let our kids sleep with us; our bed is for us. We make a point of having a date night, even if it's a glass of wine watching a movie in our room. Our decision has made all the difference. The position our partner holds on our priority list will determine the health of the relationship.

Idea for Action

If you have a partner, ask him or her to list relationships in priority order: parents, siblings, friends, coworkers, children. List what you think his or her priorities are. Switch and prioritize your relationships. Share and discuss your results. If misaligned, what will you adjust?

Parent/Teen Conflict

"When your children are teenagers it's important to have a dog so that someone in the house is happy to see you." – Nora Ephron

For several years I coached students to help with their career path. Sometimes parents struggled to see the talents of their kids in a positive light because their talents were a source of frustration. Frustration often stemmed from a child's weakness being a strength of the parent.

A common cause of parent/teen strain is the teen's uncertainty who he or she is and a need to establish a sense of identity. When we, as parents, make seemingly harmless comments such as, "Did you finish your homework?" the teen's own self-doubts of who they are, as they transition from childhood, are triggered.

Much upheaval can be experienced in the family as the teen's behavior is interpreted as rejection, rebellion, or a deteriorating relationship. In reality, the teen, perhaps unknowingly, wants his parents to acknowledge who he is becoming, even if he is uncertain.

Idea for Action

One way to support your teen is to help him or her build their identity. Three ways are to encourage self-discovery, acknowledge their natural talents, and value their uniqueness.

As a mom of two college boys, helping my sons understand who they were reduced tension. Learning about themselves increased confidence and certainty.

Self-Development

The following topics are covered in Self-Development:

Trying to Change People
Unmet Expectations
Taking Things Personally
Taking Responsibility
Preferences
Emotional Intelligence
Introspection
Curiosity
Diversity
Humility
Trust
Flexibility
Approachability
Approval Seeking
Assertiveness
Dependability
Jealousy
Loyalty
Rejection
Reputation
Social Anxiety

Trying to Change People

"If you don't think it's nearly impossible to change someone who is not willing to change, just think how hard it is to change yourself, and you are willing." – Charles F. Glassman

One of my former coworkers, Belinda, shared the best relationship advice she's ever received:

"Accept people as they are. Don't try to change others into who you think they should be. It can be hard, but living with that wisdom helped me be a better mom and helped me save my sanity and leave bad relationships before I felt stuck."

Instead of a person having the freedom to be who they're designed to be, we impose our will and expectations and try to force them into a charade of acting like someone else.

At its core, attempting to change someone is selfish.

Ideas for Action

9 ways to stop trying to change people by pickthebrain.com:

1. Let go of ideals.
2. Respect their individuality.
3. Focus on their good sides.
4. Put yourself in their shoes.
5. Be compassionate.
6. Be grateful for having them.
7. Remember why they were important to you in the first place.
8. Accept them and everything they do.
9. Stop comparing.

Read the detailed list here: bit.ly/stopchangingpeople.

Unmet Expectations

"I'm not in this world to live up to your expectations and you're not in this world to live up to mine." – Bruce Lee

Many disappointments stem from unmet expectations. Many issues develop from placing expectations on others.

1. Expectations are often not communicated. We assume people "should just know." They don't because they think differently than we do.
2. Expectations are not clearly defined.
3. Expectations are natural for us but a challenge for a person who differs from us.
4. Expecting more from others is unrealistic. We let people down too.
5. Expectations are a form of opinion. Our preferences are not the "right way," as hard as it is for us to accept.
6. We set ourselves up for constant disappointment.

The answers to our problem are not in other people's hands. Yes, we should have boundaries, but expectations undermine our happiness.

Ideas for Action

- Be honest with yourself regarding your motives.
- Suspend judging others. Accept people are flawed.
- Don't take letdowns personally. Have a Plan B.
- Resist the need to control people. Learn to let go.
- Adjust and decide if the person belongs in your life.

Taking Things Personally

"By taking things personally, you set yourself up to suffer. The impact on you and the ripple effects on those around you are unhealthy." – Suzanne Mayo Frindt

When you allow someone to control your emotions, you give them more power than they should be permitted.

We make assumptions what a person said or did concerned us, when that's rarely true. Most people don't spend time devising ways to hurt us. It's probable they weren't thinking. People say and do stupid things. To avoid assumptions, directly ask for clarification, but only if the relationship matters to you.

Instead of choosing a hurtful reaction, create a buffer around yourself. Imagine a gated fence encircling you. Only you can open the gate to allow access. Create your power and freedom.

Explore someone's actions with curiosity. Does this person's action align with what I know to be true of me? Does it align with feedback from the people who know and care for me?

The more you know yourself, the less you rely on others to tell you who you are.

Idea for Action

When you find yourself taking something personally, ask, "Do I need this person's approval?" If not, let it go and remind yourself, "I don't require this person's approval for my happiness."

If you continue to be upset, ask, "Why am I giving my power away?"

Taking Responsibility

"All blame is a waste of time. No matter how much fault you find with another, and regardless of how much you blame him, it will not change you." – Dr. Wayne Dyer

Conflict in relationships is inevitable.

A challenge I've observed in conflict resolution workshops is lack of ownership.

Each person focuses on the faults of the other. Choosing this approach escalates conflict, putting each other on the defensive, instead of promoting a commitment to reach a resolution.

When we're unwilling to take ownership in conflict, resolution is impossible. Absolving ourselves of wrongdoing, expecting the other person to do the work to repair the relationship, is unrealistic.

While it's possible the other person could be introducing unhealthy behaviors, conflict resolution is a collaborative effort. Blame is never productive.

Idea for Action

How hard is taking responsibility to you? Mark it below. Ask a close friend or partner to rate their perception of you.

|---|

Easy   Moderate   Difficult

If you scored moderate-to-difficult, increase responsibility by owning your thoughts, words, and actions. Reflect how your thoughts, words, and actions impact people in your life.

Preferences

"You'll always be disappointed when you expect other people to act as you would." – Unknown

Sometimes we expect people to cater to our preferences. When they don't act or do things the way we would, they're doing it wrong—right?

The ability to differentiate preference from necessity leads to happier relationships. Perhaps you've debated how to fold laundry, spend time or money, or celebrate special occasions.

One partner might believe recreational purchases should never exceed 20 percent of savings, while the other believes saving for the expense is sufficient.

One partner might believe weekends should be spent relaxing, while the other considers the weekend time to complete projects around the house.

Our values, personalities, and experiences shape our preferences. If we're task oriented, we value getting stuff done. If our partner is relational, he or she will value quality time together. No one is right or wrong in these scenarios, though you might side with yourself!

You don't have to give up all your preferences. Decide what's worth your sacrifice. Letting go helps you become flexible in relationships.

Idea for Action

Reflect on the big picture of what you want a specific relationship to be instead of preferences controlling the relationship. List areas where you can be more flexible.

Emotional Intelligence

"Emotional Intelligence is making your emotions work for you instead of against you." – Justin Bariso

Emotional Intelligence, also known as EQ, requires not only recognizing your own emotions but those of others. EQ consultant Kris Macchiarola suggests the following questions to improve your EQ:

"When you're delivering your message, you should be looking for the cues of the people receiving it," she says.

- What is their body language saying?
- What is the tone of their voice?
- What is their facial expression?
- What are the words they've selected to say to you?
- Is your message being received the way you intend?
- Are you listening more than you speak?

Ideas for Action

For a practical EQ guide, pick up Justin Bariso's book, *EQ Applied*.

Positive Psychology offers ideas to boost your EQ at positivepsychology.com/emotional-intelligence-exercises.

Introspection

"Everything that irritates us about others can lead us to an understanding of ourselves." – Carl Jung

Introspection helps us become aware of our own emotions. Without awareness, when triggered we'll act out in response to those stimuli. Our emotions will control us instead of us controlling our emotions.

Introspection should be a regular habit, but introspection without action to change is wasted effort.

Idea for Action

When you're upset, or before entering a potentially volatile situation, reflect:

Is this person pushing my buttons? Why do I react that way? Am I more emotional than the situation justifies? Why?

Look at your back story. What personal history is this situation triggering?

Practicing this exercise helps you enter conversations or situations knowing you bring a heightened emotional state with you. The trigger might even have something to do with someone from your past and not the person in front of you.

Curiosity

"The ability to observe without evaluation is the highest form of intelligence." – Jiddu Krishnamurti

Curiosity creates a needed pause in our interactions with others.

The space curiosity provides places us in learning mode. When we are in learning mode, we avoid jump-to-conclusion or assumption mode. Employing curiosity strengthens our relationships and builds empathy.

When we encourage others to clarify their thoughts, we reduce the risk of misunderstandings.

Curiosity also influences how others view us. Because inquisitiveness fosters deeper thinking and more rational decisions, we gain respect, build trust, and encourage collaboration.

Idea for Action

One simple statement can create a curious pause to show others we are interested in them and what they have to say:

"Tell me more about … ."

Some examples are, "Tell me more about …"

… what you think.
… your idea.
… your concerns.
… your problem.
… why you feel this way.
… how you reached your decision.

Diversity

"In our work and in our living we must realize that difference is a reason for celebration and growth, rather than a reason for destruction." – Audre Lord

Diversity in relationships has helped me grow. I grew up in a town of 23,000 people. Diversity in thought, economic status, and culture was not prevalent.

After entering the workforce and becoming active on LinkedIn, my world opened up.

Two main phases exist in relationships. The first phase involves discovering common ground and the ways we're alike. We discuss music, hobbies, or political opinions.

The second phase focuses on how we're different and where we disagree. Conflict can arise. Yet, no one is at fault for being different.

In the second phase, our goal is not to return to harmony, agree on everything, and do things the same. The goal is to learn to accept differences, resolve conflict, yet retain who we are as individuals. We can develop spiritual and emotional maturity, which allows us to care about people who differ.

Ideas for Action

1. Read about people, cultures, and viewpoints.
2. Read or watch balanced sources of media.
3. Shop at specialty ethnic stores and try new foods.
4. Talk with people of varied backgrounds: Be curious.
5. Travel or learn a language. I use the free Duolingo app.

Humility

"True humility is not thinking less of yourself; it is thinking of yourself less." – Rick Warren

Humility lets one's accomplishments speak for themselves. Humility is also not thinking ourselves more special than we are. It is not a low opinion of self; it is a realistic opinion of self.

An example of humility is a manager willing to clean up an overflowing toilet rather than being too important for the task.

Another example of humility is giving your team credit rather than taking the credit. People who are humble don't tell people they are humble. It is evident.

Humility comes down to where our attention is primarily focused: on ourselves or on others.

Research suggests humble people handle stress better and report higher levels of physical and mental well-being. They also show greater generosity, helpfulness, and gratitude—all things to enhance relationships.[98]

Ideas for Action

Three ways to increase humility:

1. Listen more than you talk.
2. Choose being at peace over appearing right.
3. Journal or reflect daily actions against the signs of pride: argumentative, defensive, opinionated, unteachable, boastful, judgmental, self-focused, humble bragger, low esteem, and easily offended.

Trust

"Breaking someone's trust is like crumpling up a perfect piece of paper. You can smooth it over, but it's never going to be the same again." – Unknown

Trust can't be pursued directly. Trust is an outcome. As an example, falling in love is an outcome. It requires a mixture of elements like attraction, compatibility, and common interests which *lead* people to fall in love.

What ingredients lead people to trust? This is largely opinion. If you research trust, you will find articles and research outlining three, four, five, and six keys to earn trust.

A consistent element is one factor alone can't build trust, but violating one factor can cause you to lose it.

Honesty – If you lie, trust is lost. A no-brainer.

Caring – People mistrust those who neglect, ignore, or disregard them.

Competency – No matter how nice you are, if you are incapable and ineffective, people can't lean on you.

Reliability – If you aren't consistent, people won't know what to expect from you and trust won't be granted.

Idea for Action

Discover level of trust with coworkers, family, or friends. Ask them to rate you on honesty, caring, competency, and reliability. Be gracious receiving feedback.

1 = almost never, 2 = rarely, 3 = sometimes, 4 = often, 5 = almost always. What areas, if any, do you need to develop?

Flexibility

"If you can't be flexible in life, you become irritable with life."
– Unknown

People who are flexible can easily adapt and respond to others, as well as to circumstances. Traits correlated with flexibility include confidence, tolerance, empathy, positiveness, and respect for others.[99]

When people lack flexibility, correlated traits are rigidity, competition with others, discontentment, unapproachability, and difficulty dealing with ambiguity.[100]

These negative traits can create challenges retaining employment or maintaining healthy relationships.

Ideas for Action

Tips to increase your flexibility:

1. Begin saying, "Tell me more about that" instead of shutting down suggestions and ideas.
2. Practice the "Yes and … ." approach. "Yes … and" is a protocol which allows everything on the table. Regardless what someone suggests, instead of disagreeing you respond with, "Yes, and … ." Accept the suggestion presented, then add to it. The method doesn't work every time, but it's a good way to keep an open mind.
3. Expand your willingness to experiment and learn.

Approachability

People: "You look so unapproachable."
Me: "And yet, here you are." – Anonymous

Approachability is the quality of being accessible, easy to meet or deal with.

When you are approachable it puts people at ease and builds trusted relationships. Trust leads people to be open and honest with you, so you hear good and bad news.

To be more approachable, smile, express interest, remember people's names, exhibit a friendly demeanor, laugh at yourself, initiate conversation, and act professionally personable by finding common ground.

Idea for Action

How approachable are you? Rate yourself at bit.ly/approachabilityquiz.

Ask five people you trust to candidly rate you on these approachability statements based on their experiences:

1. People can talk to me about anything, even hard topics.
2. I seldom come across as critical, defensive, or disinterested.

Ratings:

1 = almost never
2 = rarely
3 = sometimes
4 = often
5 = almost always

Approval Seeking

"An amazing thing happens when you stop seeking approval and validation: You find it." – Mandy Hale

When you habitually seek approval from others, you place the beliefs, opinions, and needs of people above your own. Consequences can include stress, lower confidence and self-esteem, and reduced levels of achievement and fulfillment.[101]

How do you know if you engage in approval-seeking? Here are eight signs:

1. Backing down from a position when someone disapproves or disagrees.
2. Complimenting people insincerely so they'll like you.
3. Stating agreement, even when you disagree.
4. Doing things you don't want because you can't say no.
5. Failing to speak up when you've been wronged.
6. Reflexively apologizing for yourself a lot.
7. Fear of admitting you don't know something.
8. Asking permission that isn't required.

Ideas for Action

Reflect where the need for approval comes from. How have childhood or early influences contributed to approval-seeking? Were you taught never to question authority? Did you believe you must earn affection through compliant behavior?

Reframe rejection as a positive. It means you're being true to yourself when you aren't pleasing everyone.

Assertiveness

"Every time we speak we choose, and use, one of four communication styles: assertive, aggressive, passive, and passive-aggressive." – Jim Rohn

Being assertive means you know how to communicate what you want in a clear and respectful manner. You are neither aggressive nor passive.

Assertiveness enables you to stand up for yourself and others in a calm and positive way. Behaving this way always respects the rights of others.

To be assertive, you must open up, listen, maintain self-control, and admit mistakes. Assertiveness is a skill and can be developed.

Idea for Action

Practice these steps to build assertiveness: [102]

1. Believe in your rights. Speak it as an affirmation.
   "I have a right to have an opinion."

2. Describe your concerns using specifics with "I" statements to express the impact on you.
   "I feel _____, and I'm concerned because _____.

3. Role play assertive responses with a trusted person.
   Ask a partner to act out likely responses.

4. Start small by practicing in safe, real-life scenarios.
   Start with low stress situations.

Dependability

"If your actions don't live up to your words, you have nothing to say." – DaShanne Stokes

Are you reliable? No one is perfect, and forgiveness should always play a role in relationships. Yet we build our reputation by what we do and do not do. Here are three things we must do consistently to be considered dependable.

Deliver on promises – If you say you will do something, do it. Excuses won't cut it. If a serious situation arises, let the person know you can't deliver. If you broke your leg and can't help a friend move, they will understand. Communicate proactively and timely so they can adjust their plans.

Be honest – When honesty goes out the door, trust goes with it.

Be there – Do you back out of plans at the last minute or fail to show up at important times? In relationships, if you're rarely there for people, they won't believe they can depend on you.

Idea for Action

Ask five people you trust to candidly rate you on these statements based on experiences with you.

1. I deliver what I promise.
2. I show up on time and meet deadlines.

Ratings:

1 = almost never
2 = rarely
3 = sometimes
4 = often
5 = almost always

Jealousy

"My wife's jealousy is getting ridiculous. The other day she looked at my calendar and wanted to know who May was." – Rodney Dangerfield

Jealousy is an emotion which combines desire and insecurity but not love. That's not to say if you struggle with jealousy you don't love someone. Jealousy is not a *demonstration* of love.

The irony of jealousy is it's deeply rooted in fear and insecurity of losing another person. However, jealousy creates a self-fulfilling prophecy because the very behaviors which bubble up from jealousy push the other person away.

A competent and secure person is almost incapable of jealousy.

Ideas for Action

1. Arrest jealous thoughts to prevent spiraling into conflict.
2. Refrain from acting on jealousy. Practice self-control by first working through your emotions internally.
3. Be honest about your feelings in a calm and gentle way. You might say, "I'm struggling with insecurity about your trip. I trust* you. I'm just feeling overwhelmed and want to be open with you."

*If you have rational reasons not to trust your partner, have an open, mature discussion to explain why you have difficulty trusting him or her, or speak with a professional for guidance.

Loyalty

"Trust is earned, respect is given, loyalty is demonstrated. Betrayal of any one of those is to lose all three." – Ziad K. Abdelnour

Allegiance. Faithfulness. Fidelity. A loyal friend sticks with you in good times and bad. They don't talk behind your back, hide things from you, or lie to you.

We generate loyalty when we consider other people's feelings, listen, make them a priority, keep confidences, are there emotionally and physically, and keep our word.

Loyalty is important in all relationships, from significant others, friendships, coworkers, and clients. Loyalty creates security and trust. The result is deeper emotional connections and more satisfying relationships.

Remember to also be loyal to yourself. Loyalty to self includes honoring your values, beliefs, and morals. It also includes setting and honoring your boundaries and prioritizing your needs and responsibilities.

Ideas for Action

Are you a loyal person? If you want to build your loyalty, do these three things immediately:

1. Refuse to participate in gossip.
2. Be honest and straightforward about your feelings.
3. Follow through on your commitments.

Rejection

"As I look back on my life, I realize that every time I thought I was being rejected from something good, I was actually being redirected to something better." – Steve Maraboli

Everyone experiences rejection. You might think it's personal, but it isn't. Think of screws and screwdrivers. They go to together, right? Often, no, they don't. Each screw has a different pattern. If you attempt to turn a square-headed screw with a slotted screwdriver, they're incompatible. No matter how persistent you are, you won't succeed because they aren't designed to work together. You'll strip the screw.

Some say, "You were rejected because they failed to see what you offer!" or, "They're flawed, not you!" You see, it's not that. Imagine you had a gift to know what everyone wanted. You could change to fit everyone's preferences, from romantic relationships to job interviews. You'd change until you lost sight of who you are.

In all situations, we can have peace despite rejection. If you're not right for them, by default they aren't right for you. It's a gift they figured it out before you did, far more painfully.

Ideas for Action

Face your emotions if you feel rejected. Treat yourself kindly and keep rejection in perspective. Ask, "What can I gain from this experience?" Rejection is a reminder you're putting yourself out there. Rejection isn't failure. Failure is giving up.

Reflect on times you were rejected then got something better.

Reputation

"Worry about your character, not your reputation. Your character is who you are. Your reputation is who people think you are." – John Wooden

We can't control our reputation. Our reputations are created and live in the minds of others. Trying to regulate our rep burns us out and leaves us stressed. We can influence opinions only through our character.

If we consistently focus on our character, unfair, inaccurate, or fabricated accounts of us will be difficult for others to believe. Inaccurate stories won't align with their experiences. We don't need to defend ourselves. Our character speaks for us. What an incredibly empowering and liberating truth!

Our character is our responsibility and where focus is wisely placed. Our duty is not to attend to what people think of us.

Why is this so important? If we keep our eyes fixed on our reputation, we won't do the work of developing our character. We'll be distracted defending ourselves in the court of public opinion.

If you take care of your character, your reputation will take care of itself.

Idea for Action

People don't care about us as much as we think they do. Remembering this can help us keep perspective. Flip your interpretation of a situation into a positive. Look for the silver lining, and keep moving forward.

Social Anxiety

"No one can make you feel inferior without your consent." – Eleanor Roosevelt

Feeling shy or uncomfortable in certain settings is not the same as social anxiety. Social anxiety usually disrupts a person's normal routine and often doesn't begin until the teen years.

Anxiety tends to run in families but can also result from an over-active amygdala. A hyperactive amygdala hijacks your body's normal response to fear. Anxiety can also be learned from past traumatic social situations.

Risk factors for social anxiety include family history, negative experiences, new social demands, temperament, and having an appearance or condition that attracts attention.

Ideas for Action

1. Get help as soon as possible – Consider seeing a doctor or mental health professional if you avoid and fear day-to-day social situations because they cause embarrassment, fear, or alarm.

2. Track your progress – Write down everything that makes you feel better or worse.

3. Manage your time and energy – Spend time doing things you enjoy.

4. Avoid unhealthy substance use – Alcohol, drugs, and caffeine can worsen anxiety.

5. Check out Mark Metry's book, *Screw Being Shy*.

CAREER

"Build your own dreams, or someone else will hire you to build theirs."

Farrah Gray

Helping people find career fulfillment is my greatest professional passion.

I wrote my third book, *YouMap,* to help people recognize their true potential to move into roles where potential is best lived out.

The *Career* chapter has something for everyone, whether unemployed, happily employed, self-employed, or mis-employed. We often place ownership of our careers into the hands of others instead of taking a proactive approach to shape the work we want to do. We are the architect of our careers. One of my favorite quotes by author, Alice Walker, says, "The most common way people give up their power is by thinking they don't have any."

The chapter is organized into the categories Self-Discovery, Career Management, Entrepreneurship, Job Search, and Professional Development.

Self-Discovery

The following topics are covered in Self-discovery:

Four Pillars of Career Fit ™
Ideal Day Exercise
Failure or Poor Fit?
Discovering Your Strengths
Strengths Statements
Shadow Side of Strengths
Discovering Your Values
Discovering Your Skills
Discovering Your Career Interest Type
Occupation Research
Transition Careers
Unique Contribution

Four Pillars of Career Fit™

"Being in a poor job fit isn't a personal failure. If you bought shoes that didn't fit, you wouldn't consider that a failure. You'd get new shoes." – Kristin Sherry

How, why, what, and who are key questions to ask yourself to find your Four Pillars of Career Fit™.

How do you want to work? The question reveals *priorities*.

We prioritize one or more of the following: relationships, influencing others, getting results, and challenging our mind.

Why do you work? The question reveals what's *important*.

Do you value growth, success, making a difference, meaningful work, achievement, learning, balance, collaboration?

What is your ideal day? The question reveals preferred *skills*.

Do you enjoy administration, managing people, selling, leading, research and analysis, conceptualizing or creating, working with people, managing projects?

Who are you? The question reveals your personality *preferences*.

Are you a doer, a creator, a thinker, a helper, an influencer, or an organizer?

Idea for Action

List things you enjoyed in the jobs you've held. Even if you hated a job, you probably liked something. Add your answers from your how, why, and who. What a great starting point for an ideal job description! Share with trusted advisors for their thoughts. See the next page, *Ideal Day Exercise*, for guidance.

Ideal Day Exercise

"Whenever I don't have to wear makeup, it's a good day." – Cameron Diaz

Have you ever sat and thought long and hard about your ideal day at work? It sure seems most people don't, at least not people I've talked to.

My Ideal Day exercise is instructive and oftentimes eye-opening. We can clearly see how far we've drifted from spending our time in fulfilling ways. Sometimes we're promoted farther and farther away from a job we truly enjoyed into a day we don't enjoy at all.

I think now is a good a time to discover your ideal day.

Think of every job you've ever had and list the things you enjoyed. Include your experiences, people you impacted, and accomplishments you were proud of. Even if you disliked a job, likely you enjoyed things or experiences in each position.

Idea for Action

Complete your ideal day exercise.

If you're employed, discuss opportunities to incorporate aspects of your ideal day into your job with your manager. If you don't have a trusted relationship with your manager, how can you use your ideal day to find a role better suited to you?

If unemployed, use your results to compare against job descriptions. If you work for yourself, how might you adjust your role to better align with your ideal day?

Failure or Poor Fit?

"Figuring out what you do best isn't just about work. It's about inviting your authentic self to come into the light instead of remaining in the shadows of what everyone else wants you to be." – Kristin Sherry

In our careers, when we are in a role or culture which doesn't tap our strengths, align with our values, leverage skills we enjoy, or fit our personality, we take it personally when we don't thrive.

I've met many people in a bad job fit, and it killed their confidence.

Do you know people who tie their identities to their work? If you're struggling in your career, you're probably planted in the wrong soil. Just as a plant or tree cannot survive, let alone thrive, in the wrong environment, neither can you. Let go of the idea you should succeed in a position where you don't fit.

Idea for Action

Answer these questions to assess fit:

1. Do you believe you fully use your strengths at work?
2. Are you burned out or exhausted in a typical week?
3. Are your values honored at work?
4. Do you like your work but not the culture you do it in?

If you don't use your strengths or you're burned out, a career transition might be needed. If your job violates your values or you like your work but not the culture, you might need to leave your manager or organization.

Discovering Your Strengths

"Everyone is born with natural talents, but not everyone realizes the talents they have or actively works to develop them." – Kristin Sherry

Never get between a person and their strengths; you'll lose every time. Strengths set our priorities. By nature, most of us find focusing on our weaknesses unpleasant because our weaknesses are not aligned to our priorities.

In *Four Pillars of Career Fit*™ on page 238, I shared the four keys to career fulfillment. The first key is aligning your strengths to your work. I cannot overemphasize the impact this has on your career.

Not only will you experience higher engagement at work, but you will have better jobs for the rest of your life. Sounds like a big guarantee, doesn't it? Gallup has conducted a large body of global research on career satisfaction and found a direct link to using one's strengths at work and career satisfaction and performance.[103]

Ideas for Action

1. Complete a *Reflected Best Self* exercise: Ask 5-10 people who know you to write and email you a story about a time you were at your best.
2. Highlight the most commonly occurring themes.
3. Brainstorm ideas and ways to use your top strengths more frequently, such as stretch projects or task forces at work.
4. *Optional*: Get your own personalized YouMap® to discover your strengths at bit.ly/OrderYouMap.

Strengths Statement

"I know what I bring to the table, so trust me when I say I'm not afraid to eat alone." – Unknown

Once you have a clear picture of your abilities and strengths, it's time to share your value in a brief strengths value statement. Understanding what we do best is important, but if we can't explain it to others, we'll struggle in networking, marketing ourselves, and making a strong impression in job interviews.

I received several job offers when I didn't have direct experience because I tied my strengths to the needs of the role. If you don't have a lot of formal work experience, the ability to explain what you do well, naturally, is even more necessary.

If you haven't identified your strengths, read *Discovering Your Strengths* on page 241, or complete the Top 5 CliftonStrengths assessment at gallup.com/cliftonstrengths. You don't need the "full 34" strengths. Plus, it costs more.

Idea for Action

Use the keyword list from the *Reflected Best Self* exercise in *Discovering Your Strengths* on page 241 or your Gallup Top 5 strengths to build a strengths value statement.

I [*action* or *characteristic* of one or two strengths] by [brief statement of *how*] to [*value* or *result delivered*].

Example: I **adapt to change** (action or characteristic) by **problem-solving** and **anticipating needs of others** (how) to deliver **personalized solutions for customers** (value/result delivered).

Shadow Side of Strengths

"Too much of anything is bad, but too much Champagne is just right." – F. Scott Fitzgerald

We are, thankfully, steadily shifting in the business world from focusing on weaknesses to homing in on strengths. Gallup research shows strengths interventions positively impact employees and the company's bottom line.[104]

Yet a person can have too much of a good thing. When talking about strengths, address the dark side of talents. During certification, YouMap® coaches are trained to guide clients to reflect on the positives and the barriers people might see with each strength.

I once worked for someone who had the Achiever talent. Our team was incredibly productive, but success came with a cost. Sometimes our manager didn't push back on unrealistic customer expectations, resulting in team members working 70-hour weeks.

When strengths are overused, engagement and productivity are sure to plummet.

Idea for Action

When discovering your strengths, as part of development, ask several people who know you in different contexts to offer feedback on positives and barriers of your strengths.

1. What do I do well when using this strength?
2. What one thing should I change when I use this strength?

Discovering Your Values

"The only thing worse than being blind is having sight, but no vision." – Helen Keller

Values are your judgment on what's most important to you in life. Knowing your values:

- Guides your boundaries and helps you hold them.
- Helps you create a vision for your life.
- Aids decision-making aligned to your vision.
- Keeps you focused on what's important to you.

Despite the importance of values, most people go through life without identifying them. It's no wonder we end up in jobs where we don't feel honored. Our values don't align with the work we're doing, the culture, or whom we're working for.

Values are also critical for relationship choices. People often focus on personality differences. Incompatible values are a bigger deal breaker.

Idea for Action

Get your own personalized YouMap® to discover your prioritized values at bit.ly/OrderYouMap.

For a free manual option to identify and prioritize your top 5-10 values, go to myyoumap.com/worksheets.

Reflect on your work. Pinpoint which values your job, manager, company, or clients are violating, and why.

Create a plan to address each violation.

Discovering Your Skills

"Transferable skills are a versatile set of skills that you can apply to more than one job. These are the skills that add to your marketability as a candidate and help you assimilate from one job to another." – Trish Freshwater

The YouMap® career profile reveals fifty-five skills displayed by skill category.

"Most preferred" skills are defined as:
- A skill you're good at and enjoy using.
- A skill you haven't used but think you would enjoy.

"Least preferred" skills are defined as:
- A skill you're good at but do not enjoy using.
- A skill you're not good at and do not enjoy using.
- A skill you haven't used and think you wouldn't enjoy.

Ideally, you should spend a minimum of 80 percent of your day aligned to your preferred skills. Otherwise you are under-utilized. You should commit less than 20 percent of your day using your least preferred skills. Otherwise you can burn out.

Do your preferred skills align with your current role? Are your least preferred skills limiting your effectiveness?

Idea for Action

Get your own personalized YouMap® to discover your most and least preferred skills at bit.ly/OrderYouMap.

Download a manual skills discovery worksheet at no cost by visiting myyoumap.com/worksheets.

Discovering Your Career Interest Type

"My personality traits don't determine my destiny, they inform it." – Anne Bogel

Do you know how personality influences your career interests? Six personality types shape your needs and preferences at work.

Realistic – **Doers** prefer work involving practical, hands-on solutions to problems.

Investigative – **Thinkers** are intellectual, curious, and reserved. They like to solve problems and engage in challenges in their work.

Artistic – **Creators** are imaginative, creative, original, independent, and expressive. They avoid highly structured or routine work activities.

Social – **Helpers** are interested in serving society and making a difference. They like to help people, and their work is centered around people.

Enterprising – **Persuaders** often deal in business, leadership, or politics and are involved in making decisions, starting up and carrying out projects, and selling ideas or things.

Conventional – **Organizers** provide structure, process, and order businesses need to run well.

Idea for Action

Discover your career interest type at bit.ly/CareerInterestTest at no cost.

Occupation Research

"Research is what I'm doing when I don't know what I'm doing." – Wernher von Braun

If you are a student or stay-at-home parent returning to work, seeking a career change, or looking for a promotion, occupation research is a must.

Our idea of what a job entails might not be anything resembling a typical day. You must gain a realistic understanding of tasks and detailed work activities, technologies, and knowledge, skills, and abilities required for a role. What are the general education requirements and median salary for your geographic area? How does the work align with your values?

These are questions you can answer when you research occupations. I studied neuroscience in university and discovered I didn't want to be a neurologist after speaking to one.

I enjoyed the rigor of a science-based education. Dissecting brains was amazing. However, I value a healthy personal life apart from work. One question he asked was if I planned to have a family, because the work wasn't family friendly. That was a deal breaker for me.

Idea for Action

On the next page, *Transition Careers*, I outline how to find career options. Use an occupation research tool such as onetonline.org and set up informational interviews with people in roles you're considering for feedback.

Transition Careers

"The most difficult thing is the decision to act, the rest is merely tenacity. The fears are paper tigers. You can do anything you decide to do. You can act to change and control your life; and the procedure, the process is its own reward." – Amelia Earhart

If contemplating a career change, consider these steps:

1. *Discover your Four Pillars of Career Fit*™ – Pinpoint your strengths, values, preferred skills, and interests to help you move in the right direction.
2. *Write out your ideal day* – Envision what you want your day to look like.
3. *List deal makers and deal breakers* – Know what you need to have and want to avoid; stay honest with yourself.
4. *Assess feasibility/desirability* – Evaluate viability and level of desire for the options before choosing.
5. *Align with your target* – Tailor your networking pitch, resume, LinkedIn profile, and interview stories to the new career/role target.

Idea for Action

Use job boards and informational interviews to research roles. See *Creative Job Board Search* on page 286.

1. List career options which appeal to you.
2. Rank feasibility for each role. Consider finances, time, ability to close skill gaps, and education needed.
3. Rank desirability (low, medium, high) for each role.
4. Assess your passion or interest for each option, and research if the field is growing or shrinking.

Unique Contribution

"Let go of who you think you're supposed to be. Embrace who you are." – Brené Brown

Everyone does something better than most. Our secret sauce is our unique contribution. Three challenges exist:

1. We don't realize our talents are unique.
2. We lack an ability to explain our unique value clearly and succinctly without stumbling.
3. We try to be someone we're not or believe we should be doing what we see works for others.

Idea for Action

Draft your unique contribution statement:

1. List your strengths, traits, values, skills, and key experiences.
2. Select 5-10 key words which resonate most. Include words from across all areas (strengths, traits, values, skills, experiences).
3. Draft 1-2 sentences to explain who you are, what you do best, and the value you bring. Ask people who know you for feedback.

Example:
A possibility-focused bridge builder who finds a way for opposing perspectives to come together. Able to work independently to research, evaluate and strategize, yet work collaboratively to implement change, programs, or solutions to problems.

Career Management

The following topics are covered in Career Management:

Adversity Quotient
Bad Bosses
Brag Folders
Career Planning
Career Success
Finding a Mentor
Company Loyalty
Giving LinkedIn Recommendations
Asking for LinkedIn Recommendations
LinkedIn Headline
LinkedIn About (Summary)
Managing Your Email
Managing Your Power
Missed Goals
Prioritization
Promotions
Questioning Authority
Sharing Your Expertise
Zone of Genius

Adversity Quotient

"Without adversity, we can never unleash our greatness." – Paul Stoltz

Adversity Quotient (AQ) affects your drive and motivation. People high in AQ are resilient and turn obstacles into opportunities. Are you a quitter, a camper, or a climber? Paul Stoltz, author of *Adversity Quotient*, says 90 percent of the workplace are campers.

Quitters: Resentful complainers who retired years ago, but they didn't tell anyone and keep going to their jobs.

Campers: Employees who worked hard to get to a goal or spot and now stay camped there.

Climbers: They never stop learning and growing and continuously pursue goals. They inspire others to see their own potential and act from a place of purpose.

Unlike quitters, campers still have a flame inside. With a meaningful vision, the camper will climb once again.

Idea for Action

Five steps to unleash your inner climber:

1. Uncover what you care about (values).
2. Itemize your abilities (strengths).
3. Set goals supported by your values that use your talents.
4. Craft a unique contribution statement to showcase what you do best.
5. Share your statement with others for feedback.

Bad Bosses

"Having a bad boss isn't your fault. Staying with one is." – Nora Denzel

If you're unhappy with your manager, give feedback instead of suffering silently. Feedback isn't easy, but it's worth the discomfort and requires less work than a job search. After you navigate the conversation, note what went well and what to improve upon. Don't give up if the first attempt is unsuccessful. Relationships are a journey.

Idea for Action

Try the following framework to offer feedback:

1. Briefly explain the situation you experienced or are currently experiencing.
2. Address observable actions and behavior. Leave out your interpretations of the behavior, accusations, or assumptions of motive.
3. Briefly explain the impact the situation or behavior has on you. Don't take a victim's stance or whine—be objective and mature.
4. Suggest an alternative approach for the future:

   "It's a challenge to prioritize my workload with the number of projects I have. Yesterday when you assigned the quarterly analysis of our customer feedback data, I was uncertain where my projects fit on the priority scale. It would help me if we could meet weekly for project prioritization so I can deliver as expected." See *Giving Feedback* on page 163 in the *Relationships* chapter.

Brag Folders

"I hope your life is full of 'I can't believe I did it' than 'I should've done it.'" – Unknown

When I wrote associate performance reviews, I started capturing successes and accomplishments of the team to create more substantial write-ups for their reviews. I remember Charlene had an impressive quarter, creating a lot of process improvements.

After I shared her review with her she responded, "Wow, I didn't remember I had done all of that." And therein lies the point. Someday, you might need to provide accomplishments, either as a business owner or a job seeker on a resume or in an interview.

We think we'll remember the details of our successes, but we won't. We especially won't remember numbers and figures. Then we kick ourselves when we need details. I have a friend who had a 20-year career with a company and resigned. When he needed to update his resume, he had no metrics of his success. He called Human Resources, and they refused to release his performance reviews.

Ideas for Action

1. Save kudos to a brag folder as you receive them. Label the folder whatever you want.
2. Save accomplishments on your personal computer. If you're terminated, you won't have access at work.
3. Download or screenshot your performance reviews ASAP! If you don't have a review, ask for feedback.

Career Planning

"If you don't design your own life plan, chances are you'll fall into someone else's plan. And guess what they have planned for you? Not much." – Jim Rohn

A common approach people take to their careers is work hard and wait to get promoted or rewarded.

Employees own their careers. Managers should give support. Companies should offer career development resources.

To create a simple career plan:

Discover – Know your strengths, values, skills you enjoy, and what you want more of.

Define career goal(s) – Uncover options for your next career move based on the discovery step plus the following questions:

- Where is my organization or the market growing?
- What are my top skills, and how can I leverage them?
- What skills do I need to build?
- What are my development options?
- What opportunities fit my values and needs?

Create a plan – Identify desirable skills you want to develop to close gaps between where you are and where you want to be. List actions in the *Act* section at the back of the book, including skill development ideas.

Idea for Action

Think of one or two mentors to expand your network and support your development. See *Find a Mentor* on page 256.

Career Success

"I want to look back on my career and be proud of the work and be proud that I tried everything." – Jon Stewart

Career success hinges on clarity of purpose and direction. Successful people know what they want. No one can define your career success but you. Most people who are successful know what they're good at and what they enjoy, and they demonstrate it regularly.

If you seek success by copying others, their paths are unlikely to work for you and your unique gifts. If you pursue what society considers success, it probably won't align with your values. Each decision can drive you farther from what matters to you if you don't create your own definition of success. Also consider how you will measure success. What has to happen?

Idea for Action

1. Write five of your proudest achievements in life.
2. List successes that did not make you happy.
3. List reasons the five achievements fulfilled you and the other achievements did not.
4. Write a success mantra or statement that aligns with why these were your most fulfilling successes.

Here is an example to inspire your success statement:

"I will use my gifts of creativity and innovation to cultivate awareness and confidence in children and adults. My books and programs will change lives around the world." See *Finding Your Purpose* on page 103 in the *Spirituality* chapter.

Finding a Mentor

"A mentor is someone who sees more talent and ability within you, than you see in yourself, and helps bring it out of you." – Bob Proctor

Whenever I had a mentor in my life, I experienced exponential growth. Mentors helped me step up my career and personal life unlike other experiences, aside from participating in a mastermind. See *Masterminds* on page 311 for more.

When seeking a mentor, start by identifying your goals. Are you interested in becoming a best-selling author? Do you want a promotion to management? Do you plan to start a business? Are you looking to build certain traits, such as executive presence?

List people who have achieved the goals or possess the traits you wish to develop.

Idea for Action

Create a list of the characteristics, skills, knowledge, or experiences in your ideal mentor. List people who are potential mentors or who could help you find one.

If a potential mentor declines your request, ask if they would recommend someone else based on the goals you shared and the reasons why you chose him or her.

Company Loyalty

"Companies never love you back." – Judith C. Spear

One of the best pieces of advice my mother gave me was, "Companies never love you back." In the past, I sacrificed moments I'll never get back because of work.

In 2019, I took my daughter's picture the moment she spotted me at her first-grade costume parade. I used to say, "I can't make it sweetie, Mommy has to work." I decided to make her events a priority. No one ever looked at me like she did when I walked into a meeting at work.

New parents feel pressure to rush back to work after the birth of a child. Those precious early weeks and months can never be relived. Do you have to miss events, games, and recitals because of your job?

We don't pen the book we long to write, start the podcast, or learn a new skill because we are just too busy with work.

We must be accountable, but where do we draw the line to avoid sacrificing our lives and the people we love? The COVID-19 pandemic showed us how disposable we are with job losses surpassing those in the 2008 financial crisis.

Idea for Action

What is a goal or dream you've placed on the back burner? Create a plan, and start taking steps to achieve it. Start the side hustle, learn a language, write that book!

Asking for LinkedIn Recommendations

"Don't be shy asking for help. It doesn't mean you're weak, it only means you're wise." – Unknown

I'm most often asked for LinkedIn recommendations when people need them. They've started a business, lost a job, or are interviewing.

Asking for recommendations all at once creates an odd look on your profile. When you amass 12 recommendations in one week, they appear forced. It seems you asked for a recommendation instead of someone willingly writing one.

The best time to ask for a recommendation is before you need it. Make a practice of periodically asking for recommendations, so your profile appears organic.

Make is easy to write you a recommendation by sending the request through "Request a Recommendation" under "More" on his or her profile. Include a personal note instead of sending the impersonal default message to avoid appearing entitled to it.

Idea for Action

List experiences, skills, and abilities you want to be known for. Capture names of people who have knowledge of those things. Hide recommendations that are off focus or request an update.

When making a request, advise the person of areas of focus. "Would you be willing to write a recommendation for me? You have a valuable perspective on my ability to manage people, solve problems, and create innovative ideas."

Giving LinkedIn Recommendations

"Give and it will be given to you." – Luke 6:38 NIV

Consider giving recommendations before you ask, and give at least as many recommendations as you receive.

A friend's manager spoke to her in a condescending and disrespectful manner. I was curious to see her manager's background, so I looked at her LinkedIn profile.

All of her recommendations were from her previous job, written at the same time (which means she likely asked for them). No one had written her recommendations in her years at the new company. Despite having 17 recommendations, she had written exactly zero for anyone.

It painted a picture of a taker, not a giver. That's an assumption, but I found it notable she accepted 17 recommendations to post to her profile without returning the favor to anyone who took time to write one for her.

To receive recommendations and not give any is a bad look. If I noticed it, a recruiter or hiring manager who is looking for clues about the kind of person you are could notice it too.

Idea for Action

Review your career. Think of people you've worked with. View each profile to see if they're doing similar work or if they've transitioned. If they're in the same role, write a recommendation. If they've transitioned, write one, but first ask what areas of focus would be most relevant in the recommendation.

LinkedIn Headline

"You never get a second chance to make a first impression." – Will Rogers

The world's largest professional networking site, LinkedIn, reported 675 million monthly users in 2020. Standing out online isn't easy, but a powerful headline helps.

Users choose one of three basic headlines on LinkedIn:
1. Default headline: job title at company name
2. Keyword headline
3. Slogan headline

Avoid the default headline. If you begin a job search, removing your employer from your headline could draw unwanted attention. Your profile is *your* brand, not your employer's.

Keyword headlines focus on areas where you excel that are in demand for your target role. Recruiters search keywords, so this is a great option for job seekers. This example showcases skills, results, and desired industry:

Operations Manager | Process Improvement | New Product Launches | Top 1% Performing Team | Healthcare

Slogan headlines are memorable and ideal for sales and entrepreneurs. My headline is *Creator of the Award-Winning YouMap® Profile | Author, Amazon #1 Bestseller YouMap | Children's Book, You've Got Gifts! | Maximize 365.*

Idea for Action

Review ideal job descriptions. Select keywords for your headline or write a slogan that conveys your superpower.

LinkedIn Summary (About)

"Inside each of us is a natural-born storyteller, waiting to be released." – Robin Moore

Your LinkedIn *About* section is a 2,600-character summary of your professional story. The section elaborates on your headline. Your LinkedIn profile is not an online resume.

Here's a simple four-part formula for writing your LinkedIn summary:

1. Brief introductory paragraph expounding on the thing(s) in your headline you do best; focus on the core problem you solve; your *why*.
2. Brief success story or list of accomplishments to back up your introductory paragraph and demonstrate what you do best; your *how*.
3. Call to action, such as requesting people connect with or contact you.
4. Keyword summary of skills you enjoy or services you provide and want to be known for. Adding keywords in your summary is important because it's searchable, like the headline.

Idea for Action

Review LinkedIn profiles of people in your industry or role for inspiration, but don't copy their text. What elements might you implement in your profile? LinkedIn strategy coach Andy Foote has helpful articles on his profile to assist you with your profile. Follow Andy at *linkedin.com/in/andyfoote*.

Managing Your Email

"Email is having an increasingly pernicious effect. Not only is it having a perceptible effect on productivity, it's skewing what it is we focus on. The immediate increasingly crowds out the important." – Noreena Hertz

Twenty-three minutes and 15 seconds. That's the amount of concentration you lose when interrupted, according to Gloria Mark, who studies digital interruption.[105] Returning to your task takes almost 25 minutes. Imagine the effect on productivity in a week, month, or year. I calculated wasted time assuming only three daily interruptions:

Weekly: (23.25*3)*5=348.75 minutes / 5.8 hours

Monthly: 1,395 wasted minutes or 23.25 hours

Yearly: 16,740 wasted minutes or 279 hours; assumes four weeks' vacation

"I can't wait 24 hours. What if it's important?!" Email is not the best method for urgent communication. Retrain people to expect a 24-hour turnaround on email. Then your email becomes a to do list instead endless daily interruptions.

Idea for Action

Try the Yesterbox email method by Zappos CEO, Tony Hsieh:

1. Set a daily calendar time to manage yesterday's email.
2. Use your email's filters to see yesterday's email.
3. Respond to important email first. When finished, you're done with email for the day.
4. Repeat each morning.
5. Read Tony's method in detail at yesterbox.com.

Managing Your Power

"Leadership is not wielding authority, it's empowering people." – Becky Brodin

Even if you are not a high-level leader, a power differential exists between you and your associates. Two factors influence the power gap: the actual control you have and your associates' past experience with people in authority.

You can't control either of those factors—the power you have is the power you have, and you can't control what associates think about your authority. What you can control is your behavior.

When you *magnify* your power, by saying no without explanation or blaming or declaring your power, you lose trust.

When you attempt to *eliminate* your power by developing friendships with your team and not holding them accountable, you create a leaderless atmosphere.

When you *balance* your power, you build trust and create a healthy environment.

Idea for Action

Review the following list of behaviors. Are you engaging in these? Ask your team for feedback if you're uncertain.

- Solicit team opinions and listen.
- Empathize with, and care about, your team.
- Be direct and respectful to hold people accountable.
- Be accessible: Avoid unresponsiveness and keeping your door shut.

Missed Goals

"Shoot for the moon. Even if you miss, you'll land among the stars." – Les Brown

In early 2020 I gave a talk to 140 women on how to get your goals back on track. I presented five drivers leading to goal attainment: Belief, desire, persistence, having a plan, and taking action.

Belief – Do you believe the goal is possible, and have you abandoned excuses? Our thoughts become actions.

Desire – Do you have a burning desire to reach the goal? If not, it's probably the wrong goal. Find your motivation behind the goal.

Persistence – Do you treat a temporary defeat as a permanent failure? Setbacks aren't failure until accepted as such. Keep going.

Plan – Are you breaking the larger goal down into manageable steps, setting smaller goals for each week, and celebrating wins?

Action – Have you translated your plan into clear, prioritized actions? Are you eliminating distractions?

Idea for Action

Conduct an examination of a goal you aren't achieving against the five drivers of goal attainment. Where do you need help?

Prioritization

"People who can focus, get things done. People who can prioritize, get the right things done." – John Maeda

The enemy of getting the right things done is time bandits. A time bandit is a time waster. Picking up my phone while writing to scroll social media is too easy. Before I know it, I've burned through 30 minutes looking at pictures of people's kids.

You'll find a plethora of prioritization advice online, but you have to pinpoint your time bandits.

Do you struggle to say no? Are you addicted to a device? Do you allow the wheel that squeaks the loudest to pull you off task? Do you fail to delegate? Do you over-analyze or seek perfection? Do you multi-task? Do you fail to set boundaries? Do you tackle tasks at the worst time of day for you?

Gaining victory over time bandits helps you focus on tasks to yield the most impact.

Idea for Action

For one day, track your time bandits. What or who took you off task? List strategies to better manage time bandits.

For example, set office hours, ask people to email if something isn't urgent. Set times to check email and turn off notifications so you're not pulled into email reflexively. Say no to things misaligned with your priorities. Schedule social media breaks to avoid FOMO (fear of missing out). Do the hardest thing first. Procrastination isn't laziness, it's an escape.

Promotions

"People don't get promoted for doing their jobs really well. They get promoted by demonstrating their potential to do more." – Tara Jaye Frank

At various points in my career I wanted a promotion and didn't get one. In 2011, I was selected for an eight-month leadership program. The executive coach who facilitated the program pulled me aside and gave me career-changing advice.

She told me I should report to a vice president, not a senior manager, because a manager has less influence opening doors in my career.

She explained 10 percent of getting promoted is attributed to hard work, 30 percent to our brand or reputation and 60 percent to the visibility we have in the organization.

Immediately, I set out to find a mentor to help me advance my career. I made sure to ask someone at an executive level so they could expand my network. Within seven months, a senior executive offered me a role with a skip level to the president.

Working hard alone will not get you promoted. You must be seen and have a reputation for showing potential to do more.

Idea for Action

Proactively prepare yourself for your next career move. What role do you want next? Study the job description, identify required skills, and look for chances to build the skills now. Take courses to close your skill gaps. Find a mentor to support you.

Questioning Authority

"Think for yourself. Know what you're doing. Question authority." – Timothy Leary

A power differential exists between you and your manager, however small. That does not mean your manager is always right, or you should do what they say without question.

Early in my career, I worked as a software developer. We were releasing a new website which gathered credit card data upon account creation. For reasons I can't recall, we were unable to operate in New Jersey. My boss gave direction to collect credit card data for all registrations.

I was opposed. I expressed concern we could put the company in hot water to collect credit cards from people we can't do business with. I believed the practice was unethical, and we should avoid storing sensitive data of people who can't choose to be customers.

Thankfully, my boss agreed, and we put a residency check in place before storing customer financial data. Even without agreement, I would have stood my ground on the issue. Don't be afraid to take your concerns as high as you must.

Idea for Action

Is someone in authority:

- Giving you direction misaligned with your values?
- Offering unfair, biased, or unsupported feedback?
- Treating you with disrespect?

Question authority by speaking with authority. Be direct with respect.

Sharing Your Expertise

"In vain have you acquired knowledge if you have not imparted it to others." – *Deuteronomy Rabbah*

The internet is a great vehicle to share your expertise in an accessible, evergreen way. Posting articles on your LinkedIn profile is one example.

Status updates on LinkedIn disappear quickly unless you save the link to each post. Articles stay on your profile for all to see. You can showcase link, articles, videos, and media in the "Feature" section of your profile.

If you have expertise in sales, engineering, marketing, management, process improvement, or geology, sharing your expertise on your profile benefits you and others.

Others benefit from your experience when your articles contain tips or action items, or helps them see something in a new way.

Here are five ways you benefit:

1. Attract the right people to connect with you.
2. Demonstrate knowledge to others, leading to jobs or clients.
3. Position yourself as a leader in your field.
4. Share your content easily by providing a link.
5. Create opportunities such as a collaboration or speaking engagement.

Idea for Action

List knowledge areas where you're confident. What stories can you tell with tips, lessons, and ideas for others?

Zone of Genius

"Your genius will show up to the extent you woo it." – Gay Hendricks

Author and psychologist, Gay Hendricks, created the concept of *The Genius Spiral*.

Zone of GENIUS!	Zone of Excellence
Zone of Competence	Zone of Incompetence

Zone of Incompetence – things most others do better than we can.

Zone of Competence – things we do well, as many others. We probably shouldn't be doing these things.

Zone of Excellence – things we do better than most others. We persist in them long after we've achieved mastery, and the work becomes routine. Many people stay here.

Zone of Genius – the place of flow. We are energized and excited by what we're doing. We are fully absorbed, using the full range of our gifts.

We live more powerful, fulfilled, and happy lives when we spend as much time as possible in our zone of genius.

Idea for Action

Give yourself permission to discover your areas of genius. Make a commitment to spend time in this zone by identifying one thing you enjoy most. Be open to failure, and schedule 15 minutes daily devoted to this area of genius. Check out *The Big Leap* and *The Joy of Genius* by Gay Hendricks to go deeper.

Entrepreneurship

The following topics are covered in Entrepreneurship:

Entrepreneurship: Is It for You?
Niches: Finding Yours
Risk Taking
Free Isn't Valued
Prospect Calls, Giving Away Too Much
Prospect Conversions
Pitching Your Ideas
Passive Income
Writing a Book: Know Why
Writing a Book: 3 Mistakes to Avoid
Writing a Book: Stay on Track

Entrepreneurship: Is It for You?

"Using your own personal resources is the easiest way to start a business. You don't have to convince investors about the merits of your idea. You just have to convince yourself." –Ryan Holmes

Some people dislike being an employee. Ten reasons why:

1. They value their autonomy.
2. They desire flexibility over their schedules.
3. They believe people frequently misunderstand them.
4. They prefer working on things they want to work on.
5. They want to make all decisions affecting them.
6. They have ideas and are frustrated when they're shot down.
7. They cannot stay motivated on other people's missions.
8. They think a lid is placed on their potential.
9. They see the path and have low patience for consensus.
10. They sense a pull to something greater.

What natural strengths and skills do you enjoy? What's a problem in your life your strengths and skills can solve?

Idea for Action

Consider these steps:

1. Set up a budget, and save six months of expenses.
2. Cut spending, such as eating out.
3. Read books to find your calling.
4. Hire an expert who specializes in niches. Get referrals and read testimonials. See *Niches: Finding Yours*.
5. Start a side business! See *Thrifty Entrepreneurship* on page 388.

Niches: Finding Yours

"If everybody is doing it one way, there's a good chance you can find your niche by going exactly in the opposite direction." – Sam Walton

Know who you are and the problems you solve to attract the right people. Here are six factors to determine your niche:

Your motivation – Who are you passionate to help? Your purpose attracts different people.

Your personality – Are you funny, serious, vulnerable, conscientious? Let your personality shine in all you do.

Your story – In what industry did you work? Target the same struggling people.

Your background – What elements of your backstory can you share? Your religion, industry, and where you grew up are part of your story the right people will relate to.

Your network – Who knows you by name, engages with you online, or lives near you? What are the needs within your network?

Your values – What kind of impact do you want to have? Working with people with similar values often seems right.

Your Unique Contribution – What do you do best that others need most? Your superpowers are also differentiators.

Idea for Action

Go through the considerations, and list your answers. Then watch *How To Find A Profitable Niche Market In 3 Easy Steps*: bit.ly/findnichemarkets.

Risk Taking

"If you dare nothing, then when the day is over, nothing is all you will have gained." – Neil Gaiman

People who are great at risk-taking are comfortable with ambiguity, take a rational approach to decision-making, and embrace challenges.

Reentering the workforce after a long absence carries risk. Quitting your job is a risk. So is staying. Asking for things you want might be a risk. Stepping out in a new direction is a risk. Starting a business is a risk.

For some, taking risks is unnatural. Our brains are wired to protect us, so when we consider doing something we believe is risky, our brains instantly try to shield us from harm through self-doubt and thoughts to talk us out of taking risks.

Many struggle with fear and self-doubt, and thoughts of doubt and failure leave them stuck.

Willingness to take risk does not promote recklessness. Risk implies one can't be 100 percent certain of the outcome; the potential for both failure and reward exists.

You won't be completely comfortable taking a risk because comfort is safety. *Safety is the domain of underachievement.*

Ideas for Action

To increase risk tolerance, trust you can figure things out.

Journal your successes. Include how and why you succeeded. Next, create pro and con lists for not taking a specific risk. Do the pros or cons motivate you more?

Free Isn't Valued

"Understand that people value what they pay for. You're not doing them a disservice by charging them, you're actually doing a profound service for the people who want to take action." – Ramit Sethi

Ramit Sethi wrote an article explaining the culture he grew up in mandates doing free favors for family and friends. For example, a doctor is expected to give a free second opinion.

Sethi had a course with a $2,000 fee. He was often asked by family and friends to provide the course at no charge. Sethi didn't mind helping people for free, but he noticed something interesting. When he reviewed usage reports of the training, no one with free access logged into the course. Not once.

When people requested free access, he shared this fact, and some people then chose to pay. Those who originally asked for free access but ended up paying completed all course modules.

I've had similar experiences. Clients who didn't pay for their own coaching were less committed, more likely to not complete the program, and most commonly canceled appointments.

Idea for Action

Instead of offering free services or products, consider setting a standard discount, such as 10 or 15 percent for friends or family. Create fairness in how you apply discounts and give people a chance to have skin in the game.

Prospect Calls, Giving Away Too Much

"When you start seeing your worth, you'll find it harder to stay around people who don't." – Anonymous

When starting a coaching practice, I made two big mistakes. I coached people in discovery calls and let the call run over the scheduled time.

After I started certifying coaches, I learned other coaches were making the same mistake of coaching prospects in the discovery call. The purpose of a discovery call is to determine if you are a fit to work together. Can you solve the customer's problem, and do your values and personality align?

Generally, two reasons cause coaching during discovery calls: being a natural helper or a need, even subconsciously, to prove our abilities to the prospect.

Eventually, I learned to respect both my time and my prospective customer's time by using discovery calls for the intended purpose. Set discovery calls to 15 minutes where 10 minutes is for the prospect to share their need, and five minutes is reserved for you to share the outcomes a customer can expect and answer any questions. Avoid getting deep into the "how."

Idea for Action

At the beginning of discovery calls, outline the expectation 10 minutes is reserved for the prospects to share their need, and the remaining time is reserved to discuss what they can expect to receive and answer questions. If discovery calls are longer, practice saying, "We have five minutes left so I want to make sure we cover _____ ."

Prospect Conversions

"Human beings are social creatures. We look to others to determine what actions we should take." – Neil Patel

Two small changes increased my prospects converting to paid clients. After completing a discovery call, tell prospective clients you will send a proposal. In the follow up, give prospective clients a one-page pdf of testimonials addressing problems you solved similar to those of the prospect.

Consider offering three packages, such as "Platinum," then "Gold" and "Silver" with value increasing in each. Marketing research shows people are more likely to buy when they have multiple options. Too many options yields the opposite effect.

If a client is price conscious, consider counter-offering a scaled-down package if they say your proposal is out of their budget. For example, if they can't afford your full program, offer a mini version, such as a one-hour session instead of three sessions. You might still offer assistance. Some help is better than none.

For example, a resume writer could offer a critique service in addition to resume writing services. Don't lower your price. It's unfair to clients who paid full price, and you undervalue yourself. Prices change only if value is added or removed.

Idea for Action

For more ideas, read Neil Patel's article, *15 Psychological Triggers to Convert Leads into Customers*: bit.ly/npateltriggers

Pitching Your Ideas

"There are limits to the human attention span, which is why a pitch must be brief, concise, and interesting." – Oren Klaff

A friend once told me two main reasons people don't pitch their ideas. The first is they're afraid their manager will take credit for the idea. The second is people think if their idea were good, someone would already have thought of it.

I want to address the latter concern. You have a unique point of view because you are a one-in-eight-billion person. No one on Earth is endowed with your specific talents, values, skills, personality, and experiences. It's quite possible no one came up with the idea before because no one has your perspective.

Having a great idea and getting people to pay attention to your ideas are not the same. Garnering interest requires knowing what matters to others and placing them in the position to consider the idea. Get people to care by getting them to feel. Evoking their emotions causes them to connect with your idea.

Idea for Action

I'm a big Sam Horn fan. Read her article titled "Confused People Don't Say Yes" for great insights to making a better pitch at bit.ly/confusedpeopledontbuy. I also recommend clicking follow within the article to access Sam's valuable insights.

Passive Income

"The greater the passive income you can build, the freer you will become." – Todd Fleming

My mother always impressed upon me to create passive income, and I took her advice to heart. When starting my business, I offered only career coaching services. Coaching is a competitive space.

I broke down what I naturally did best into a framework, or method, others could follow. Next, I wrote books about my methods to create avenues of self-help. Then, I created training programs to teach other coaches to use my methods.

I listed the programs in the back of my books on a "Work with the Author" page.

I created standalone products such as the YouMap® profile recruiters buy to submit with a candidate or job seekers take to an interview to stand out. I created a do-it-yourself Mini-YouMap® for parents to complete with their children.

Finally, I created a Master Trainer program to teach YouMap® coaches to train others in the YouMap® framework. My approach is transferable to other roles and industries.

Have you considered creating intellectual property and developing a formal process for what you do well?

Idea for Action

Get your process or idea into the world. Create a course, video, book, or product to sell. Dream a bit! List values-aligned goals for how you would use the freedom passive income creates.

Writing a Book: Know Why

"If there is a book you want to read but it hasn't been written yet, then you must write it." – Toni Morrison

Writing a book is daunting. With a routine, a topic you're passionate about, and consistency, you can do it. If you don't know why you want to write a book, you will quit. You're also likely to be disappointed with the result. An average book sells 250 copies in a year. You could have similar results, unless you have a large, supportive network.

If your goal is making money, you could be disheartened. Authors who earn sizable revenue publish multiple books. Breaking even after paying an editor and cover designer is a realistic goal for beginners. I don't mean to deter you. Writing a book opens doors and can catapult your career. Books can generate revenue. Solid reasons to write a book are to:

- Boost credibility
- Offer copies to prospective clients
- Generate leads
- Sell services
- Position yourself as an authority
- Generate speaking opportunities
- Gain media attention
- Help more people
- Create diverse, passive income strategies

Idea for Action

Review your reasons for writing a book to get clear on your goal. Knowing the goal helps you feel successful, regardless of sales figures.

Writing a Book: 3 Mistakes to Avoid

"No matter how many mistakes you make or how slow you progress, you are still way ahead of everyone who isn't trying." – Tony Robbins

Here are three book writing mistakes to avoid:

Editing as you write – A book is an iterative process. After you write it, you can edit it with a fresh perspective. Beta readers will give feedback. Your editor will make suggestions. Get the words out. They can be changed and improved through the process. Just write, even if it stinks.

Failing to set daily writing goals – If you don't set daily goals, you lose sight of progress. Reaching small goals helps you stay motivated. Writing a book is a large goal: break it down.

Trying to do too much – Before writing my first children's book, *You've Got Gifts!*, I met with a consultant, Wendy Gilhula, author of the PIKA bunny series. After I explained my book she said, "That's four books." Her advice was priceless. Cramming multiple books into one is a common mistake.

My first book took four times longer to write than this one, despite being a third the size. Lessons learned make each book easier.

Idea for Action

Set a daily writing goal. An average nonfiction book is 50,000 words. Avoid books over 80,000 words—it's a sign of bloat. To determine a daily goal, use a formula:
Total words ÷ days until due = daily goal (for writing daily)

Example: 50,000 ÷ 90 = 555.5 words per day

Writing a Book: Stay on Track!

"A professional writer is an amateur that didn't quit." – Richard Bach

Consistency is key with most success. Writing a book is no different. Many points in the process will make you want to quit. I thought each book I wrote was awful when writing it. *Maximize 365* was no exception, but I kept at it.

Here are tips to stay on track:

Find the intersection where you're most passionate and where you can help, entertain, or inspire people. Don't write books you don't have a desire for. You'll procrastinate.

Determine a due date. I use Excel to create formulas to track when my book is due, today's date, and how many words I must write daily to meet the deadline. I open the spreadsheet daily to assess progress. My goal is usually 1,000 words daily.

Schedule your writing and write even if you don't want to. Motivation *follows* action. By the time you get into the swing of writing, you'll be motivated and surpass the daily goal.

Pick a friend or two as accountability partners to share how many words you've written. Embedding a bit of potential shame in the process works well (just teasing).

Idea for Action

Choose a time to write when you're at your best. Following an outline makes writing easier. See *Timing Matters* on page 20 in the *Health & Wellness* chapter to find optimum times to write.

Job Search

The following topics are covered in Job Search:

8 Steps After Job Loss
Returning to Work After an Absence
Networking Pitch
Creative Job Board Search
Keeping Resumes Updated
Unqualified? Apply Anyway
Stories in Interviews
Panel Interviews
Performing in Interviews
Preparing for Interviews
Presentation Interviews
Qualifying/Screening Interviews
Tell Me About Yourself
Salary Negotiation
Assess Job Offers
Declining Job Offers
Counter Job Offers

8 Steps After Job Loss

"I needed to lose you to find me." – Selena Gomez, "Lose You to Love Me"

A job search is a job. Eight steps to take after a job loss:

1. *Order* YouMap, a step-by-step guide to land a job, at bit.ly/YouMapBook.
2. *Deal with your attitude.* Being upset is normal; your mindset must not block progress. Replace negative emotions by taking a perspective of provision. "I have what I need. Things will work out." Repeat daily.
3. *Update your budget.* If you don't have one, create one.
4. *Review your online presence.* Search your name, scan your social media, and set posts to private. Edit privacy settings on past posts, and delete questionable posts.
5. *Get recommendations.* Ask for, and give, LinkedIn recommendations.
6. *Update job search materials.* Tailor your resume to target jobs and update your LinkedIn profile.
7. *Nail your pitch.* Be able to explain what you're seeking.
8. *Leverage your network.* Share the role you want and value you offer.

Entries to help with the above list are upcoming!

Ideas for Action

Use a tracker such as Excel to manage leads and applications with contact names, follow-up dates, and statuses. Set and celebrate goals weekly to stay encouraged. Enlist help to avoid getting stuck.

Returning to Work After an Absence

"You don't have a career. You have a life." – Cheryl Strayed

Repeat after me: Career gaps aren't bad. They're opportunities!

If you took a break to care for sick or aging relatives, you have a story of dedication, sacrifice, and service.

If you took a break to raise children, you had clear priorities and values and intentionally aligned your life to them.

If you have a gap due to incarceration, you have an opportunity to show dependability and willingness to work hard. Express gratitude for second chances and share lessons leading to your growth.

Shift your perspective from negative to positive. Your attitude will take you far. Be unapologetic about your gap. It shaped who you are. Whatever the gap, you had experiences and learned skills and character-building lessons. Focus on that!

Idea for Action

Feel like an underdog? People love underdogs! Use it to your advantage.

What did you learn in your career gap you can connect to the job? Examples: consistency, tenacity, empathy, organization, multi-tasking, prioritization, managing ambiguity, change, improvising, planning, mediating. Marketable skills!

List knowledge and skills gained, plus innate abilities. Turn the list into 4-5 stories to use in cover letters, your resume, your LinkedIn profile and interview answers.

Networking Pitch

"No great deed was ever accomplished without focus—a defined direction and purpose. Olympic athletes win by focusing on one sport, not several." – Steve Woodruff

When I facilitate workshops for career explorers, I commonly see two areas of struggle for participants. The first is clarity in their next career move. The second is succinctly explaining why they are a good fit for an opportunity.

You must be clear what you're looking for and your knowledge, skills, and abilities which make you a great person to hire.

A solid 60-second pitch contains three elements:

1. Role or customers you're targeting
2. Strengths and experience you bring
3. Value you offer the employer or customer

Idea for Action

Write your pitch and practice saying it aloud until it's natural.

Role targeted:

"I'm an accountant with 10 years of experience seeking a process improvement role in a medium-sized financial services company."

Strengths and experience and value employer will receive:

"I recently acquired my Six Sigma green belt and transformed the accounting function in my current role through process reengineering and improvements, saving the company $100,000 annually."

Creative Job Board Search

"Well, it's not easy to find something that you do not know exists." – Patricia Nedelea

Have you used a job board, such as Indeed or CareerBuilder®?

Most users search job boards by using job titles. If you're seeking a project manager role, you might search "Project Manager Healthcare" to include the desired industry. Let's look at a creative way to find jobs you might not have thought of.

If you've read my book *YouMap*, you'll know I share 85 percent of skills are transferable to other jobs, which means you can perform jobs you might not have considered.

I'm a believer in starting a job search from the inside instead of the outside. What are you good at? What skills do you enjoy? Look inward to what you do best. Discover what fits you rather than stuffing yourself into what's out there. Get creative with your searches using keywords to see who needs what you do best!

Idea for Action

Create a list of keywords for job board searches. The *Ideal Day Exercise* is a perfect source for your list. Combine 3-4 of your strengths and skills to search. If you're *strategic* and enjoy *project management*, search "strategic project management" on a job board.

If you're *analytical*, a *problem solver*, and enjoy *process improvement*, enter those terms in the search. You can even add certifications as keywords.

Keeping Resumes Updated

"The biggest mistake that you can make is to believe that you are working for somebody else. Job security is gone. The driving force of a career must come from the individual." – Earl Nightingale

Getting comfortable in a job is easy to do. Human beings are creatures of habit. Always remember, companies will make decisions best for the company above all else.

You've certainly heard of, or witnessed, loyal employees laid off after many years of service, top executives swiftly replaced, and entire divisions purged. It's a mistake to believe jobs are secure. Everyone is expendable. Even founders of companies have been removed and replaced.

You don't want to compound a job loss with the harsh reality of being unprepared for a job search. During the shock of losing your job is not the best time to prepare job search materials.

When you are secure and confident in your position is the time to capture success stories and update your job search materials without the high stakes pressure.

See *Brag Folders* on page 253 for tracking all of your accomplishments. Ask for feedback regularly if you don't have formal performance reviews at work.

Idea for Action

Set a recurring calendar appointment every three months to review your resume and LinkedIn profile and update a master resume with your accomplishments, kudos, and awards.

Unqualified? Apply Anyway

"All our dreams can come true—if we have the courage to pursue them." – Walt Disney

Men will apply for a job with 60 percent of the qualifications. Women will apply if they meet 90 percent or more.

When people don't apply for a job, the top reason cited for men and women is, "I didn't think they would hire me since I didn't meet the qualifications, and I didn't want to waste my time and energy."[106]

Eighty-five percent of skills transfer from job to job. Knowing this helped me get offers four times when I didn't meet requirements—by connecting transferable skills and experience to the position.

Research reveals top reasons a candidate was hired are the decision maker believed the person would fit the team and had an appealing personality. I've also hired people who didn't meet all of the requirements for those reasons.

I hired Megan to conduct new hire orientation because I would want her as my "first friend" at work. She had no experience with Learning Management Systems. I knew she could learn, but I couldn't train attitude.

If you meet all qualifications, you're probably ready for a promotion! If you believe you can do the job, apply.

Idea for Action

Go through the position description and write stories of your transferable skills for each role. If you don't have a skill, write a story about learning a similar skill quickly in a prior role.

Interview Stories

"Tell me about a time you didn't have information or resources you needed to complete a task. What did you do?" – Interviewer

S.T.A.R. stories are used to answer behavioral interview questions. The S.T.A.R. format is as follows:

1. What *Situation* did you face? Be brief. Give the minimum background for context.
2. What was the *Task* to be accomplished, i.e., What did you set out to do? Use one or two sentences.
3. What *Actions* did you take? Be brief. The interviewer might zone out if you don't get to the point.
4. What *Results* did you achieve? The result is the highlight of the story. Outcomes are key!

List 4-5 achievements in your career, then use the 4-step process to describe successes in two minutes or less. Draw from multiple sources for S.T.A.R. stories:

- Past experiences
- Strengths
- Job description requirements
- Values employers seek such as honesty, dependable, strong work ethic, self-motivated, positive, adaptable

Idea for Action

Practice writing stories. Visit a job board, such as Indeed.com, and search jobs you think you would enjoy. Highlight requirements where you have knowledge, skill, or ability. Write a S.T.A.R. story for each.

Panel Interviews

"If your palms start to sweat before a one-on-one interview, you can imagine the nerves that come when a potential employer says you'll be meeting with not one, but four people—all at the same time!" – Nicole Lindsay

Panel interviews are conducted by a group of two or more interviewers. The advantage of a panel interview is you have a chance to see how the group interacts.

Panel interviews can be nerve-wracking. Try to frame a panel interview as speaking with a group of peers if the thought of a panel interview makes you nervous.

As interviewers ask questions, avoid looking only at the person asking. Address your answers to everyone in the room by shifting your glance across each person every 4-to-5 seconds. Taking this approach projects confidence.

Bring a copy of your resume for each member of the panel. Shake each person's hand and thank them at the end of the interview. Pay attention to the quietest person: They might be the final decision maker.

Idea for Action

Note the names of each person in the panel interview in a notebook. When a person asks a question, use his or her name once when you respond to their question. People are attentive to the sound of their own names, and they'll be impressed you remembered each of their names in the interview.

Performing in Interviews

"Death will be a great relief. No more interviews." – Katharine Hepburn

1. Arrive five minutes early.
2. Be friendly to all, even people who won't interview you.
3. Greet interviewer with a warm smile and firm handshake.
4. Look people in the eyes, tell them you're glad to meet.
5. Walk with purpose, and smile with confidence.
6. Speak clearly enough to be heard: Vary your pitch and pace.
7. Look for clues about the person to make a connection.
8. Ask questions or comment on items of mutual interest.
9. Listen closely to what the interviewer says.
10. Observe the interviewer, and match their style and pace.
11. Answer interviewer's questions confidently and honestly.
12. Limit answers from 20 seconds to two minutes.
13. Pause to arrange your thoughts when needed.
14. Ask for clarification if you don't understand a question.
15. Be confident, not overconfident.
16. Keep answers positive and constructive.
17. Ask questions about the role and the work to be done.
18. Ask what a top performer looks like in the role.
19. Share you enjoyed hearing about the role. Thank them.
20. Ask for next steps and timing.
21. Send a thank you note in the mail, as well as by email.
22. Tell them you're interested in the position, if so.
23. Never burn bridges with anyone, no matter the situation.

Idea for Action

Share five accomplishment stories with a friend for feedback.

Preparing for Interviews

"During job interviews, when they ask: 'What is your worst quality?', I always say: 'Flatulence'. That way I get my own office." – Dan Thompson

Quick tips to prepare for an interview:

1. Research the team, what they do, and roles within the department.
2. Make a list of questions to ask and points to make.
3. Go through the job description. Prepare 4-5 success stories linked to the top 4-5 requirements.
4. For in-person interviews, know the location. Make a test run beforehand, if needed.
5. Dress neatly and professionally to keep focus on what you say instead of your appearance.
6. Bring a pad and pen to take notes and capture the names of the interviewers for sending thank you notes.
7. Bring information about the job, copies of your resume, and any research in a folder with the company/position on the tab.
8. Bring work samples, if appropriate.

Idea for Action

Review the job description and highlight all requirements. Write your experiences, strengths, and personality traits and map them to each requirement with a brief story. See *Interview Stories* on page 289.

Presentation Interviews

"If you have an important point to make, don't try to be subtle or clever. Use a pile driver. Hit the point once. Then come back and hit it again. Then hit it a third time – a tremendous whack."
– Winston Churchill

For some interviews, you may be asked to give a presentation followed by a question and answer period. A format like this is common for sales and training roles and gives you a chance to show your communication abilities.

While you want your presentation to be unforgettable, avoid using gimmicks or being too cute. Follow the instructions given.

Begin the presentation with a hook. Share an interesting fact or statistic or ask a question. Questions pull your audience in right at the outset.

Create a structure for your talk such as:

- Engaging hook
- Three key points
- Discussion or activity
- Wrap-up

Finally, practice! Execute a dry run using the technology in front of a mirror to ensure you're ready for prime time.

Idea for Action

Conduct enough research on the company, role, products, or services and their customers to select a topic most relevant to the audience. Seek to incorporate and demonstrate skills you have required by the job.

Qualifying/Screening Interviews

"Excellence is to do a common thing in an uncommon way." – Booker T. Washington

Phone screens are 15-60 minutes by phone. Have your resume and notes on the employer and role in front of you. Find a quiet place with no distractions. Consider standing during a phone interview to project confidence.

If an interviewer calls without an appointment, ask for a few minutes to call back or schedule for another time.

Interviewers focus on your experience, education, skills, and personality in an early screen. If the interviewer asks about salary and you aren't clear on the role, try to delay money talk until you have an understanding of the position. You can say, "I'd like to learn the responsibilities before discussing salary."

A recruiter might insist on your expected salary in the first conversation. Determine the salary range for the area and position and give the interviewer a range. "I've researched the market for similar positions in Charlotte, North Carolina, and the range is $75,000-$85,000. My salary expectations are in this range."

Ask what the manager wants to accomplish through the job. The screening interviewer might not have all the answers.

Idea for Action

For salary discussions, search glassdoor.com to find reported salaries for a company. Search salaries on job boards for similar roles in the target geographic area.

Tell Me About Yourself

"Know thyself." – Socrates

Following is my practical formula to wow interviewers when answering, "Tell me about yourself."

1. Select three strengths related to the job.
2. Add the value you bring with these strengths.
3. Tell a story to back it up by reviewing the posting and choosing three things they want where you excel.

Let's say you chose these keywords from a posting:

Disciplined/organized
Relationship-builder
Accountable

Example:

"I'm a relationship-builder, a disciplined organizer, and an accountable person (your strengths). These qualities create unwavering trust in customers (value you bring). For example … ." Share a story from your experience to back your claims.

Get noticed by sincerely sharing what the employer needs most and demonstrating how you do it best while everyone else rattles off their work history (yawn).

Idea for Action

Ask three people you've worked with, or who know you well, to share their opinion of your top three strengths.

You can take the CliftonStrengths assessment at gallup.com/cliftonstrengths. Choose the Top 5 Strengths option from the assessment store. You don't need the full 34.

Salary Negotiation

"Diplomacy is the art of letting someone else have your way."
– Sir David Frost

Ideally, you should research salary prior to applying and interviewing for a position. Once you've interviewed and understand the position requirements, you might need to reevaluate your salary expectations. If you're past this point and haven't completed this step, don't worry. It's not too late to negotiate up until the offer is accepted.

You don't want to be unprepared with an offer on the table and no time to research salary information. If you receive an offer, request 24 hours to review the offer in detail. During this time, you can prepare a counteroffer if you haven't already negotiated and agreed upon the salary.

Following are some reputable tools for salary research:

www.salaryexpert.com (global salary and cost of living data)
www.salary.com
payscale.com
www.onetonline.org
www.glassdoor.com

Idea for Action

Need help preparing the exact words to say to ask for the salary you want? Read this article for guidance:
bit.ly/negotiatesalarytips

Assessing Job Offers

"Trust the vibes you get. Energy doesn't lie." – Unknown

Things to consider before accepting a job:

Does your research show fair market salary for the job? Not the title—actual responsibilities.

Have they communicated benefits? Hold accepting until then.

Is the offer in writing? Don't resign your current job, yet.

Have you discussed the offer with a trusted mentor?

Is the salary too high? Inflated salary can be a red flag. Ask why the salary is higher than market rate. Research the culture.

Is the job something you picture yourself doing daily?

Is your partner supportive of you accepting the position?

Do you understand work hours, travel, dress code, schedule flexibility, the culture, and personality of your manager?

Is the position a dead end? Does the job offer a career path?

Is the company and role aligned with your values?

Is the job a step down? Be prepared to explain your decision in a future job search.

Do you have gut instincts about the job? Don't ignore them.

Idea for Action

Crossroadscareer.org offers a free "Understand the Offer" exercise to help you make a decision to accept or decline a position: bit.ly/evaluateanoffer.

Declining Job Offers

"Refuse to attach a negative meaning to the word 'no.'" –
Anthony Iannarino

Declining an offer is awkward. If the position isn't right, you'll
be looking for another one in no time, by your choice or the
employer's.

"No" is best for everyone involved. If you don't think a role is
a good fit, your manager will likely come to the conclusion
before long.

If an offer doesn't match your needs, the first question is, "Can
I negotiate what I want?" If you don't ask, you don't get.

If the reason a role is not a fit has nothing to do with offer
details—the position just isn't what you thought—
communicate your decision quickly.

Idea for Action

When declining an offer:

- Be prompt in sharing your decision.
- Express appreciation for the offer.
- Offer a reason, without burning a bridge.
- Leave the door open for the future.

"Thank you for extending an offer for the project manager
position at Acme. Upon interviewing, I understand this role
will not have direct contact with external clients, which I enjoy
most. If a client-facing opportunity opens in the future, I would
enjoy a chance to discuss the role. I sincerely appreciate your
time."

Counter Job Offers

"Never accept a counteroffer. If they weren't good to you the first time, they've lost their chance to gain your loyalty and trust. What makes you think it will be better the next time?" – Christine Bray

When I was career coaching, I heard stories from clients who regretted accepting a counteroffer from their employer after they attempted to resign. It happened to me too. My employer never followed through on promises made, and I was gone in a year. Eighty-nine percent of people who accept counteroffers are gone within six months.[107]

Either the employer doubts your loyalty and starts seeking your replacement, or the things that made you want to leave still exist and weren't worth the pay increase. Research on counteroffers shows the effect of a raise lasts five weeks before you become dissatisfied again.

Remember, your employer should have done right by you from the beginning, not when their back was against a wall.

Idea for Action

Before submitting a resignation, list reasons you want to leave your job, prioritized by most to least important. Your list will help you resist counteroffers that don't resolve your reasons for leaving.

Professional Development

The following topics are covered in Professional Development:

Failure ... Or Temporary Defeat?
Learn from Failure
Weaknesses
Consistency
Don't Ask, Don't Get
Lifelong Learning
Concentration
Persistence
First Impressions
Stop Apologizing
Masterminds
Owning the Room
Public Speaking
Volunteer Work

Failure ... Or Temporary Defeat?

"Remember when your plans fail that temporary defeat is not permanent failure." – Napoleon Hill

When my book, *Your Team Loves Mondays ... Right?* released in 2020, I had a setback.

Forty-eight LinkedIn content contributors created videos and posts to support the launch and drove a lot of attention. No one could buy the e-book from Amazon.

An issue with Kindle delayed purchase of the book for two days. My first reaction was devastation. I quickly bounced back and remembered failure is only failure if accepted as such.

I chose to see the hiccup as a temporary defeat. Failure is final. Setbacks are temporary.

Eventually, the book hit number one on Amazon two weeks later in the Human Resources and Organizational Learning category.

What appears to be failure is almost always a temporary setback unless we choose to make it final. Perseverance, despite setbacks, can lead to eventual success and increase our self-esteem.

Idea for Action

Remind yourself setbacks are temporary. Brainstorm ideas to move beyond a current setback to reach your goal with a new approach. Ask a friend or family member skilled at idea generation to help, and get feedback from people you trust.

Learn From Failure

"You have to see failure as the beginning and the middle, but never entertain it as an end." – Jessica Herrin

If at first you don't succeed, try, try again isn't sage advice.

It's true the majority of people who experience success do so after repeated attempts; however, they don't just try again. They examine their failure. And *then* try again.

How do you examine failure?

Write:

1. *What went well?* Leverage and expand on things which worked instead of reinventing the wheel.

2. *What could be done differently or better?* Open your mind to possibilities instead of criticizing yourself.

3. *What got in your way?* Expose barriers so you can plan for them next time, including objections you faced, something you didn't prepare for, or a mistake you made.

4. *What one thing should be changed?* Prioritize and focus on the most important things first. Use these questions if a product failed, your pitch was rejected, or you didn't ace the interview. You can apply them to any setback. Have you ever examined your failures?

Idea for Action

Examine a setback by working through the four questions. Ask a mentor to help you, or independently, to adjust your plan.

Weaknesses

"Never be afraid to expose a weakness in yourself. Exposing a weakness is the beginning of strength." – Robert Anthony

Have you reached a point of comfort in admitting your weaknesses? Spending time doing things you're not good at keeps you outside your zone of genius—the place where you do things better than most.

Are you wondering, "Should I work on my weaknesses?"

I'm frequently asked this question.

The answer is yes, and no.

My greatest weakness is being inconsistent. I'm not a routine person and struggle to put my kids to bed at the same time every night. Consistent sleep is important, so my husband handles bedtime because routine comes easy for him.

Ask yourself these questions to determine if you should invest time developing a weakness:

- Does the weakness create issues for you or others?
- Must you be involved? Can someone else handle the task or situation?

An interpersonal weakness should almost always be developed. Not listening will not serve you well, for example.

Idea for Action

List your top weaknesses. Indicate any problems the weakness causes and possible solutions to try.

Consistency

"What you do every day matters more than what you do once in a while." – Gretchen Rubin

Doing things once in a while doesn't shape our lives. Consistent effort gets us where we want to be. For example, make it a practice to spend time in this book daily. Capture actions to take in the *Act* section at the back of the book. Prioritize goals and actions by scheduling them in your calendar.

At the end of a year, you can expect measurable results in areas of focus.

You can learn to be more consistent. I'm not consistent by nature, so if you're like me, be encouraged. It's possible to be consistent by setting up simple routines. I write one or two books yearly by creating a deadline, estimating the total word count, choosing days of the week to write, and estimating the number of words to write each day to meet the goal.

To ensure I write, I connect it to another routine. Each morning I make myself a protein shake. I sit down to write as I drink my shake and write even if I don't want to. I put my phone out of reach to eliminate distractions.

Consistency isn't sexy, but it's the difference between failure and success. It is my number one productivity tip.

Writing half an hour daily might not seem like much, but if you do, you'll end up with two 50,000-word books within a year. That's pretty sexy.

Idea for Action

Isolate a desired goal. Link new activities to existing ones.

Don't Ask, Don't Get

"A lot of people are afraid to say what they want. That's why they don't get what they want." – Madonna

We can explain what we want in life. We temper it by caring about the needs of those we're in relationship with.

Speak up and voice your needs instead of silently hoping someone will step in and know what you want. Your request gives people a chance to meet your needs or help you in meaningful ways that feel good to them.

If you want to shadow a coworker to learn a new skill, tell your manager. Ask to include it in your performance goals, and share ideas how you'll help the team.

If you want a promotion, talk to a mentor and your manager. Develop a plan to make it happen. If you work too many hours, explain you must cut back for your well-being.

Staying silent and wishing for the best is less effective than discussing how your needs and desires can become reality. If your manager isn't interested to help you, that's good information to know.

Idea for Action

Reflect on what you want. Plan a conversation, soon, with a person who can give it to you. Ask as if you expect to get it. Not with entitlement but confidence. Be clear, specific, and heartfelt. Explain what's in it for them. If the answer is no, consider asking, "What would it take to make this happen?"

Lifelong Learning

"Anyone who stops learning is old, whether at twenty or eighty. Anyone who keeps learning stays young." – Henry Ford

Have you ever used Adobe Photoshop? It's an intimidating software to learn. I once had to learn Photoshop, and it made my brain hurt. I was impressed when my grandfather learned to use it—in his eighties!

Lifelong learning involves curiosity across a range of topics, seeking knowledge through formal and informal learning opportunities, and continually stretching oneself to broaden horizons.

To be a lifelong learner, you must take responsibility for your own learning. Create a learning toolbox that works for you based on how you learn, such as reading, listening to audiobooks and podcasts, or taking courses. The best way to learn is by application of what you learn. Keeping up with the future of work will require continuous learning.

Other ways to encourage lifelong learning are through your career choices, projects, and hobbies. You also increase learning by asking questions. If you don't know something, ask! To admit we don't know something is a sign of humility.

Idea for Action

Start a "to learn" list based on your career or industry. Each year, search new and in demand skills for your position, such as *"project manager in demand skills."* Add skills to your learning list to stay relevant. Set due dates to ensure follow through. Look into your company assisting with any costs.

Concentration

"Surprising results are possible. Concentration is a decisive factor." – Carlo Ancelotti

In our distracted, digital world, concentration is a lost art. Experts say constant disruptions erode an ability to concentrate.

Dr. Glen Wilson at London's Institute of Psychiatry found those distracted by their phones and emails experienced a 10-point drop in IQ. From his research, he claims constant interruptions have the same effect as the loss of a night's sleep.[108]

An issue with digital distractions is they're difficult to ignore, as they have us in an addicting grip. Reaching for a device is a subconscious grab at a digital fix.

According to research from RescueTime, one of several apps for iOS and Android created to monitor phone use, people spend an average of three hours and 15 minutes on their phones every day, with the top 20 percent of users spending upwards of four and a half hours.

Increase concentration by training your brain with crossword or jigsaw puzzles and wordsearches. Exercise is known to increase focus, as is listening to classical music and avoiding processed foods and sugars.[109]

Idea for Action

Keep a daily distraction list. Add distractions as they enter your mind to address during a scheduled break. Distractions include calls, texts, online searches, email, and social media.

Persistence

"Enthusiasm is common. Endurance is rare." – Angela Duckworth

Despite setbacks, a persistent person remains determined to achieve. If I had to pick one quality most correlated to success, it would be this one.

Persistence doesn't mean you keep beating your head against a wall doing the same thing over and over to get the same disappointing results. Thomas Edison is credited with the invention of the incandescent light bulb, yet it took many iterations of creating, testing, tweaking, and retesting before his team succeeded.

When I wrote my first book, it was hard. I didn't have a book coach and learned a lot the hard way. Many times I wanted to give up. *Maximize 365* is more work than my other books, yet I never struggled with wanting to give up.

I pushed past the point where the masses give up by outlining a realistic daily goal: I would write four entries in the book seven days per week, with set times to write. At this pace, the project would take just over three months. Some days I wrote four entries, others six or ten. I wrote on days I didn't want to. Sometimes motivation kicked in after I began. Sometimes it didn't. I never missed a day and finished two days early. I learned the secret to persistence is having a routine.

Idea for Action

Develop a routine to make persistence easier. Watch *Routines: The Key to Persistence* at bit.ly/routineandpersistence.

First Impressions

"If you want to make a good first impression, smile at people. What does it cost to smile? Nothing. What does it cost not to smile? Everything, if not smiling prevents you from enchanting people." – Guy Kawasaki

With each encounter, we create an impression within seconds of people meeting us. First impressions set the tone for the relationship and are difficult to change.

Experts say first impressions are often wrong. We have lazy brains that make snap judgments on assumptions.[110]

You won't be everyone's cup of tea. Be okay with that. You attract the right people based on who you are. Make sure not to alienate those who might be the right people. How?

- Be on time.
- Be yourself.
- Smile with sincerity.
- Dress appropriately for the situation.
- Be confident without being cocky.
- Be open and approachable.
- Be attentive to others.
- Be courteous and polite.
- Be positive.

Idea for Action

You can't control others' first impressions, but you can control yours. Challenge the lazy part of your brain by giving people a chance. Ask questions and be curious before writing them off.

Stop Apologizing

"Stop apologizing for who you are, for your laugh, for 'looking crazy', for the way you eat or sleep. Stop being sorry for being yourself." – Alex Elle

It might seem contradictory to have a *Stop Apologizing* entry in a book along with an *Apologies* entry (page 181).

These are times when apologies are the right thing to do:

1. You've over-stepped a boundary.
2. You discover you hurt someone with your actions.
3. You were incorrect about something.

Reflexive apologies are often empty fillers, which can make them appear disingenuous. Insincere apologies stem from approval-seeking and could diminish your reputation.

You should not apologize for: taking up space, crying, being upset, saying no, asking for something, asserting yourself, being different, not living up to people's expectations, expressing your thoughts, making choices that work for you, being yourself, or taking time to yourself.

Apologies suggest approval matters more than self-respect.

Idea for Action

Pause before responding. If you reflexively apologize, adjust, and say, "What I meant to say is … ." Repeat until hollow apologies are no longer a habit. "I'm sorry. I'm tired" becomes, "I've had a crazy week and can't make it. I appreciate your understanding."

Masterminds

"Every mind needs friendly contact with other minds, for food of expansion and growth." – Napoleon Hill

I have long been a proponent of mentoring but didn't join a mastermind until 2018. I joined a second mastermind in early 2020. I can say with confidence belonging to a mastermind group has been the single best action I've taken to increase my career success.

Surround yourself with other people who value investing in the success of others and who strive to have an abundance mindset.

The mastermind creates almost infinite knowledge when the minds of multiple people are brought together. Far more ideas or solutions can be conceived in a group than in any one person's mind.

A mastermind also creates accountability and reinforces motivation to reach your goals. Exposure to the ambition, persistence, self-belief, and successes of your fellow mastermind participants is a strong motivator.

Idea for Action

Start talking to your network: colleagues, business connections, clients, and friends who might know of a mastermind group you can join or might be interested in starting a group with you. Give careful thought to the members of the group. Who participates matters. You should share values with members of the group.

Owning the Room

"You can never leave footprints that last if you are always walking on tiptoe." – Leymah Gbowee

The following tip comes from Lila Smith, creator of the Say Things Better™ method of intentional communication.

Lila shares the importance of not being timid to take your place at the table.

"I walk into every room I'm in like I have a right to be there, which I do. After that, calling attention to things like technology failing or stuttering or making excuses for taking a break from social media or for the way we look only serves to show our insecurities, not our intellect. Don't apologize or make excuses for the gift of sharing your time and presence with others. Just focus on making that gift valuable."

What excuses do you make for yourself that might erode your confidence or affect how people perceive you? Does your body language in a job interview convey you don't believe in yourself? Does your posture on the podium tell the audience you aren't confident in your knowledge?

Idea for Action

Speak positive affirmations before entering a meeting or giving a talk. Remind yourself you deserve your seat at the table, such as, "My presence is my power."

Public Speaking

"Speakers who talk about what life has taught them never fail to keep the attention of their listeners." – Dale Carnegie

Public speaking is a common fear. Chris Guillebeau, author of *The $100 Startup*, gave one of the most enjoyable talks I've ever heard.

When I spoke at the Career Thought Leaders national conference, Guillebeau was there to promote his new book, *Born for This*. I remember sitting in the audience curious about his talk because he appeared to be an introvert.

Almost immediately, Chris had the audience laughing and hanging on his every word. He didn't use grand gestures; he wasn't full of energy and charisma. He leveraged his authentic personality, sense of humor, and the ability to tell a story.

Great public speakers have a few things in common: knowing their audience, clear purpose in the message, authenticity instead of trying to be someone else, and influence through narration.

Idea for Action

If you have an upcoming talk, before putting your audience to sleep with slides and statistics, make your point through a story. You lived it, you know it, you felt it. Now help others feel it and move *them* with it. At the end of your talk, distill your experience into 1-3 practical lessons, tips, or actions the audience can apply to their lives. Consider a Toastmasters club to practice public speaking. Visit toastmasters.org to find a club.

Volunteer Work

"The best way to find yourself is to lose yourself in the service of others." – Mahatma Gandhi

Aside from offering a testing ground for a new career, volunteer work can help fend off depression by focusing on others, create a sense of purpose, provide meaningful stories to tell in interviews when asked what you've been doing while unemployed, build new friendships, keep you involved in your community, and expand your skills.

I owe my career to volunteering. While working in the corporate arena, I started volunteering in a career ministry to help unemployed, underemployed, and misemployed job seekers. I became hooked on helping people in their careers.

Volunteer work led to coaching full time, which led to writing career books and my pre-career children's book series, *You've Got Gifts!*, *You've Got Values!*, *You've Got Skills!*, and *You've Got Personality!*

Volunteering helps others and can take you to new places!

Idea for Action

Consider your goals and how volunteer work could dovetail with them. Are you considering a new career path? Where might you volunteer to get an idea of the environment or typical day?

Are you interested in gaining new skills? What volunteer opportunities could help you gain these skills?

Are you currently unemployed? What volunteer work would an employer find relevant for positions you're seeking?

FINANCES

"The rich rule over the poor, and the borrower is slave to the lender."

Proverbs 22:7 NIV

Financial ignorance is costly.

According to the *S&P Global Financial Literacy Survey (FinLit, 2014)*, consequences include spending more on transaction fees, running up bigger debts, incurring higher interest loans, borrowing more, and saving less. Those who are financially literate, on the other hand, do a better job of saving for retirement and have lower financial risk due to greater diversification in their finances.[111]

On average, 56 percent of young adults age 35 or younger are financially literate, compared with 63 percent of those age 36 to 50. Financial literacy rates are lower for adults older than 50, and rates are lowest among those older than 65.[112]

The chapter is categorized into Saving Money, Managing Debt, Building Wealth, Financial Planning, and Family Money Matters. I'm not a financial expert and have curated advice and expertise from others. I hope the abundant resources ahead help you achieve better financial health.

Saving Money

The following topics are covered in Saving Money:

Ideas to Save Money
Emergency Fund
Paying Yourself
Impulse Buying
Money Buddy
Needs vs. Wants
Financial Calendar
Cash Envelope System
Frugal Living
Credit Unions
Beauty on a Budget
Ideas for Free Entertainment
Holiday Spending
Experiences Over Things
Saving Money on Rent

Ideas to Save Money

"The goal isn't more money. The goal is living life on your terms." – Chris Brogan

Are you ready to think like a saver? Many creative ways to save are available. Some ideas you might not have considered. Others you've considered but haven't implemented, then some you might already be practicing.

Let's look at eight small ways to make a big impact in a year!

1. Throw nickels, dimes, and quarters into a container. Keep a separate container for pennies. Just fifty cents daily is $182.50 annually.
2. Save automatically. Set up an automatic transfer on payday to move money to savings.
3. Don't carry the debit card to your savings account.
4. Calculate purchases by hours worked rather than cost. For example, if you want $150 shoes and make $10/hour, ask if they're worth working 15 hours for.
5. Unsubscribe from emails to avoid impulse buys.
6. Borrow books and movies for free from the library.
7. Purchase store brands instead of name brands.
8. Bag your lunch and plan meals weekly. Create a shopping list to lower grocery costs.

Ideas for Action

Choose three ideas from the above list or create your own savings ideas. Begin implementing them now.

Incorporate new tips from the list once you have achieved a goal or the new habit has become an established routine.

Emergency Fund

"If you have debt, I recommend saving a starter emergency fund of $1,000 first. Then, once you're out of debt, it's time to beef up those savings and build a fully funded emergency fund of three to six months of expenses." – Dave Ramsey

Your household size determines the size of your emergency fund. If you have a two-income household with stable employment, three months of expenses should be fine. If you are single, or if someone in your family has a chronic illness, financial experts recommend saving six months of expenses.

Emergency funds should be in cash to be easily accessible and should be used only for true emergencies, such as a car accident, medical emergency, or necessary home repair, like a leaking roof.

Ideas for Action

Consider trying these five emergency fund steps:

1. List all income and expenses.
2. Determine your needs for 3-6 months of expenses.
3. Decide on an amount to set aside monthly to reach the goal.
4. Use emergency funds for the unexpected, necessary, or urgent.
5. Replenish funds immediately by repeating the steps.

Paying Yourself

"A cardinal rule in budgeting and saving is to pay yourself first." – John Rampton

Once your paycheck hits your account, financial experts suggest you should pay yourself even before you pay bills. For example, move whatever you can, even a small amount, into an emergency savings fund.

I interviewed Rob Morgan, a chief investment officer and financial commentator. Morgan speaks on finance on CNBC, Fox Business News, and Bloomberg TV. He suggests you pay yourself through a retirement plan such as an employer 401(k). He recommends making the payment automatic so you can "set it and forget it."

If you already contribute the maximum to an employer 401(k) and want to contribute more, you can contribute to a Roth IRA and a 401(k) at the same time. Hire a financial services company of your choice to set up your IRA.

Idea for Action

If you're not paying yourself first, start now. Commit to an amount to set aside every week to pay yourself. Even twenty dollars every week, at the end of a year, would provide over $1,000. If invested, your $1,000 will grow over time.

Roth IRA accounts have historically delivered between 7 and 10 percent average annual returns, compared to 1-2 percent with a traditional savings account.

Revisit the amount you pay yourself, annually, and increase the amount each year if possible.

Impulse Buying

"...our impulses are too strong for our judgement sometimes."
– Thomas Hardy

When my sons Tristan and Justin were little, I decided to teach them about impulse buying. One day we went to Home Depot for a new trash can after losing ours in a storm.

While shopping, my sons saw a backyard fire pit and asked if we could have one. I told them, "I'd like to have a firepit, but we came for a trash can. We can plan for this purchase and come back for it if we still want one, later."

I did go back to buy the firepit a couple of weeks later.

When my sons asked for something at a checkout, I gently reminded them it was an impulse buy, and impulse buying will lead them to poor finances. I bought each of them a wallet to carry their own money so they could learn to make planned, versus impulsive, purchases. My sons, now 23 and 19, are not impulsive spenders.

Ideas for Action

Is impulse spending a challenge for you? Try these five ideas:

1. Create a list to track planned purchases.
2. Implement a 30-day wait for purchases over a set limit.
3. Give yourself a free treat for evading an impulse buy.
4. Avoid online shopping sites except to make planned purchases.
5. Avoid using credit cards.

Money Buddy

"Anything is possible when you have the right people there to support you." – Misty Copeland

Want to crush your financial goals, or any life goal? Have an accountability buddy. People trying to lose weight are more successful when they have an exercise buddy or if other adults in the house are also eating healthily.

When you are headed off the rails, your buddy can keep you accountable and vice versa. If you want to save more and spend less, a money buddy might do the trick. A money buddy can be especially helpful for people who aren't naturally disciplined.

Sharing your money goals with others makes them harder to ignore. Your money buddy can hold you accountable to monthly savings goals, creating a budget, and not overspending when shopping.

A 2014 study by Dr. Gail Matthews at the Dominican University of California found participants who sent weekly progress updates to a friend were far more likely to achieve their goals.[113] I sent weekly writing goal updates to two friends, so I know this works with more than finances.

Ideas for Action

Consider people in your life who have reached your financial goals or are disciplined and not afraid to hold you accountable. Ask them to be your money buddy to report your weekly progress. Check in with them before and after a shopping trip. You could also join a financial support group for accountability.

Needs vs. Wants

"You can't always get what you want. But if you try some time, you find, you get what you need." – The Rolling Stones

Financial needs are essential to live and work: housing, food, clothing, insurance, transportation, fuel, and electricity.

Wants typically include things like a gym membership, entertainment, eating out, drive-thru lattes, designer clothes, travel, and brand-new cars.

NerdWallet recommends a 50/30/20 rule of thumb where 50 percent of your income is allocated to needs, 30 percent to wants, and 20 percent to savings and debt repayment. If you don't have emergency savings or have stressful debt, I recommend flipping wants and savings/debt repayment to 20 and 30 percent, respectively.

Idea for Action

Organize your budget with needs at the top followed by wants listed at the bottom. If you haven't created a budget, see *Household Budget* on page 365 in this chapter.

If you've already created a household budget, use the amount of your take home pay (after taxes) to allocate needs, wants, and savings/debt repayment.

Example with $3,400 monthly take home pay:

Needs = $3,400 x 0.50 = $1,700/month
Wants = $3,400 x 0.30 = $1,020/month
Savings and Debt repayment = $3,400 x 0.20 = $680/month

Financial Calendar

"A plan is what, a schedule is when. It takes both a plan and a schedule to get things done." – Peter Turla

As you begin to proactively manage your finances, managing and monitoring your financial picture will be easier using a financial calendar.

Ten activities and reminders to place on a financial calendar:

1. Schedule debt repayments for all loans each month.
2. Set reminders to review progress toward financial goals.
3. Schedule review of retirement investment.
4. Schedule review of your household budget.
5. Add dates of emergency fund goal milestones.
6. Add dates for renewals, such as insurance policies.
7. Set reminders to download free annual credit reports.
8. Schedule tax payment dates.
9. Set reminders to monitor accounts for suspicious activity. See *Reviewing Your Accounts* on page 393.
10. Add schedule of bill payment dates.

Automate what you can to avoid a lot of manual management.

Idea for Action

Consider downloading an app, such as *Mint*, to create a clear picture of your financial status.

Cash Envelope System

"When you pay cash for everything, your credit score becomes irrelevant." – Steven Magee

People overspend with no established limitation to stop them. An envelope system creates boundaries. Here are the steps:

1. Label a series of envelopes based on your spending categories. For example, create an envelope for groceries, gasoline, entertainment, car maintenance, gifts, health, etc.

2. Figure out your budget amount for each envelope.

3. If you get paid twice monthly, put half of the money in when you get paid and the other half from your next paycheck. For example, if you budget $150 each month for gasoline, take $75 from your bank account, and put the cash in an envelope and label it "Gas." When you get your second paycheck, do the same thing again, and put the other $75 in the envelope for a total of $150.

4. No money comes out of an envelope except to pay for purchases in that category. Put any change you get back in the envelope. Once the money is gone, it's gone. Do not borrow from other envelopes. Find creative ways to stretch your money.

Idea for Action

If you have money remaining in any of the envelopes at the end of the month, contribute the cash to debt pay off instead of spending it. Every amount helps.

Frugal Living

"The greatest wealth is to live content with little." – Plato

Being frugal is a great way to save money, but you can take it too far. Spending an entire day searching and clipping coupons to save $20 is not valuing your time.

Pulling out a calculator to itemize each penny your friends owe at dinner is tacky. Filling a container in your purse at an all you can eat buffet treads into the unethical.

Here are 10 ideas to save money and pay off debt:

1. Ditch cable or satellite television.
2. Get a library card to borrow movies and books.
3. Adjust the thermostat to save money on energy.
4. Cut out or reduce alcohol, smoking, and junk food.
5. Replace costly nights out with a weekly game night.
6. Get your hair cut at local cosmetology schools.
7. Reduce meat in your diet to lower the grocery bill.
8. Plan meals around the grocery store's weekly sales.
9. Bag your lunch and make your own coffee.
10. Shop on Craigslist and in consignment stores.

Idea for Action

You might be surprised by how many unplanned or unnecessary expenses you don't recall making.

Review your expenses for the prior month. Go through credit card and bank statements to find areas to cut back or cut out.

Credit Unions

"Before the arrival of the credit union, people who were from a poor background or a working-class background couldn't borrow from banks." – John Hume

Credit unions are nonprofit, member-owned financial cooperatives. Banks are accountable to stockholders, while credit unions answer to their members.

Credit unions can help you in a number of ways. First, they offer similar products and services to banks, but the fees are often more reasonable than from traditional banks.

Also, credit unions invest resources back into the institution instead of paying out to shareholders to continue to better serve their members.

You are more likely to receive favorable credit card and loan rates from a credit union, as well as less stringent rules to qualify for a loan. Credit unions also often provide personalized credit assistance and guidance.

Finally, credit unions focus on the local community. They often cooperate with organizations offering discounts to members on services and products they might already need.

Idea for Action

Think you might want to try a credit union?

The National Credit Union Administration (NCUA), the agency that oversees federal credit unions, provides a credit union locator online at mapping.ncua.gov.

Beauty on a Budget

"True beauty in a woman is reflected in her soul." – Audrey Hepburn

Beauty is a 90-billion-dollar-a-year business. Beauty products aren't cheap! Here are a few ideas to save money.

Update your eyewear using online optical shops like Zenni or Warby Parker instead of picking out glasses at the eye doctor's office. You'll spend a fraction of the cost for prescription eyewear online.

Drink water for healthy, glowing skin. Aim for 64 ounces daily. Take a stainless-steel water bottle everywhere you go. I wear less makeup from this tip alone.

Add beauty products to the online cart of your favorite website and leave them. Companies send reminders, often with discounts, to encourage you to buy.

DIY your manicures and pedicures. YouTube videos can help you look like you stepped out of a salon. Find coupons for beauty services such as haircuts and waxes on Groupon. Try generic store brand products instead of name brands.

Consider getting haircuts and beauty services from cosmetology schools. Shop online at Overstock.com for hairdryers and flattening and curling irons instead of paying retail price.

Idea for Action

Take advantage of free samples from freeflys.com and birthday freebies from companies like Sephora and Aveda.

Ideas for Free Entertainment

"The best things in life aren't things." – Art Buckwald

Entertainment can be expensive, especially for a family. Eating out, going to a movie, or attending a sporting event can take a big bite out of your take home pay.

Here are some low cost or free ideas:

1. Host a potluck. Create a theme like Mexican, favorite comfort food, appetizers, or breakfast for dinner. Extend the theme to costumes to add more fun.
2. Plan a morning or afternoon at the park. Pack a cooler bag and have a picnic; bring a ball to toss.
3. Check the local library for author readings and speakers.
4. Visit local attractions you've taken for granted or haven't seen in a while.
5. Go for a weekend hike, bike ride, or fishing adventure.
6. Take courses online. Free Zoom webinars are cropping up from universities and culinary schools.
7. Plan a weekend movie marathon, puzzle competition, or game night.
8. Goodhousekeeping.com, smithsonianinstitute.com, travelandleisure.com, and others, offer virtual tours you can take on your couch!

Idea for Action

Search these keywords online: "Free things to do in [city/town]." Free events, concerts, and festivals are possibly available in your area you might not be aware of.

Holiday Spending

"Sharing the holiday with other people, and feeling that you're giving of yourself, gets you past all the commercialism." – Caroline Kennedy

Holidays can get us into debt if we aren't careful. Parents, especially, want to make birthdays or holidays memorable for children. I can't remember gifts I received for Christmas or my birthday. If it weren't for photos, I wouldn't remember any of them.

Remember how excited you were the first time you bought something you wanted? Then within a short period of time the newness wore off. The new car was a delight, then before too long you got inside and drove without the thrill.

Things aren't what make holidays special. Imagine a holiday where you receive everything you dream of but spend it alone.

Take control of holiday spending to eliminate financial stress tainting our joyful times with family and friends.

Ideas for Action

1. Set a holiday spending budget, and stick to it.
2. Make a list; don't impulsively buy unplanned items.
3. Commit to paying cash for holiday purchases.
4. Devise a plan in advance to repay when you use credit.
5. Purchase items during the year to spread the cost.
6. Shop during sales through the year to spend less.
7. Track items purchased and how much you spent.
8. Give experiences over things. Give a coupon for a homemade dinner and massage, a day at the beach, or personalized homemade gifts.

Experiences Over Things

"Fill your life with experiences not things. Have stories to tell not stuff to show." – Unknown

The science of happiness is clear. Well, sort of. We derive more satisfaction from experiences than things. Experiences are more integral to who we are than material goods.

There is a caveat, however. Lower income individuals who often don't have much beyond basics have a different response. They are similarly happy to receive things and experiences.[114]

Here are five reasons to fill your life with experiences over things, besides better finances:

1. Excitement for things fades fast.
2. Experiences form who we are.
3. Experiences can be connected to passion and purpose.
4. Anticipation of experiences causes excitement, while anticipation of things can cause impatience or stress.
5. Experiences are social, connecting us to others; social connection is better for our well-being.

We trade hours of our life working in a job we don't enjoy buying stuff we don't need.

Idea for Action

Before buying things ask, "What value will this add to my life?" and, "What am I giving up in exchange for this?"

Saving Money on Rent

"It's not how much money you make, it's how much you keep, how hard it works for you, and how many generations you keep it for." – Robert Kiyosaki

Housing is our number one budgeted monthly expense. For renters, it can be hard to save for home ownership while paying rent. Here are a few ways to save on rent.

A landlord would rather have one renter for three years than three renters in the same time period. See if you can negotiate a lower monthly rent payment by signing a longer lease if you know you won't be going anywhere.

You can also negotiate your rent when your lease comes due. If you're a good tenant, your landlord might be willing to lower your rent to keep you instead of leaving the apartment unoccupied or taking the risk of a renter who doesn't pay on time.

Look for a roommate. The more people you live with, the lower your costs. You will have less privacy, but it's a temporary sacrifice to achieve your longer-term financial goals.

Be mindful of your utility costs. Conserve water and electricity to lower your overall monthly housing costs.

Idea for Action

Consider looking for an apartment during the slow months of the year. A landlord might be open to negotiate the monthly rent to have the apartment occupied rather than sitting empty.

Managing Debt

The following topics are covered in Managing Debt:

Overspending
Revolving Debt
Monthly Credit Card Payoff
Credit Card Interest
Credit Reports
Credit Scores
$5 a Month on Your Mortgage
Debt-to-Income Ratio
Loan Cosigning
Loan Forgiveness
Loan Refinancing
Medical Debt
Student Debt
Debt Collection
Consolidation Loans
Payday Loans
Bankruptcy
Auto Leasing

Overspending

"Beware of little expenses. A small leak will sink a great ship."
– Benjamin Franklin

When we think of overspending, we might think larger purchases like $1,000 shopping sprees and $500 shoes. For most of us, the devil is in the details. Those small expenses like stopping by the Starbucks drive through five days a week costs $1,300 a year. Eating dinner out for a family of four at $10 per person is $2,080 annually.

Most people overspend because they don't have a sense of how much money is leaving their wallets. To keep overspending in check, look at your spending triggers. Do you spend money to feel better? Do you give in to temptation and impulse? Are you attempting to fill a need? Are you unsure where your money is going because you aren't tracking expenditures?

Finally, beware of social media luring you to spend. Your smart phone tattles on you by sharing your activity. If you have been searching products online, you'll soon seen ads on Instagram and Facebook prompting you to impulse buy, not to mention the influence social media has on comparison behavior.

Idea for Action

Make a list of items you plan to buy and stick to the list. Avoid stores triggering you to overspend. For example, if shopping for toiletries, head to a drug store instead of box stores or the mall if you're tempted by the clothing section.

Revolving Debt

"Today, there are three kinds of people: the have's, the have-not's, and the have-not-paid-for-what-they-have's." – Earl Wilson

Revolving debt is credit that allows customers to access money up to a predetermined limit, known as the credit limit. When the customer pays down an open balance on the revolving credit, that money is once again available for use.

TV news financial commentator, Rob Morgan, explains:

"Fixed debt is backed by an asset such as a home or a car, but the first thing you have to do is get your revolving debt under control. If you can, eliminate it. Every time you reduce your revolving debt, such as credit cards, it's effectively savings."

Idea for Action

Dave Ramsey is the author of *Total Money Makeover* and founder of Financial Peace University. He recommends the debt snowball method to repay debt:

1. List credit card debt from smallest to largest payoff balance. Don't worry about interest rates.
2. Make minimum payments on all credit cards except the smallest. Attack the smallest card with the most tenacity.
3. Pay off the smallest credit card and close the account.
4. Take the money you paid on the smallest credit card and roll it into paying off the next smallest balance.

Monthly Credit Card Payoff

"The whole point of credit cards, the way they are rendered most profitable, is that we dig ourselves into debt and stay trapped there forever." – Brett Williams

Credit reporting company Experian offers this advice:

If you are trying to establish a strong payment history, you can do so by making small purchases on your credit card each month, paying the balance in full, and making sure payments are made on time.

If you cannot pay the balance in full, keep the balance as low as possible. You should never carry a balance over **30 percent of your credit limit** on any one card or in total. The lower your balances, the better your credit scores.

Rob Morgan agrees you should pay your monthly credit card balance in full. Making the minimum payment on your credit card is financially toxic. A $2,000 credit balance with an 18 percent annual rate and a minimum payment of 2 percent of the balance or $10, whichever is greater, would take over 30 years to pay off!

Idea for Action

Calculate the percentage of your credit card limit you are using. If you're using over 30 percent of your total credit, review and categorize expenditures for the past three months to determine if you are using credit for nonessential purchases such as eating out.

Adjust your spending habits, pay more than the minimum, and restrict charges to essential bills to lower balances.

Credit Card Interest

"A cash advance on a credit card is one of the worst types of borrowing because the interest rate is typically 21 percent or more." – Suze Orman

When you pay credit card interest, you end up paying more for an item than what you borrowed.

To avoid paying interest, pay the balance in full each month. If you're unable to pay the balance, you are overspending. Credit cards should not be treated as cash, as this gives an inflated sense of your available financial resources.

If you are unable to pay the balance, pay what you can and commit to not billing more charges to the card, or you'll dig yourself into a hole.

If you have a balance of $7,800, an interest rate of 15 percent, and you make a 3 percent minimum payment of $234 monthly, you will take three-and-a-half years to pay the debt. However, you won't pay $7,800. You'll pay a whopping $10,153 with interest.

Finally, avoid cash advances. Interest accrues immediately on cash advances, so you can't avoid paying interest.

Idea for Action

Read the fine print on your credit card contract. Be cautious with "interest-free," and "same-as-cash," offers. These are deferred interest financing plans which require you to pay a balance in full by the end of the promotional period. If you don't pay in full, the interest rate is ridiculously high.

Credit Reports

"If you don't take good care of your credit, then your credit won't take good care of you." – Richard Wagner

A credit report is a report card that tells people how you manage your finances. Your report reveals your timeliness paying bills, how much debt you have, if you've filed for bankruptcy, automobile repossessions, tax liens, and if an account has been turned over to a collection agency.

The information on your report is given to credit reporting agencies from financial institutions and companies you do business with.

Reviewing your credit reports can help you discover identity theft. Items listed on your report could affect mortgage rates, apartment rental applications, or even a job application.

Idea for Action

In the US, obtain a free copy of your credit report every 12 months from annualcreditreport.com. The government mandated site allows free reports from the three major credit reporting bureaus, TransUnion, Experian, and Equifax.

In Canada, the UK, and other countries, request a free report by contacting the credit reporting bureau in your country.

Verify the information on your report is accurate. Submit a dispute for incorrect information or suspicious activity.

Credit Scores

"I don't have a FICO score because I don't borrow money. Because not being in debt is the fastest way to becoming wealthy." – Dave Ramsey

According to myfico.com:

"A FICO Score is a three-digit number based on the information in your credit reports. It helps lenders determine how likely you are to repay a loan. This, in turn, affects how much you can borrow, how many months you have to repay, and how much it will cost (the interest rate)."

The following is a general breakdown of FICO scores.

Very poor credit: 300 – 579
Fair credit: 580 – 669
Good credit: 670 – 739
Very good credit: 740 – 799
Exceptional credit: 800 – 850

Dave Ramsey points out a very good or exceptional credit score indicates you've incurred a lot of debt you've been paying off on time, for a long time.

Ideas for Action

Listen to Dave Ramsey's insightful take on FICO credit scores here: bit.ly/ramseyfico.

If you want to know your FICO credit score and your credit card does not include this information, you can purchase your score at myfico.com.

$5 a Month on Your Mortgage

"Freedom from debt is worth more than any amount you can earn." – Mark Cuban

I'd like to share an idea I learned a decade ago. Before I do, remember your primary financial goal is to build an emergency fund. See *Emergency Fund* on page 318.

Once you have an emergency fund, the next step is to pay down debt, starting with credit cards since interest rates are likely the highest on revolving credit.

Let's say you have a 30-year mortgage of $235,000 and a fixed interest rate of 3.42 percent. If you pay the monthly payment, you'd pay $141,123.93 in interest over 30 years.

If you added just $5 to the monthly payment, you wouldn't have to make the last two payments, and the payment prior would be $25.20. You're unlikely to miss $5 per month, yet it wipes out almost three full months of mortgage payments!

You might not want to put too much extra down. You'll earn more investing, benefiting from compound interest, which is often a higher rate than mortgage interest. Add extra to your mortgage once your emergency fund and credit card debt is paid. You might be able to save interest on car payments too. Doubling my monthly car payment saved $3,000 in interest. Check to make sure your loan doesn't have pre-payment penalties.

Idea for Action

Use a payoff calculator to try various extra payment amounts to see how much interest you can prevent paying. daveramsey.com/mortgage-payoff-calculator

Debt-to-Income Ratio

"One of the greatest disservices you can do a man is to lend him money that he can't pay back." – Jesse Jones

In personal finance, debt-to-income (DTI) ratio compares an individual's monthly debt payment obligation to their monthly gross income before taxes.

The DTI is used by lenders to determine your ability to repay a loan. For example, if you are looking for financing for your business, a mortgage loan, or to purchase a vehicle, the lender will have you fill out an application with information they use to calculate your DTI.

The lower your DTI, the more attractive you are as a borrower. A DTI of 43 percent is typically the highest ratio a borrower can have and still qualify for a mortgage, but lenders generally seek ratios of no more than 36 percent.[115]

To calculate DTI, total your monthly debt payments such as rent or mortgage, student loans, personal loans, auto loans, credit card payments, child support, alimony, etc. Then divide the debt payment total by your monthly income.

For example, if your monthly debt equals $2,500 and your gross monthly income is $7,000, your DTI ratio is 35.7 percent: $2,500 ÷ $7,000 = 0.357.

Idea for Action

If you are planning a home purchase, know your DTI before applying for a mortgage. An online calculator can help: zillow.com/mortgage-calculator/debt-to-income-calculator.

Loan Cosigning

"You are not helping a friend or family member by co-signing a loan." – Dave Ramsey

Years ago, I cosigned a loan for my first husband during our marriage. A couple of years later, we divorced. After my divorce, I read *Total Money Makeover* by Dave Ramsey and decided to pull my credit report.

I discovered delinquent automobile payments even though my car was paid off. The cosigned loan was on my report. My ex-husband had lost his job and was behind on the payments.

I took back the car to pay the loan, and he drove my car that was paid off. I made the final payment and closed the loan, but the damage was done. I had a delinquency reported for seven years.

Good reasons exist not to cosign. You're the first person the creditor sues if the individual making payments defaults, and you will be making the payments. The relationship could become damaged as a result. Someday you might require a loan, and the cosign could prevent you from getting funds.

Creditors require a cosigner because they know, statistically, the borrower is unlikely to pay.

Ideas for Action

Alternatives to cosigning are to get the loan yourself, so missed payments won't affect your credit. Be sure to set up a repayment schedule with interest. You might also offer to make one emergency payment to prevent a loan default.

Loan Forgiveness

"May your college memories last as long as your student loan payments." – Unknown

Public Service Loan Forgiveness (PSLF) is a federal program to encourage students to enter relatively low-paying careers such as firefighting, teaching, government, nursing, public interest law, and the military.

Once you've made loan repayments for 10 years while working for the government or a nonprofit, you can qualify for tax-free forgiveness. Tax-free means you won't have to claim the discharge amount on your taxes as income. PSLF is an option for graduates who pursue careers in public service.

Federal education loan forgiveness is also available for certain volunteer work such as the Peace Corps, AmeriCorps, or VISTA. You can earn $4,725 for 1700 hours of service.

Students who are in the Army National Guard might be eligible for the Student Loan Repayment Program, which offers up to $10,000.

Students who become full-time teachers and serve low-income students can have a portion of their Stafford or PLUS loans forgiven under The National Defense Education Act. The program forgives up to $17,500 of a loan balance.

Many law schools will also forgive loans of students who go into public law service, such as a public defender.

Idea for Action

Review the complete list of your loan forgiveness options at bit.ly/loanforgivenessnerdwallet.

Loan Refinancing

"Refinancing your mortgage payment makes sense if you can lower your interest rate by at least two points. But the most important question to ask yourself is, how long will it take you to break even?" – Barbara Corcoran

Loan refinancing refers to "the process of taking out a new loan to pay off one or more outstanding loans." Borrowers refinance to obtain lower interest rates or to reduce their overall repayment amount.

According to Dave Ramsey, first do the math to make sure you don't refinance just to lower the monthly payment. In the long run, you could end up paying more. You should refinance only if you will end up paying less over the entire period of the loan.

NerdWallet advises to "refinance loans as soon as you have good credit and a stable income to get a lower rate that saves you the most money."

Wait to refinance until interest rates are down. If you aren't sure if a refinance will benefit you, speak with a financial counselor. If you need a financial counselor to help you decide if refinancing is right for you, seek an organization that offers budget counseling and savings and debt management classes.

Ideas for Action

Before refinancing a home, review your credit for issues, prepare for a home appraisal, and get quotes from several lenders to get the best offer. Freshen your home's paint, clear clutter, and point out hidden features for the best appraisal.

Medical Debt

"My doctor gave me six months to live, but when I couldn't pay the bill he gave me six months more." – Walter Matthau

Nearly one in three Americans have delayed getting care because they're afraid of the cost, according to the *American Journal of Medicine.*[116]

According to the Consumer Financial Protection Bureau, one in five credit reports include one or more medical collections.[117] The average unpaid medical debt on credit reports is $579. However, the average debt for households that experience medical bankruptcy is $44,622. Fifty-four percent of consumers with medical debt have no other debts listed on their credit reports.

Investopedia strongly advises against placing medical bills on a credit card. Consumer debt is subject to penalties and fees. Consumer debt also hinders the ability to get a mortgage and pass a background check for a job and expands the debt.

Your best bet is to negotiate manageable payments with your provider or the hospital. You should obtain a copy of the bill and examine it carefully.

I've read statistics about billing errors and overcharges, and it's far more common than we realize.

Avoid going to the emergency room except for true emergencies. Make an appointment instead to avoid larger medical bills.

Idea for Action

In need of medical debt relief? Visit bit.ly/medicalbillhelp.

Student Debt

"Student debt is a product that has been sold to us with such repetition and intensity that most people believe they can't live without it." – Dave Ramsey

The negative effects of student debt are far-reaching. Debt limits choices. You might take jobs you don't want, forgo your dreams, live longer with parents, endure the inability to purchase a home, and miss out on jobs with background checks if you missed payments.

According to the Project on Student Debt, seven in ten college graduates leave school with debt. In the US, over 44 million people have outstanding student loans.[118]

A decade ago, average student debt in the US was approximately $17,000. As of 2019, it's closer to $30,000. In the UK, average debt in 2018 was £36,000.

Researchers at the UCL Institute of Education in London and the University of Michigan found large student debt leads to lower job satisfaction, affects lifelong finances, and harms mental health.[119]

Ideas for Action

Is college right for you? Alternatives exist. Exhaust all options before taking loans, like grants and scholarships. Enroll at a less expensive college. If you must attend a specific school, take general electives at a less expensive school, and transfer for major classes. Assess fees and credits to ensure a transfer won't extend graduation, or you could pay more. Use tuition payment plans instead of loans. Work part-time. Pay interest while in school to keep what you owe from blowing up.

Debt Collection

"You can't get out of debt while keeping the same lifestyle that got you there. Cut out everything except the basics." – Dave Ramsey

The average person carries around $38,000 in personal debt.[120]

If you default, the company will often use a collection service after 90 days to recover the debt, or sell the debt for pennies on the dollar. A potentially large profit is why collection agencies often use intimidating or aggressive tactics to get you to pay.

Once you are in collections, the agency will call you regularly and persistently and won't cease until the statute of limitations for your debt is reached (between three and ten years) or until you agree to pay.

Some people avoid debt collectors because it's stressful. Don't ignore your debt! The problem will get bigger and harder to solve. Though debt collectors can be aggressive, they want to be paid and will probably work with you. Try to set up a repayment plan or settle the debt for a lower amount. Note the IRS considers settled debt over $600 as income and will require you to report the settled amount on your taxes.[121]

Idea for Action

If you have a debt sent for collection, learn your rights according to the Fair Debt Collection Practices Act. If you don't know your rights, debt collectors could push beyond their legal boundaries. Visit bit.ly/fairdebtcollection to learn more.

Consolidation Loans

"Debt sucks. But the truth is debt consolidation loans and debt settlement companies suck even more." – Dave Ramsey

The term *debt consolidation* refers to the act of taking out a new loan to pay off other liabilities and consumer debts. Debt consolidation companies offer you a loan to cover multiple debts so you pay a single creditor. You still owe your debts but in a single payment.

Be aware the debt consolidation industry is full of scammers. Search "debt consolidation scam," and read to your heart's content.

Even aboveboard debt consolidation firms end with you getting the short end of the stick. Ultimately, you end up paying on your debt longer than if you had left your debt unconsolidated. You will most likely have a longer repayment period, which means you will pay more total interest on your debt than if you had not consolidated.

Idea for Action

Investigate these options before using a debt consolidation service:

1. Can you pay your debts on your own by getting your finances and payment schedules organized?
2. Have you tried using a credit counseling service?
3. Have you tried to settle your debts for less than you owe with your creditors?

Payday Loans

"The decision to go into debt alters the course condition of your life. You no longer own it. You are owned." – Dave Ramsey

Payday loans are short-term loans designed to trap people in a cycle of debt. They prey on people with bad credit and no savings.

In a nutshell, here is how a payday loan works:

1. You have an emergency. Say your car breaks down. The repair costs $800, and you don't have the money.
2. A payday loan storefront verifies your bank account and income.
3. The company loans your $800, and you must write a post-dated check for $920. Eight-hundred dollars pays for the original loan, and you incur $120 in interest.
4. A post-dated check is cashed on your next payday to ensure funds are available, thus, payday loan.
5. In two weeks, when the loan is due, if you don't have the funds, you apply for another loan to cover the $800 and are required to pay the $120 interest fee.
6. A viscous cycle continues until you have paid $1,120 in interest and still owe the original $800.

Payday loans are predatory.

Idea for Action

Research earnin.com as an alternative to payday loans. The community-supported platform seeks to create financial fairness. It charges no fees or interest and encourages users to tip for using the service. Tips are not required.

Bankruptcy

"Know what happens when an individual declares bankruptcy and how it affects his or her life." – Marilyn vos Savant

Bankruptcy is a court proceeding where you seek to prove to a judge you are unable to pay your debts. The court will examine the assets you own and your financial liabilities to make a determination to dismiss your debts. If the court finds you don't have the means to repay your debts, you declare bankruptcy.

Bankruptcy can stop foreclosure on your house, repossession of property, and garnishment of your wages by creditors. Bankruptcy will cancel many, but not all, of your debts.

Bankruptcy does not release you from student loans, child support, alimony, any government debt such as taxes, or purchases made immediately prior to filing for bankruptcy, such as a new car and expensive luxury items.

If you choose to pursue bankruptcy proceedings, it becomes public record. Future employers, banks, your clients, or anyone can access the details. You will also pay expensive attorney and court fees. A bankruptcy is likely to make buying a home difficult.

Filing for bankruptcy is complicated and involves a lot of paperwork, so consider bankruptcy counseling to help you through the process.

Idea for Action

If you haven't filed for bankruptcy, consider retaining a financial coach to investigate alternatives to bankruptcy.

Auto Leasing

"Leasing is suited for power users who need to keep up with technology." – Roger Kay

When you lease a car, you're paying to drive a new vehicle, not own it. If you ask, "Should I lease a car?" you will receive "yes," "no," and "it depends" answers.

Strictly speaking, leasing is the worst financial option to obtain a vehicle. However, not all financial decisions are clear cut. Some people's priorities are based on preferences rather than the best financial decision. The best financial choice to obtain a vehicle is to buy a used car with cash.

Two reasons people are attracted to leases are lower monthly payments over buying and driving a new car every three years. However, you never own a leased vehicle. Leasing contracts also have strict mileage and wear and tear limits, and you will be making payments forever. When buying a car, you can benefit many years without a car payment.

Leasing might make sense for business owners who write off the expense and care about the image they project to clients by driving new luxury cars. For everyone else, leasing is unwise. Dave Ramsey says rich people ask, "How much?" Broke people ask, "How much down and how much a month?"

Idea for Action

Still not sure if you should buy or lease? Dave Ramsey explains buy versus lease in this video: bit.ly/ramseybuyvslease.

Building Wealth

The following topics are covered in Building Wealth:

Saving Early
Compound Interest
Investment Ideas for Beginners
Your Financial IQ
Financial Apps
Financial Vision Boarding
Money Mindset
Money Mantras
Employee Retirement Plans
Earning Extra Income
Bitcoin
Real Estate

Saving Early

"Do not save what is left after spending; instead, spend what is left after saving." – Warren Buffet

You might put off building savings because you think you can't afford to save. You can't afford not to save. Some day you will no longer be working. If you haven't saved money, you could be headed toward a crisis in retirement. *Always pay yourself first.*

A Chinese proverb says, "The best time to plant a tree is 20 years ago. The second-best time is now."

Let's say you have $1,000 with a five percent return on your investment.

One person invests $1,000 at age 40, and a second person invests $1,000 at age 30.

The 30-year-old saver will end up with over 60 percent greater return by saving 10 years earlier.

If you haven't been saving, don't fret. Start now, and your ten-years-older self will thank you.

Idea for Action

If you haven't been saving, start immediately.

Calculate an amount to invest monthly and contribute to some form of retirement plan such as an IRA or 401(k). Traditional savings accounts have low rates of return, so you want to invest in the magic of compound interest.

See *Needs vs. Wants* on page 322 and *Emergency Fund* on page 318 in this chapter for guidance.

Compound Interest

"Compound interest is the eighth wonder of the world. He who understands it, earns it; he who doesn't, pays it." – Albert Einstein

According to Investopedia, "Interest is defined as the cost of borrowing money as in the case of interest *charged* on a loan balance. Conversely, interest can also be the rate *paid* for money on deposit."

Compound interest is calculated on the principal amount and also on the accumulated interest from previous periods and can be considered as earning "interest on interest."

The Rule of 72 calculates roughly the amount of time required for your investment to double at a given interest rate. The formula is (72 / i), where i = interest. It can be used only for annual compounding but is helpful to plan how much money you expect to have in retirement.

For example, an investment earning a 7 percent annual rate of return will double in 10 years (72 / 7%).

An investment earning an 8 percent annual return will double in nine years (72 / 8%).

Money in savings accounts earning rates of 1.5 percent will take 48 years to double. Savings accounts aren't useful to build wealth.

Idea for Action

If you aren't currently investing, consider trying a frugal lifestyle for the time being to build savings to invest. See *Frugal Living* on page 325 in this chapter.

Investment Ideas for Beginners

"Never depend on a single income, make an investment to create a second source." – Warren Buffet

Nerd Wallet recommends the following six ideas for beginning investors:

401(k) – If your employer offers a 401(k), this is the first place to invest.

Robo-advisors – Robo-advisors do the heavy lifting on investments for you. These low-cost advisors are becoming more popular and include Betterment, Wealthfront, and Ellevest.

Target-date mutual funds – Mutual funds are a basket of investments comprised of stocks and bonds. Investments are based on your target date of retirement. Examples are TD Ameritrade and You Invest by J.P. Morgan.

Index funds – An easy, hands-off way to invest in the stock market: nerdwallet.com/article/investing/how-to-invest-in-index-funds.

Exchange-traded funds – ETFs are traded like stock. You can even find commission-free ETFs: nerdwallet.com/blog/investing/what-is-an-etf/.

Investment apps – Apps such as Acorns and Stash help rookie investors easily create and build investments.

Idea for Action

Review your budget and choose an amount to invest. Some options presented allow transactions as low as $100. Set a date to open and contribute the amount budgeted.

Your Financial IQ

"An investment in knowledge pays the best interest." – Benjamin Franklin

Learning personal finance can be overwhelming. You might not be familiar with the jargon. The following resources create an easier pathway to increase your financial literacy.

A solid place to start is to read or listen to personal finance books. Personally, I've found David Bach's books enormously helpful and interesting. *Smart Women Finish Rich* is a must read for all women, and *Automatic Millionaire: A Powerful One-Step Plan to Live and Finish Rich* is a treasure for anyone. *The Total Money Makeover* by Dave Ramsey is also helpful. I read it in 2009 to rebuild my finances after a divorce.

If books aren't your jam, here are a few top blogs and podcasts:

Blogs:

Jim Collins, *The Simple Path to Wealth*: jlcollinsnh.com

Michael Piper, *The Oblivious Investor*: obliviousinvestor.com

Lauren Bowling, *Financial Best Life*: financialbestlife.com

Podcasts:

So Money with Farnoosh Torabi – Great for finance newbies

The Dave Ramsey Show – For those wanting to get out of debt

The College Investor – For millennials, students, and grads

The Fairer Cents – For women

The Mad Fientist – For financial freedom and retiring early

Idea for Action

Block an hour weekly on your calendar for financial education.

Financial Apps

"The more you read the more things you will know. The more that you learn, the more places you'll go." – Dr. Seuss

If you have made a decision to intentionally manage your finances, financial apps can make it easier to reach your financial goals. Among these are apps for managing your budget, monitoring financial markets, tracking your investments, and more.

Prism – Integrates with 11,000 different cable, phone, insurance, and utility providers to help track your budget

Personal Capital – Tracks your budget, financial investments, and everything from mortgage and home equity loans to IRA account and credit card balances

Expensify – Tracks expenses; perfect for travelers

Stash – Teaches you how to invest

MarketWatch – Keeps you abreast of financial news. Customize your feed to track specific investments.

Robinhood – Allows you to invest and earn interest on the funds in your Robinhood account and pay no commission

Betterment – Helps you minimize investment risk and get higher returns

Acorns – Helps new investors with no minimums or trade fees

Idea for Action

Prioritize your financial goals, and download and learn to use an app designed to help with your goal. Read app reviews before downloading.

Financial Vision Boarding

"Being rich is having money; being wealthy is having time." – Margaret Bonnano

A vision board is a collection of images and words connected to your goals. A common purpose of financial goals is to achieve financial freedom, which leads to time spent on your terms.

Many financial vision boards online offer samples. Pinterest is a good resource to find examples for inspiration.

Vision boards help you prioritize where your money goes. The items you include are your most important goals. Keep in mind while material things are nice, they aren't what make people happiest. Reflect on the life you want. It's fine if you want to include a new kitchen or car, just remember you don't need to choose only things.

Perhaps "student debt" with an "X" over it appeals if you want to break free of loans. Maybe experiences, like a trip to Italy or Hawaii, motivate you to save. Savings goals might be a priority.

Idea for Action

Get a poster board, glue, magazines, or use a free site such as unsplash.com to search images to print. No printer? Magazines and flyers work. Cut out letters or words or create them in a word processing program or PowerPoint. For a small board, use construction paper, and frame it when finished. Display your financial vision board where you see it daily to stay focused on your financial goals. The imagery helps inspire you.

Money Mindset

"Money is a terrible master but an excellent servant." – P.T. Barnum

Historically, I struggled with money mindset. I often gave advice and resources away free because I felt bad asking for money.

If someone expressed interest in one of my books, I'd offer to send it for free, even though I have to purchase my books from the publisher and pay for shipping. I had to stop because my habit wasn't sustainable as my books gained popularity.

After a conversation with a colleague, Bob Sager, I uncovered I was afraid of being greedy. My parents are generous people, and I didn't realize what a strong value generosity was for me. I once believed my financial well-being couldn't coexist with generosity. Bob helped me realize money is an exchange for value creation.

Sean McCabe sent me a signed copy of his book, *Overlap*, and I've never forgotten something I read. "If you don't care about money, you don't care about your mission." Wow. If I didn't ensure the financial health of my business, I couldn't help people if I went out of business! That was an eye opener.

Have you ever reflected on your money attitude?

Idea for Action

Money mindset affects our decisions and choices. Would you like to learn your money mindset? Take a free quiz to find out! You can find it here: bit.ly/quizmoneymindset.

Money Mantras

"Bust the myth that it's not spiritual to earn for your great work." – Gabby Bernstein

Money mantras are a lot like affirmations. We think it, we speak it, then we begin to believe it. Thoughts become actions. Mantras are not to promote greed or lust for money. They set our mind right on our mental money hang ups, serve as needed reminders, and keep us focused on our financial goals.

My money mantra is, "Always buy the best you can afford." My mantra has two goals: To remind me not to buy cheap merchandise I'll have to continually replace, thereby spending more, and a reminder not to overspend.

Here are some examples of money mantras:

- "Money flows to me easily and naturally."
- "Receiving money by sharing my gifts is a birthright."
- "This won't bring me joy."
- "Money is a tool."
- "I want Italy more."
- "There's plenty where that came from!"
- "If I make meaning, I'll make money."

What are your money hang ups?

Idea for Action

Set 1-2 financial goals. Create a money mantra connected to those goals, and place it somewhere you can see it and say it daily.

Employee Retirement Plans

"Contribute the maximum to your 401(k) the second you start working. You will feel like you don't have the money, but you will always be able to make it work." – Kellan Barfield

If you work for a company contributing to your retirement as an employee benefit, take the free money you're offered.

Let's say you have a salary of $50,000. If you contribute 6 percent of your salary into the company 401(k), you will have $3,000 in the plan after the first year. If your employer offers a 100 percent match, you will have $6,000 in the plan. If your employer offers a 50 percent match (or 3 percent of your salary), you will have $4,500 in the plan. The contribution will start earning compound interest.

If an employer offers you a higher match when you contribute the maximum to your 401(k) and you don't contribute the maximum, you're leaving free money on the table. A $3,000 employer contribution annually with a 7 percent return will be worth $22,838 in five years.

Retirement creeps up quicker than we can imagine. Start preparing as soon as possible.

Idea for Action

If you aren't contributing to a retirement account, discover your options using this link: bit.ly/choosingretirementplans. Non-US residents should consult the government tax agency website for their countries.

Earning Extra Income

"Earn with your mind, not your time." – Naval Ravikant

Passive income is my favorite kind of income. I always look for ways to separate my time from my dime to allow me to spend my time as I choose. I share more in *Passive Income* on page 278 in the *Career* chapter.

Think of experiences you've had, problems you've solved, expertise you've developed, and ideas you have. List ways you can create services, resources, or products to sell such as guides, courses, books, videos, workbooks, toolkits, art, shirts, or merchandise using your ideas, experience, and expertise.

If passive income isn't an option, other possibilities are available.

Earn extra cash by taking surveys or becoming an affiliate for products you believe in. Teach others something you know by offering lessons, start a side hustle, drive for Uber or Lyft, make deliveries, or shop as a side gig with Instacart.

What skills can you offer as a freelancer?

Idea for Action

Turn ideas into income with the best resource I've read, *IDEApreneur: Monetize Your Mind* by Sam Horn: bit.ly/ideapreneursamhorn.

I've implemented moneymaking ideas for my business with this book. You can purchase the paperback on Amazon if you don't prefer a digital download.

Bitcoin

"I really like Bitcoin. I own Bitcoins. It's a store of value, a distributed ledger. It's a great place to put assets, especially in places like Argentina with 40 percent inflation, where $1 today is worth 60 cents in a year, and a government's currency does not hold value. It's also a good investment vehicle if you have an appetite for risk. But it won't be a currency until volatility slows down." – David Marcus

According to Investopedia, Bitcoin is a type of digital currency. Balances of Bitcoin tokens are kept using public and private "keys," which are long strings of numbers and letters linked through the mathematical encryption algorithm used to create them.

Bitcoin issues no physical bills or coins. The currency is decentralized, so no government, bank, or authority controls it. Owners are anonymous: Instead of using names or social security numbers, bitcoin connects buyers and sellers through encryption keys. Bitcoin is "mined" by powerful computers on the internet.

Bitcoin is legal but could be subject to future regulation since it attracts criminals due to its anonymity. As an investment, Bitcoin is high risk but also potentially high reward. One big risk lies in the fact Bitcoin value is volatile.[122]

Idea for Action

Investing in Bitcoin is not for the risk averse. If you want to know more, this article by Investopedia outlines the risks: investopedia.com/terms/b/bitcoin.asp.

Real Estate

"The major fortunes in America have been made in land." – John D. Rockefeller

Real estate is generally a good investment because investors make money through rental income as well as the appreciation of the asset.

Real estate generates cash flow. You build your asset as you pay down the mortgage using the cash from your renters. Real estate investments also offer tax breaks and deductions which help lower your tax obligation.

A downside of real estate is the difficulty of turning your asset into cash. I have a neighbor who purchased a house one street over from us. They have been trying to sell the property, without success, for a few years.

Billionaire Andrew Carnegie once said, "Ninety percent of millionaires got their wealth by investing in real estate."

New York Times Bestselling author, Grant Cardone says, "Real estate is real, and it's always a good idea to put your money in real assets. But let me be clear: That doesn't mean all real estate is a good idea.

"I only buy certain types of properties, generally multifamily ones in upscale locations that provide consistent cash flow and great potential for future appreciation."

Idea for Action

If you're considering real estate, Udemy has a slew of courses at udemy.com/topic/real-estate-investing.

Financial Planning

The following topics are covered in Financial Planning:

Household Budget
Giving
Opportunity Cost
Lifestyle Inflation
Mortgages
Insurance
Starting Over After Divorce
Calculating Your Net Worth
Wills and Estate Planning
Social Security

Household Budget

"A debt problem is, at its core, a budgeting problem." – Natalie Pace

If you're interested in financial security, having a budget is needed. People mistakenly believe living paycheck-to-paycheck is an earnings problem. In reality, it's unchecked spending or lack of visibility into where your money goes. Money issues are often an outflow issue not an inflow issue.

A 2020 poll revealed budgeting behavior by age group:[123]

18-24 years old – 76 percent use a budget
25-34 years old – 81 percent use a budget
35-44 years old – 79 percent use a budget
45-54 years old – 76 percent use a budget
55-64 years old – 79 percent use a budget
65 and older – 82 percent use a budget

Eighty percent of Americans are bound in chains of debt.[124]

A budget can help you:

- Stay focused on your goals
- Identify bad money habits
- Keep from overspending
- Prepare for emergencies
- Establish a happier life in retirement

If setting up a budget is overwhelming, tackle it in bite-sized chunks each morning or evening over a week.

Idea for Action

For guidance to create a budget, follow these steps: bit.ly/createfamilybudget.

Giving

"Whoever sows sparingly will also reap sparingly, and whoever sows generously will also reap generously." – 2 Corinthians 9:6 NIV

An abundance mindset yields abundance, while a scarcity mindset yields more scarcity. The idea of reaping what you sow applies to all areas of life. If you sow criticism, you'll reap criticism. If you sow kindness, you will reap kindness. And if you sow generosity, you will reap generosity.

Charitable giving is something to consider incorporating into your financial plan.

Five reasons giving is good for you are:[125]

1. Giving makes us happy.
2. Giving is good for our health.
3. Giving is contagious, creating ripples of generosity.
4. Giving promotes cooperation and social connection.
5. Giving evokes gratitude.

Idea for Action

Find an organization with a mission you're passionate about. It could be a nonprofit that helps children, the unemployed, education and prevention of intimate partner violence, or a local hospice organization.

List the most feasible way(s) to give to your preferred organization with your time, talents, or financial resources.

Opportunity Cost

"There is an opportunity cost for everything we do. This is why we must have the awareness to ensure that what we are pursuing is really what we value, because the pursuit leaves countless lost opportunities in its wake. We choose one experience at the sacrifice of all other experiences." – Chris Matakas

Opportunity cost is the loss of potential gain from other alternatives when one alternative is chosen. Opportunity cost applies to all resources because resources are *finite*, or limited.

Business owners fall into opportunity traps. Let's say a new consultant who charges $400/hour doesn't hire someone to help with customer service, proposals, or invoices.

Each week, she spends five hours managing these tasks. An hour daily seems small, but the opportunity cost is $2,000.

Sometimes decisions of opportunity are complex. Imagine two investment options: one has a conservative return but ties up your cash for only two years. The other option locks in your money for 10 years but pays higher interest with a bit more risk. You would make your opportunity-cost decision based on your risk tolerance *and* how available you need your money to be.

Idea for Action

When evaluating an investment, include opportunity costs in the analysis.

Opportunity cost = Return on the best option not chosen *minus* Return on the option chosen

Lifestyle Inflation

"Mo money, mo problems." – The Notorious B.I.G.

Lifestyle inflation occurs when our financial position advances and our spending increases correspondingly.

Our higher pay tempts us to purchase extra toys, take on a new car loan or two, buy a bigger house or rent a place in a pricier neighborhood, go on unbudgeted trips, or increase eating out.

We increase our lifestyle not because we have to but because we can. Most people spend more if they have more. Two common reasons for lifestyle inflation are keeping up with the Joneses and a sense of entitlement for working hard.[126]

Investopedia points out there are times it makes sense to up your spending such as new clothes to dress appropriately for a promotion at work or moving into a new apartment with an extra room if you're expecting a baby, as long as you can afford it.

Ideas for Action

Here are three ways to avoid lifestyle inflation:

1. Pay yourself first from your financial increase. Contribute a monthly amount to an emergency fund then to a retirement fund after you reach the emergency fund goal.

2. Update your budget any time your financial situation changes. See *Household Budget* on page 365.

3. Categorize expenses as needs or wants. See *Needs vs. Wants* on page 322.

Mortgages

"Potential buyers should be checking their credit reports regularly and at least six to 12 months before applying for a mortgage." – RateSupermarket.ca

My mother taught me the expression "house poor."

House poor is a term to describe a person who spends a large proportion of his or her total income on home ownership, including mortgage payments, property taxes, maintenance, and utilities.

A mortgage is a large debt, perhaps the largest you'll incur. Interest.com recommends avoiding these seven traps when getting a mortgage:

1. Committing too much income to housing costs
2. Ignoring the cost of home ownership. Budget 1-2 percent of your home's cost for maintenance.
3. Neglecting to shop around for the best loan
4. Ignoring the annual percentage rate (APR)
5. Putting too little down. Aim to save a 20 percent down payment to save on interest and avoid mortgage insurance payments.
6. Failing to check or fix your credit reports, which affects mortgage rates and loan approval
7. Forgetting to check if you qualify for a VA loan if you served in the military

Idea for Action

Enter house buying with the knowledge of what you can truly afford. Try NerdWallet's *How Much Can I Afford* calculator: bit.ly/mortgageaffordcalculator.

Insurance

"If a child, a spouse, a life partner, or a parent depends on you and your income, you need life insurance." – Suze Orman

To protect your assets, look into insurance such as auto, home, life, disability, and long-term care insurance. Periodically review your policies to make sure they meet your, or your family's, needs as those needs change.

To know how much insurance you need, you answer questions concerning your marital status, how much savings you have, your income, debt, and number of dependents.

Next, determine how much coverage you need, which is generally 10–12 times your annual income, according to Dave Ramsey.

Finally, choose a policy that meets your requirements.

It's a good idea to get disability and long-term care insurance to cover medical costs and special care if you become disabled. Also, living benefits insurance allows you to cash in on life insurance while you are still alive if you have a terminal illness.

Idea for Action

Use an insurance calculator such as the one below to determine your term life insurance needs. Term life insurance offers coverage for a specific amount of time and are more affordable than whole life insurance because the policy has no cash value until you die.

daveramsey.com/recommends/term-life-insurance/calculator/about

Starting Over After Divorce

"Divorce is one of the most financially traumatic things you can go through. Money spent on getting mad or getting even is money wasted." – Richard Wagner

I've heard it said divorce is one of the most financially devastating events we can experience. Legally uncoupling from another person is not only emotionally taxing, it takes time to get your finances in order.

Make a checklist of important things to take care of to ensure everyone is protected and nothing falls through the cracks.

You'll want to:

- Cancel joint accounts and open new ones in your name
- Change your beneficiary on financial accounts
- Download your credit report to periodically monitor your credit for anything out of the ordinary. In the United States, Federal law allows you to get a free copy of your credit report every 12 months from each credit reporting company at annualcreditreport.com.
- Create a new budget
- Consider hiring a financial planner to get you on track

Idea for Action

Consider a small lock box or personal safe for your home to keep important documentation, including your divorce decree. You will likely need to reference this paperwork in the future, so have a safe place for your documents.

Calculating Your Net Worth

"Your net worth is not the same thing as your self-worth. Your value is not based on your valuables." – Rick Warren

Your net worth is the amount your assets exceed your liabilities or, in simpler terms, what you have versus what you need to pay off. Regardless of your financial situation, knowing your net worth can help you evaluate your financial health and plan for the future.

Calculating your net worth is important for several practical reasons. First, it's a necessary step to create a will and plan what happens to your possessions and any minor children upon your death. See *Wills and Estate Planning* on the next page.

Knowing your net worth is the only way to have a handle on your finances instead of them handling you. If you plan to buy a house or apply for a loan, you should know your financial picture. Financial knowledge is power.

Knowing your net worth helps you find areas for improvement and aids your financial goal setting to ensure you are headed in the right direction. If you aren't, you can adjust course before it's too late.

Idea for Action

Download this personal net worth worksheet to build your financial picture: bit.ly/rutgersnetworthworksheet.

Wills and Estate Planning

"A will can save one's family from being put into a quagmired pit of legal conundrum, in case of death (which may even be untimely)." – Henrietta Newton Martin

A will is an important document to communicate your wishes clearly and precisely upon your death.

A will generally outlines:
1. Executor(s), who will carry out provisions of the will
2. Beneficiaries, those who inherit your assets
3. Details on how and when beneficiaries receive assets
4. Appointed guardians for minor children

Your estate is everything you own, from your house and possessions to your bank accounts and investments.

Estate planning is for everyone and is more than a plan for your assets. It includes instructions for your care if you become disabled, a plan to provide for loved ones who aren't reliable with money, and a plan to minimize taxes and court and legal fees.

Upon your death, if you don't have a plan, your state or province has one. It likely isn't what you would choose. If both parents die, the court chooses child guardianship. If you become disabled, the court, not family, decides how your assets care for you.

Ideas for Action

You can hire an attorney, use DIY software such as Quicken's *WillMaker & Trust*, or use a guidebook such as the *Quick & Legal Will Book* by Denis Clifford to create your will. Also, check out 10 steps to write a will at bit.ly/willwritingsteps.

Social Security

"Retirement security is often compared to a three-legged stool supported by Social Security, employer-provided pension funds, and private savings." – Sander Levin

Pensions, which are retirement funds paid by employers, are going the way of the dinosaur. That leaves 401(k) plans, private savings, and Social Security as sources of retirement income. Half of American workers participate in a workplace retirement program. As of 2017, only 16 Fortune 500 companies offered pension plans to new hires.[127]

The question many ask regarding Social Security is, "How much will I receive?" In 2017, women 65 and older received an average annual Social Security income of $14,353, compared to $18,041 for men. That's $1,196 per month for women and $1,503 per month for men.

These averages aren't guaranteed but are helpful to get an idea of what your financial picture would be like if you don't have savings, private investments, or an employer-sponsored 401(k).

Social Security as a sole source of retirement income is inadequate. Look to create as many revenue streams as possible for a secure retirement. If you don't have a 401(k), consider opening an individual retirement account (IRA).

Idea for Action

How much Social Security will you receive? You can get basic benefit estimates by calling the Social Security Administration at 800-772-1213. Remember, they're estimates, not promises.

Family Money Matters

The following topics are covered in Family Money Matters:

Joint or Separate Bank Accounts
Couples' Spending Habits
Money Arguments
Asking for a Raise
Cost of Raising Children
Childcare Costs
School Supply Costs
Kids and Financial Literacy
College Alternatives
College Savings for Kids
Borrowing from Retirement
Vacation on a Budget
Thrifty Entrepreneurship
Lending Money
Tax Refunds
Protecting Yourself Online
Identify Theft
Reviewing Your Accounts

Joint or Separate Bank Accounts

"At the bank, I told the cashier, 'I'd like to open a join account please.' 'OK, with whom?' 'Whoever has lots of money.'" – Unknown

Money disagreements can cause havoc in relationships, which is why couples must communicate on finances. Joint or separate bank accounts are one such conversation.

Most couples choose joint accounts to make managing money and paying bills easier. In some situations, separate accounts make sense. My husband and I have separate accounts for two reasons.

First, we have accounts at different banks. We maintain accounts at separate banks in the event of fraud or compromised accounts. If either debit card is canceled for fraud, or an account is compromised, we have access to cash.

Second, I have two children from my first marriage and two with my husband. I help my older sons with college tuition, and having separate accounts makes transactions easier when my husband's paycheck is not intermingled in the account.

There is no right or wrong decision for joint or separate accounts, only preferences. Our system works because we're in agreement with money. Discussing your needs is what matters.

Idea for Action

If you have a partner, do you know their thoughts on joint accounts? Do they know yours? Set aside time to discuss.

Couples' Spending Habits

"You can't write a story together if you're not on the same page." – Unknown

Therapists, financial advisors, and divorce attorneys have stories to tell of couples clashing over saving and spending.

Money habits are an important conversation for couples to have early in a relationship. Otherwise, your partner will likely display money attitudes that will catch you off guard. One partner may feel wrongly entitled to make the financial decisions if he or she is the primary income earner.

Another might spend money spontaneously while the partner is a staunch saver. Couples may also have different financial goals. For example, one likes to spend money on experiences, while the other wants to invest and enjoy travel and experiences in retirement.

In addition to open communication about finances, both people should have a clear picture of the finances. In the event of divorce or death of a spouse, a financially unaware spouse could be placed in a disastrous situation.

Idea for Action

Schedule a quarterly conversation with your spouse to review your financial status and progress toward financial goals to reassess them if needed. Periodic evaluation renews your

commitment and focus to achieve your goals.

If you don't have financial goals or know your financial status, use the first quarterly conversation as a discovery session.

Money Arguments

"The aim of an argument should not be victory, but progress."
– Karl Popper

Fights about money don't always lead to divorce, but they can lead to decreased relationship satisfaction and increased stress. In disagreements, seek to understand the underlying cause. Often people go back and forth about preferences and opinions, but they don't dig down to the why behind the differences to help partners understand our basis of thinking.

For example, Chris spends money spontaneously, which upsets Lilian. He can afford the expense and doesn't understand why Lilian is upset. Lilian can ask herself, "Why does it bother me when Chris spends spontaneously if he has saved the money?" Eventually, Chris and Lilian discover she values security. Spontaneous spending makes her nervous because it threatens her sense of safety.

Know why you're fighting. Be honest about the values your partner's attitudes or behaviors with money threatens, so you can get to the root of the problem instead of fighting over surface opinions.

Idea for Action

Incorporate these four steps into your money conversations:

1. Be patient with each other.
2. Try to understand where your partner is coming from.
3. Be honest and fair. Just because one partner earns more doesn't mean he or she should call the shots.
4. Seek common goals and create a plan.

Asking for a Raise

"When it comes to asking for a raise, you just have to do it in the right way. You may get a no, and that's fine, but ask and make sure you know when you can come back and ask again!"
– Alexis Maybank

If one of your financial goals is to increase your income, you have two choices: find a higher paying job or ask for a raise. Prior to asking for a raise, you'll need to prepare.

Research the financial health of the company. Are layoffs and spending cuts happening? If the company is cutting back, it's probably not the right time to ask for a raise.

Be prepared to share why you deserve a raise. Being in your role a long time without one is not a good reason. Technically, raises aren't required, so you must show how you've added value to justify a salary increase.

How, specifically, have you added value to the organization? Quantify your impact where possible. Have you implemented four improvements that saved 100 hours of manual work and $10,000 per quarter?

Proactively communicate successes throughout the year, not just when asking for a raise. If a customer sings your praises, share it with your manager.

Focus on why you deserve a raise, not why you need one. Practice your pitch and anticipate questions.

Idea for Action

Research the market salary for your job title to know where you fall in the range at indeed.com/salaries.

Cost of Raising Children

"We make the cost of raising kids higher than it has to be just because we feel they need all this stuff, like gadgets, certain schools, and activities that are nice but aren't really necessary."
– Patricia Heaton

Diapers. Daycare. Music lessons. Hobbies. The cost of raising a child is estimated at a quarter million dollars to age 17. That doesn't include college.[128]

Raising children is not a topic often discussed beyond, "How many children do we want to have?" It warrants discussion given the $250,000 commitment. Childcare is the largest expense after housing.[129]

Some conversations you should consider regarding kids:

1. How many children do we want?
2. Will we adopt or try fertility treatments if unable to conceive? What are the costs?
3. What are our education choices? Homeschooling? Public school? Private school? Other?
4. What is our financial stance on children's hobbies?
5. What is the financial plan for college?
6. What contribution will we make, if any, to post-secondary education?
7. What is our expectation for part-time employment? By what age?

Idea for Action

Consider opening an investment account for your child's education. Birthday and holiday money can be contributed to the account.

Saving Money on Childcare

"Children are not a distraction from more important work. They are the more important work." – John Trainer

Depending on where you live, annual childcare costs often exceed a year of college tuition. Affording quality childcare is a concern of most parents. Here are some ideas to save money without sacrificing quality:

Share childcare costs – Can you go in on a nanny with a friend? The nanny rate will be higher, but your split rate will be less.

Ask a homeschool or stay-at-home mom – A mom at home with her kids might give you a lower rate than a professional nanny.

Leverage family part-time – When I went back to work with my firstborn, my mother kept my son on Mondays, and a friend cared for him three days per week. If you can shift from full-time to part-time childcare costs, you'll save a lot of money.

Consider working part-time – For a brief period, you could consider working part-time and getting family to help to have zero child-care costs.

Idea for Action

Consider participating in an au pair program. An au pair is a foreign national who lives with a host family and cares for their children, and in return, the host family provides room, board, and a stipend usually less than the cost of a nanny.

School Supply Costs

"Education is not the filling of a pail but the lighting of a fire."
– William Yeats

According to the National Retail Federation, families with kids in elementary school through high school will spend an average of $696.90 per child on back-to-school necessities.[130] Ouch. That's a lot of money many families can't afford. What's worse is 94 percent of teachers end up buying supplies out of their own pockets.

A number of creative ideas can save you money on back-to-school shopping.

First, remember the dollar stores! You can save a good amount of money buying school supplies, snacks, water bottles and stationery at a discount. Also, follow your favorite stores on Facebook and Twitter to get deals or coupons for back-to-school needs. Watch for weekly sales flyers.

Keep a plastic bin or drawer to save school supplies at the end of the year. You're bound to have extra index cards and other supplies to reuse. Some items such as rulers, backpacks, calculators, and pencil cases should last multiple years.

Save money on clothes and uniforms by buying next year's sizes when they're on clearance. You can also shop at consignment stores and garage sales.

Idea for Action

Go to taxadmin.org/current-tax-rates and click "Sales Tax Holidays" to see if your state provides sales tax holidays for clothing, computers, and school supplies to save even more.

Kids and Financial Literacy

"The number one problem in today's generation and economy is the lack of financial literacy." – Alan Greenspan

You can start teaching your children about money as early as preschool.

Little ones can start saving money in a clear jar. Set an example by not impulse buying what they ask for, and let them give money to a cashier so they begin to understand things cost money.

If you have middle schoolers, give them a wallet and have them manage transactions with cashiers. I gave my sons wallets at age seven, and they had to manage their purchases from that age. They learned social skills in the process. Consider giving kids an allowance in exchange for chores, help them avoid impulse purchases, and teach them generosity and giving.

For high schoolers, let them open a bank account so they can begin saving for their educations. Teach them the importance of avoiding student loans and credit cards, help them think of ways to earn money, show them how to set up a simple budget, and start to teach them about compound interest.

Idea for Action

Does your teen show the signs of an autonomous, enterprising nature? Consider the Teen Entrepreneur Toolbox to guide teens in creating their own business. Find it here:

daveramsey.com/store/product/teen-entrepreneur-toolbox.

College Alternatives

"Some people get an education without going to college. The rest get it after they get out." – Mark Twain

Not sure college is right for you or your child? Perhaps you're unwilling to take on debt. Here are five alternatives to a degree.

1. Obtain an associate degree in a skilled position such as dental hygiene, web design, veterinary assistant, or imaging technician. After landing a job, see if your employer pays for a bachelor's degree if you want one.

2. Serve in the military. The military offers many benefits, including helping to pay for your education.

3. Attend a technical college to learn a trade. Many skilled tradespeople will be retiring soon, which will open up abundant job opportunities.

4. Complete an apprenticeship in a high-demand field. Find apprenticeships at apprenticeship.gov/become-apprentice.

5. Take a gap year if you're not ready to attend college. ParachuteBridge.org offers quality gap year summer and semester programs to build skills and real-world experiences.

Idea for Action

Before investing time and money in a degree, explore if a degree is needed. Visit nodegree.com for jobs that don't require a degree.

College Savings for Kids

"Borrowing for college used to be the exception, now it's the rule." – Arne Duncan

College costs are hard to estimate due to differences in private versus public tuition, fee increases, and unknowns of scholarship awards or financial aid qualification.

Fidelity investments recommends using a 2K rule to save for college. Multiply your child's age by $2,000 to cover half the average cost of a four-year public university.

For example, if you have a 5-year-old, you'd need $10,000, or $2,000 times 5 years, to be fairly confident you can afford half of the cost of a four-year, in-state public university. The calculation assumes you're using a state-sponsored 529 college savings plan.

If funds in a 529 are used for anything other than qualified education costs, you'll pay federal income tax and a 10 percent penalty on the earnings. If your child gets a full scholarship, the penalty is waived!

Reaching college savings goals relies on consistent contribution to a designated account. 529 plans are sold by the state or by financial advisors. Visit investor.gov/free-financial-planning-tools for details on 529 plans.

Idea for Action

Create a gift registry for family and friends to contribute to your child's 529 account for holiday or graduation gifts. Visit giftofcollege.com to set this up after opening your child's 529 account.

Borrowing from Retirement

"Making an early withdrawal from your retirement account is one of the biggest no-no's in personal finance." – Annie Nova

Dipping into your retirement starts ripple effect damage. First, you chip away at your hard work to save for retirement. When funds are cashed out, they're no longer invested, and you lose out on compound interest.

Second, you will be slapped with hefty withdrawal penalties and fees. Last, you will receive a tax bill on any money you withdraw. The process is intentionally punitive to deter people from putting themselves in a bad position down the road when it comes time to retire.

The most common reasons people dip into their retirement are medical debt, education, unexpected expenses, buying a house, and paying off debt.

Ideas for Action

Five alternatives to dipping into retirement funds:

1. Take a side job temporarily to increase your income.
2. Cut back where possible to reduce expenses (shut off cable, landline, subscriptions, eating out, etc.).
3. Sell some possessions online for extra cash.
4. Consider a home equity loan.
5. Apply for a personal loan. Make sure the total cost will be less than what you'd pay in taxes and penalties borrowing from retirement.

Vacation on a Budget

"We travel not to escape life, but for life not to escape us." –
Robyn Yong

A vacation can get expensive very quickly. It's fun to get away
but not if you blow your budget. Here are a handful of ideas
for a more affordable vacation.

- Rent an inexpensive cabin with good hiking to take
  advantage of nature for free.
- Stay somewhere in driving distance to save on airfare.
  Rent a place with a kitchen, plates, and cookware. Plan
  meals and pack a cooler to save on eating out.
- Plan a weekend getaway at an affordable bed and
  breakfast. Before you go, conduct an online search of
  free activities, festivals, and events.
- Take a camping vacation, and enjoy the outdoors.
- Snag vacation deals through Costco.com.
- Travel during the off-season. Hotels will be cheaper.
- Plan a vacation to visit a national park.
- Book far enough in advance to pay less. Vacations
  booked on short notice cost more.

Idea for Action

Browse discount vacation sites such as groupon.com/getaways.

Thrifty Entrepreneurship

"It's smart to be thrifty." – Bernice Fitz-Gibbon

If you're starting a business, or have started one, be cautious not to scale up early without the cash to back it up. When I started my business, I wanted to build an automated solution instead of creating YouMap® profiles manually.

My husband works in software consulting services and talked me out of the idea, explaining, "If we build it, they will come," is what puts entrepreneurs out of business. I disagreed but followed his advice. He was right. Client revenue paid for automation and expansion instead of bootstrapping out of my personal funds. The bottom line? *Keep overhead low.*

Crowdfunding is still an option through Kickstarter or GoFundMe. Campaigns with videos including your purpose and passion will do better than without a video. Keep the campaign to a month. Longer campaigns don't do as well.

Networking for angel investors is another option for cash-strapped startups. Make sure you have a compelling "why" to help people connect with your mission and vision.

Idea for Action

If you want to set up a business, start a dedicated savings fund. The US Small Business Association estimates most small businesses cost $3,000 to start. Start small, estimate expected costs, and conservatively project your cash flow.

Lending Money

"Quick to borrow is always slow to pay." – Proverb

A Finder survey determined people borrow $184 billion from friends and family each year. Approximately one in three individuals have borrowed money from people they know with an average loan of $3,300.[131]

Next time someone asks you for money, consider this checklist of questions to help you decide if you want to extend the loan:

- Has this person asked me for money before?
- If so, did they repay the loan?
- Did they repay me in a timely manner?
- What is the likelihood they will pay me back?
- What are the funds for?

Also, ask the person, "What is your plan to pay back the loan?"

Idea for Action

Three considerations before lending money:

1. Treat the loan as any business transaction with terms and an agreed upon repayment schedule in writing. It can be simple but should be documented.
2. Plan for the repayment to take a while. Someone who needs a loan probably won't be in a position to repay quickly.
3. Expect not to be repaid. Likely you won't be repaid, so if you don't expect it, you won't be disappointed and risk the relationship.

Tax Refunds

"Intaxification: Euphoria at getting a refund from the IRS, which lasts until you realize it was your money to start with." – Unknown

Have you ever gotten excited to receive a large tax refund? "Woo hoo! We're getting back $4,000!"

I never want to burst anyone's bubble, but getting a tax refund is an indication of poor tax planning. Essentially, you've loaned your hard-earned money to the government interest free. A tax refund is due when a person pays more through tax withholding through income than the tax amount due.

In short, you directed the government to take too much money out of your paycheck in taxes, so they are returning it to you. If you had invested $4,000 instead of loaning it to the government, you would earn $4,290 at an average rate of return of 7 percent. You actually lost money.

The ideal scenario is not to owe money and also not get a refund. If you break even on your tax return, it means your withholdings were right on the money, so to speak.

Idea for Action

If you get large tax refunds or are hit with large tax bills, you need to review your withholdings. I've included a resource to show you how to calculate your tax withholdings.

daveramsey.com/blog/how-to-calculate-tax-withholdings

Protect Yourself Online

"Treat your passwords like your toothbrush. Don't let anybody else use it, and get a new one every six months." – Clifford Stoll

Fraud and online theft are realities of a digital world. The more you know, the more you can protect yourself.

Working from coffee shops, libraries, or internet cafes is more appealing to some than working at home. If you use public Wi-Fi and shop online, you invite theft. Shop on your own network or connect your laptop to a mobile hotspot on your smart phone if you access financial sites or conduct financial transactions.

Avoid shopping on unsecured websites. Look for a lock icon at the left of the address bar and "https:" (not "http:") in the URL. The "s" indicates a secure protocol for sending data.

Don't give away too much information online. Leave non-required fields blank. Give minimum information.

Use multi-factor authentication. Multi-factor means you provide two or more pieces of data to verify your identity before logging into an account. A password plus responding to a text sent to your phone is an example. The slight inconvenience is worth the protection.

Never use the same password for email and financial accounts. If hacked, you give access to accounts with that password.

Idea for Action

Keep up with dynamic security matters by following the *Krebs on Security* blog at krebsonsecurity.com.

Identity Theft

"As a young child my mother told me I can be anyone I want to be. Turns out this is called identity theft." – Unknown

How do you know if you've been a victim of identity theft? IdentityTheft.gov offers warning signs to pay attention to:

- Your bank account shows unfamiliar withdrawals.
- Paper statements have stopped arriving in the mail.
- Merchants refuse your checks.
- Debt collectors call you for debts that aren't yours.
- Unauthorized accounts or charges appear on your credit report.
- Medical providers bill for services you didn't use.
- Your health plan rejects legitimate medical claims saying you reached your benefit limit.
- Your health plan won't cover you because medical records show a condition you don't have.
- IRS notifies you more than one tax return was filed in your name, or you have income from an employer you don't work for.
- You receive notification of compromised data by a company where you do business or have an account.

Identity theft is a dynamic and continual problem. Keep abreast of common and emerging scams to prevent your data from being compromised.

Idea for Action

Here are 10 additional tips to detect and prevent identity theft: bit.ly/identitytheftprevention.

Reviewing Your Accounts

"Money shouldn't be worshiped and it shouldn't be ignored."
– Alexa von Tobel

LearnVest founder and CEO Alexa von Tobel, swears by setting aside one minute each day to check on her financial transactions. A 60-second act helps identify problems faster and keep track of goal progress, and it sets the spending tone for the rest of the day.

I learned this daily money minding habit from my mother. Each morning I log into my personal and business bank accounts to make sure the balances are what I expect and that I recognize the transactions. I have found fraudulent transactions in my account. Someone once used my account to pay their cable bill in the amount of $195, and I was able to report it to the bank instead of being ignorant of the transaction and eating the cost.

A daily review of your accounts can prevent overdraft and insufficient fund fees and help you see impulse purchase patterns or other habits you want to deter. Most importantly, this keeps your financial goals top of mind and shapes daily behavior.

Set an alarm on your phone to remind you to check your accounts until it becomes an established habit.

Idea for Action

Bookmark your investment and bank account links in your browser or keep a secure spreadsheet with link and account details to log into each account with a quick click to immediately address anomalies or unexpected surprises.

Final Thoughts

Maximize 365 was not written to be read once. I hope you will highlight and mark it up. Work it and make it yours. Read it every year and choose areas of your life to transform. With 365 entries, it's impossible to take thoughtful action on every tip relevant to you in a single year.

Prioritization is important because you can't do it all. You will also need to practice consistency. As author Gretchen Rubin said, "What you do every day matters more than what you do once in a while."

I anticipate this book will be a constant companion on your journey to maximize and transform your life.

All my best to you!

Kristin

Reflect

Act

Action(s) to Take	Due Date

Act

Action(s) to Take   Due Date

_____

_____

_____

_____

_____

_____

_____

_____

_____

_____

_____

_____

_____

_____

_____

_____

Act

Action(s) to Take   Due Date

_____

_____

_____

_____

_____

_____

_____

_____

_____

_____

_____

_____

_____

_____

_____

References

1. Dr. Melanie Greenburg, "The 3 Most Common Causes of Insecurity and How to Beat Them," Published on December 6, 2015, https://www.psychologytoday.com/us/blog/the-mindful-self-express/201512/the-3-most-common-causes-insecurity-and-how-beat-them.

2. Fiona Buckland, "Feeling like an impostor? You can escape this confidence-sapping syndrome," Retrieved July 20, 2020, https://www.theguardian.com/commentisfree/2017/sep/19/fraud-impostor-syndrome-confidence-self-esteem.

3. Heidi Grant Halvorson, "The Cure for Loneliness," Published on October 1, 2010, https://www.psychologytoday.com/us/blog/the-science-success/201010/the-cure-loneliness.

4. "Science Agrees: Nature is Good for You," Association of Nature and Forest Therapy Guides and Programs, Retrieved June 2, 2020, https://www.natureandforesttherapy.org/about/science.

5. Kathleen Doheny, "Forest Bathing, Nature Time Are Hot Health Advice," Retrieved July 20,2020, https://wb.md/2Ko6Yi3.

6. Joshua Becker, "The Statistics of Clutter," Retrieved April 22, 2020, https://www.becomingminimalist.com/the-statistics-of-clutter/.

7. Ibid.

8. Ibid.

9. Ibid.

10. Ibid.

11. Katy Halverson, "Can Organizing Impact Your Mental Health," Published April 5, 2018, https://intermountainhealthcare.org/blogs/topics/live-well/2018/04/can-organizing-impact-your-mental-health/.

12. The Associated Press, "Analysis of Twitter yields insight into moods," Retrieved July 20, 2020, https://www.cbsnews.com/news/analysis-of-twitter-yields-insight-into-moods.

13. Evan Asano, "How Much Time Do People Spend on Social Media?," Published on January 4, 2017, https://www.socialmediatoday.com/marketing/how-much-time-do-people-spend-social-media-infographic.

14. Sarah Karnasiewicz, "7 Scary Things You Never Knew About Cell Phone Addiction," Published on February 2, 2018, https://www.health.com/condition/anxiety/cell-phone-addiction.

15. Amy Morin, "7 Scientifically Proven Benefits of Gratitude That Will Motivate You to Give Thanks Year-Round," Published on November 23, 2014, https://www.forbes.com/sites/amymorin/2014/11/23/7-scientifically-proven-benefits-of-gratitude-that-will-motivate-you-to-give-thanks-year-round/#8da9909183c0.

16. Eric Jaffe, "Why Wait? The Science Behind Procrastination," Published on March 29, 2013, https://www.psychologicalscience.org/observer/why-wait-the-science-behind-procrastination.

17. Sian Beilock, "Why Talented People Fail Under Pressure," Published on June 27, 2019, https://hbr.org/2019/06/why-talented-people-fail-under-pressure.

18. James C. Coyne and Howard Tennen, "Positive Psychology in Cancer Care: Bad Science, Exaggerated Claims, and Unproven Medicine," Published on February 10,2010, https://www.ncbi.nlm.nih.gov/pmc/articles/PMC2858800.

19. Judith Acosta, "Why Realistic Wisdom Beats Positive Thinking," Updated August 14, 2011, https://www.huffpost.com/entry/realistic-wisdom_b_875488.

20. Rawn, C. D., & Vohs, K. D. (2006). The Importance of Self-Regulation for Interpersonal Functioning. In K. D. Vohs & E. J. Finkel (Eds.), Self and relationships: Connecting intrapersonal and interpersonal processes (p. 15–31). The Guilford Press.

21. Marla Tabaka, "8 Signs You're a Perfectionist and Why It's Toxic to Your Mental Health," Published on October 31, 2017, https://www.inc.com/marla-tabaka/8-signs-youre-a-perfectionist-and-why-its-toxic-to-your-mental-health.html.

22. Elizabeth Scott, "Perfectionist Traits: Do These Sound Familiar?" About, Inc., Published on February 2, 2020, https://www.verywellmind.com/signs-you-may-be-a-perfectionist-3145233.

23. Michael Corballis, *Mind Wandering*, American Scientist, Vol. 100, No 3, May 1, 2012, https://doi.org/10.1511/2012.96.210.

24. Raj Raghunathan, Ph.D., "How Negative is Your 'Mental Chatter'?" Published on October 10, 2013, https://www.psychologytoday.com/us/blog/sapient-nature/201310/how-negative-is-your-mental-chatter.

25. MedLine Plus, "Health Risks of an Inactive Lifestyle," Retrieved July 23, 2020, https://medlineplus.gov/healthrisksofaninactivelifestyle.html.

26. Cathy Donohue, "Research Reveals Weight Worries Trouble Women For Almost Two Hours Every Day," Retrieved April 25, 2020, https://www.her.ie/beauty/research-revelas-weight-worries-plague-women-for-almost-two-hours-every-day-78919.

27. Denis Campbell, "Body Image Concerns Men More Than Women, Research Finds," Published on January 5, 2012, https://www.theguardian.com/lifeandstyle/2012/jan/06/body-image-concerns-men-more-than-women.

28. Rachel Krause, "You Think You're Worried About Your Appearance? Try Being a Man," Retrieved April 25, 2020, https://stylecaster.com/beauty/men-more-worried-about-looks-study/.

29. Megan Dix, RN-BSN, "What's an Unhealthy Gut? How Gut Health Affects You," Healthline Media, Retrieved April 9, 2020, https://www.healthline.com/health/gut-health#signs-and-symptoms.

30. Jayne Leonard, "10 Ways to Improve Gut Health," Updated May 28, 2019, https://www.medicalnewstoday.com/articles/325293#vegetarian-diet.

31. Uma Naidoo, MD, "Gut Feelings: How Food Affects Your Mood," Retrieved May 8, 2020, https://www.health.harvard.edu/blog/gut-feelings-how-food-affects-your-mood-2018120715548.

32. Elizabeth F. Sutton et al., "Early Time-Restricted Feeding Improves Insulin Sensitivity, Blood Pressure, and Oxidative Stress Even Without Weight Loss in Men with Prediabetes," Published on May 10, 2018, https://www.ncbi.nlm.nih.gov/pmc/articles/PMC5990470.

33. Jack Anderson, "10 Reasons Why the Second Half of Your Life is Better Than Your First," Updated December 6, 2017, https://www.huffpost.com/entry/why-second-half-of-life-better_b_12662164.

34. "9 Scientific Secrets to Healthy Aging," WebMD, Retrieved April 29, 2020, https://www.webmd.com/healthy-aging/healthy-aging-secret.

35. Ibid.

36. Mayo Clinic, "Skin care: 5 tips for healthy skin," Published on October 15, 2019, https://www.mayoclinic.org/healthy-lifestyle/adult-health/in-depth/skin-care/art-20048237.

37. Medical News Today, "Why Sleep is Essential for Health," May 21, 2019, https://www.medicalnewstoday.com/articles/325353.

38. Ibid.

39. "2017 Stressful Jobs Reader Survey," CareerCast.com, Adicio Inc, Retrieved April 7, 2020, https://www.careercast.com/career-news/2017-stressful-jobs-reader-survey.

40. Udemy, "Overcoming Workplace Stress Study," Retrieved April 7, 2020, https://business.udemy.com/resources/workplace-stress-study.

41. Melinda Smith, M.A., Jeanne Segal, Ph.D., and Lawrence Robinson, "Burnout Prevention and Treatment," Last updated October 2019, HelpGuideOrgInternational, https://www.helpguide.org/articles/stress/burnout-prevention-and-recovery.htm.

42. Jacob Morgan, "Top 10 Factors for On-the-job Employee Happiness," Published on December 15, 2014, https://www.forbes.com/sites/jacobmorgan/2014/12/15/the-top-10-factors-for-on-the-job-employee-happiness/#4d7ad62d5afa.

43. Marianna Pogosyan, "On Belonging," Published on April 11, 2017, https://www.psychologytoday.com/us/blog/between-cultures/201704/belonging.

44. "The Loneliness Epidemic," Health Resources & Services Administration, US Department of Health and Human Services, Last updated January 2019, https://www.hrsa.gov/enews/past-issues/2019/january-17/loneliness-epidemic.

45. Ariel Shensa, Jaime E. Sidani, Liu yi Lin, Nicholas Bowman, Brian A. Primack, "Social Media Use and Perceived Emotional Support Among US Young Adults," Retrieved April 24, 2020, https://www.ncbi.nlm.nih.gov/pmc/articles/PMC4842323.

46. J. Levenson, A. Shensa, J. Sidani, J. Colditz, B. Primack , "The Association Between Social Media Use and Sleep Disturbance Among Young Adults," Published on January 11, 2016, doi: 10.1016/j.ypmed.2016.01.001.

47. Lindsay Holmes, "This Is How Much Time You Should Spend On Social Media Per Day," Updated November 14, 2018, https://www.huffpost.com/entry/how-much-time-on-social-media_n_5be9c148e4b0783e0a1a8281.

48. Deb Knowbelman, PhD., "No One is Really Thinking About You," Published on May 6, 2019, https://medium.com/the-ascent/research-confirms-that-no-one-is-really-thinking-about-you-f6e7b09c458.

49. Ibid.

50. Brandon M. Savage, Heidi L. Lujan, Raghavendar R. Thipparthi, and Stephen E. DiCarlo, *Humor, Laughter, Learning, and Health! A Brief Review*, Advances in Physiology Education, Vol. 41, No 3, July 5, 2017, https://doi.org/10.1152/advan.00030.2017.

51. Ibid.

52. Pamela Gerloff, "You're Not Laughing Enough, and That's No Joke," Published on June 21,2011, https://www.psychologytoday.com/us/blog/the-possibility-paradigm/201106/youre-not-laughing-enough-and-thats-no-joke.

53. Matt Davis, "Why a Sense of Humor is an Essential Life Skill," Published on April 16, 2019, https://www.weforum.org/agenda/2019/04/why-humor-is-an-essential-life-skill/.

54. Lowri Dowthwaite, "A Sense of Humor Could Mean You're a Healthier, Happier, and Smarter Person," Published on October 17, 2017, https://www.businessinsider.com/a-sense-of-humor-could-mean-youre-healthier-happier-and-smarter-2017-10.

55. Nadia Whitehead, "People Would Rather Be Electrically Shocked Than Left Alone With Their Thoughts," American Association for the Advancement of Science, Published on July 3, 2014, https://www.sciencemag.org/news/2014/07/people-would-rather-be-electrically-shocked-left-alone-their-thoughts.

56. Roland Bénabou and Jean Tirole, "Self Confidence and Personal Motivation," Updated June 2001, https://www.princeton.edu/~rbenabou/papers/papers/CONFQJE2.pdf.

57. Mandy Oaklander, "Why Waiting Actually Makes You Happy," Published on August 26, 2014, https://time.com/3182382/why-waiting-actually-makes-you-happy/.

58. "Wisdom," Retrieved April 19, 2020, https://www.psychologytoday.com/us/basics/wisdom.

59. Robert Biswas-Diener, "The Three Types of Complaining," Published on June 13, 2017, https://www.psychologytoday.com/us/blog/significant-results/201706/the-three-types-complaining.

60. Ibid.

61. Emily C. Bianchi and Kathleen D. Vohs, "Social Class and Social Worlds: Income Predicts the Frequency and Nature of Social Contact," Published on April 11, 2016, https://journals.sagepub.com/doi/full/10.1177/1948550616641472.

62. Science News, "Generous People Live Happier Lives," Published on July 11, 2017, https://www.sciencedaily.com/releases/2017/07/170711112441.htm.

63. GoodTherapy, "Shame," Updated September 27, 2019, https://www.goodtherapy.org/learn-about-therapy/issues/shame.

64. Shirley Davis, "The Neuroscience of Shame," April 11, 2019, https://cptsdfoundation.org/2019/04/11/the-neuroscience-of-shame/.

65. Stephanie Pappas, "Hard-working and Prudent? You'll Live Longer." Published on March 15, 2011, https://www.livescience.com/13258-hard-workers-live-longer.html.

66. Denise Mann, "Social Ties Can Add Years to Your Life," Future US Inc., Posted July 27, 2010, https://www.webmd.com/balance/news/20100727/social-ties-can-add-years-your-life#1.

67. Marsha L. Richins and Scott Dawson, "A Consumer Values Orientation for Materialism and Its Measurement: Scale Development and Validation," American Psychological Association, Retrieved May 4, 2020, https://psycnet.apa.org/record/1993-16069-001.

68. Josh Hafner, "Does Money Equal Happiness? It Does, But Only Until You Earn This Much," Published on February 26, 2018, https://www.usatoday.com/story/money/nation-now/2018/02/26/does-money-equal-happiness-does-until-you-earn-much/374119002/.

69. Jason Marsh and Dacher Keltner, "How Gratitude Beats Materialism," Published on January 8, 2015, https://greatergood.berkeley.edu/article/item/materialism_gratitude_happiness.

70. Mike McHargue, "How Your Brain is Wired for God," Published on July 1, 2014, https://relevantmagazine.com/god/how-your-brain-wired-god.

71. Ibid.

72. Ibid.

73. Ibid.

74. Summer Allen, "Eight Reasons Why Awe Makes Your Life Better," Published on September 26, 2018, https://greatergood.berkeley.edu/article/item/eight_reasons_why_awe_makes_your_life_better.

75. "Benefits of Mindfulness," Retrieved April 17, 2020, HelpGuideOrgInternational, https://www.helpguide.org/harvard/benefits-of-mindfulness.htm.

76. Alexandra Carley Spanier, "Why Is Music So Important?" Published on October 22, 2015, https://sites.psu.edu/siowfa15/2015/10/22/why-is-music-so-important/.

77. Shoba Sreenivasan, Ph.D., and Linda E. Weinberger, Ph.D., "Do You Believe in Miracles?" Published on December 15, 2017, https://www.psychologytoday.com/us/blog/emotional-nourishment/201712/do-you-believe-in-miracles.

78. Shoba Sreenivasan, Ph.D., and Linda E. Weinberger, Ph.D., "Do You Believe in Miracles?" Published on December 15, 2017, https://www.psychologytoday.com/us/blog/emotional-nourishment/201712/do-you-believe-in-miracles.

79. Rohini Venkatraman, "You're 96 Percent Less Creative Than You Were as a Child. Here's How to Reverse That," Published on January 18, 2018, https://www.inc.com/rohini-venkatraman/4-ways-to-get-back-creativity-you-had-as-a-kid.html.

80. May Wong, "Stanford Study Finds Walking Improves Creativity," Published on April 24, 2014, https://news.stanford.edu/news/2014/april/walking-vs-sitting-042414.html?hn=.

81. Emily Esfahani Smith, "Masters of Love," Published on June 12, 2014, https://www.theatlantic.com/health/archive/2014/06/happily-ever-after/372573/.

82. Real Life Counseling, Retrieved July 21, 2020, https://reallifecounseling.us/predict-divorce-gottman.

83. Eric W. Dolan, "Couples Who Communicate More About Sex Tend to Have Better Sex, Study Finds," June 21, 2019, https://www.psypost.org/2019/06/couples-who-communicate-more-about-sex-tend-to-have-better-sex-study-finds-53916.

84. Nicole Beasley, "How Long Does It Take For a Man To Get Over Divorce? 10 Factors that Affect Healing" Published on February 27, 2020, https://www.regain.us/advice/divorce/how-long-does-it-take-for-a-man-to-get-over-divorce-10-factors-that-affect-healing/.

85. Leon F. Seltzer, "Don't Let Your Anger 'Mature' Into Bitterness," January 14, 2015, https://www.psychologytoday.com/us/blog/evolution-the-self/201501/don-t-let-your-anger-mature-bitterness.

86. Healthy Aging®, "Why Healthy Aging is Good for the Soul," Retrieved May 11, 2020, https://healthyaging.net/healthy-lifestyle/why-volunteering-is-good-for-the-soul/.

87. Frank Newport, PhD., "Religion and the COVID-19 Virus in the U.S.," Published on April 6, 2020, https://news.gallup.com/opinion/polling-matters/307619/religion-covid-virus.aspx.

88. Ibid.

89. Gad Saad, PhD., "How Often Do People Lie in Their Daily Lives?" Published on November 30, 2011, https://www.psychologytoday.com/us/blog/homo-consumericus/201111/how-often-do-people-lie-in-their-daily-lives.

90. Jeremy Adam Smith, "What's Good About Lying?" Published on February 8, 2017, https://greatergood.berkeley.edu/article/item/whats_good_about_lying.

91. Barton Goldsmith, PhD., "10 Things Your Relationship Needs to Thrive," March 24, 2013, https://www.psychologytoday.com/us/blog/emotional-fitness/201303/10-things-your-relationship-needs-thrive.

92. Beverly D. Flaxington, "Say What You Mean; Mean What You Say," Published on July 26, 2016, https://www.psychologytoday.com/us/blog/understand-other-people/201607/say-what-you-mean-mean-what-you-say.

93. Renee Garfinkle, "What's So Tough About Apologizing?" Published on June 2, 2013, https://www.psychologytoday.com/us/blog/time-out/201306/what-s-so-tough-about-apologizing.

94. Study.com, "How Healthy Conflict Leads to Team Commitment," Retrieved July 22, 2020, https://study.com/academy/lesson/how-healthy-conflict-leads-to-team-commitment.html.

95. Karina Schumann and Michael Ross, "The Benefits, Costs, and Paradox of Revenge," Retrieved May 2, 2020, https://web.stanford.edu/~omidf/KarinaSchumann/KarinaSchumann_Home/Publications_files/Schumann.SPPC.2010.pdf.

96. Briar P., "HardTalk: How to have difficult conversations featuring Dawn Metcalfe," Published on September 25, 2018, https://www.meetup.com/deals-in-high-heels/events/252891522.

97. Barbara Wilson, "The Five Levels of Intimacy," Published on March 9, 2020, https://www.familylifecanada.com/blog/the-five-levels-of-intimacy.

98. Vicki Zakrzewski, "How Humility Will Make You the Greatest Person Ever," Published on January 12, 2016, https://greatergood.berkeley.edu/article/item/humility_will_make_you_greatest_person_ever.

99. Tony Alessandra, "Do You Have Adaptability," November 3, 2016, https://www.success.com/do-you-have-adaptability/.

100. Ibid.

101. Carthage Buckley, "13 Approval Seeking Behaviors You Need to Stop," Retrieved July 22, 2020, https://www.liveyourtruestory.com/13-approval-seeking-behaviours-you-need-to-stop-confidence.

102. Clay Tucker Ladd, Ph.D., "Building Assertiveness in Four Steps," Updated July 8, 2018, https://psychcentral.com/blog/building-assertiveness-in-4-steps/.

103.   Peter Flade, Jim Asplund, and Gwen Elliott, "Employees Who Use Their Strengths Outperform Those Who Don't," Published on October 8, 2015, https://www.gallup.com/workplace/236561/employees-strengths-outperform-don.aspx.

104.   Susan Sorenson, "How Employees' Strengths Make Your Company Stronger," Published on February 20, 2014, https://news.gallup.com/businessjournal/167462/employees-strengths-company-stronger.aspx.

105.   Gloria Mark, "The Cost of Interrupted Work: More Speed and Stress," Institute of Psychology Humboldt University Berlin, Germany, Retrieved April 20, 2020, https://www.ics.uci.edu/~gmark/chi08-mark.pdf.

106.   Tara Sophia Mohr, "Why Women Don't Apply for Jobs Unless They are 100 Percent Qualified," Published on August 25, 2014, https://hbr.org/2014/08/why-women-dont-apply-for-jobs-unless-theyre-100-qualified.

107.   Tammy Stone, "Counter Offers. It's Never Just About the Money," April 8, 2016. http://thepsychologyofbusiness.com/counter-offers-its-never-just-about-the-money/.

108.   Martin Wainwright, "Emails Pose Threat to IQ," Retrieved April 26, 2020, https://www.theguardian.com/technology/2005/apr/22/money.work andcareers.

109.   Pushpak Pawar, "Tips to Improve Concentration," Published on November 24, 2019, https://thriveglobal.com/stories/practical-tips-to-improve-concentration.

110.   Karla Starr, "Why Your First Impression of Others is Often Wrong," Published on August 14, 2018, https://www.fastcompany.com/90217778/why-your-first-impression-of-someone-else-is-often-wrong.

111.	Leora Klapper, Annamaria Lusardi, and Peter van Oudheusden, "Financial Literacy Around the World," Retrieved March 30, 2020, https://gflec.org/wp-content/uploads/2015/11/3313-Finlit_Report_FINAL-5.11.16.pdf?x22667.

112.	Ibid.

113.	Sarah Gardner and Dave Albee, "Study focuses on strategies for achieving goals, resolutions," Retrieved July 22, 2020, https://scholar.dominican.edu/cgi/viewcontent.cgi?article=1265&content=news-releases.

114.	Alessandra Melito, "Sorry, Millennials: Not Everyone is Happier Spending Money on Experiences Over Stuff," Published on October 8, 2018, https://www.marketwatch.com/story/sorry-millennials-not-everyone-is-happier-spending-money-on-experiences-over-stuff-2018-10-05.

115.	Chris B. Murphy, "Debt-to-Income (DTI) Ratio," Published on March 30, 2020, https://www.investopedia.com/terms/d/dti.asp.

116.	Willis Towers Watson, "Retirement Offerings in the Fortune 500: A Retrospective," Published on February 27, 2018, https://www.willistowerswatson.com/en-US/Insights/2018/02/evolution-of-retirement-plans-in-fortune-500-companies.

117.	Consumer Financial Protection Bureau, "Consumer credit reports: A study of medical and non-medical collections," Retrieved July 21, 2020, https://files.consumerfinance.gov/f/201412_cfpb_reports_consumer-credit-medical-and-non-medical-collections.pdf.

118.	Lydia Smith, "How Student Debt Can Affect Your Mental Health," Published on November 9, 2019, https://finance.yahoo.com/news/how-student-debt-can-affect-your-mental-health-060033659.html.

119.	Ibid.

120.   Save Your Dollars, "How Does Debt Collection Work? A Helpful Guide," Published on April 29, 2020, https://saveyourdollars.com/how-does-debt-collection-work-a-helpful-guide/.

121.   Ibid.

122.   Justin Jaffe, "What is Bitcoin? Here's Everything You Need to Know," Published on February 12, 2018, https://www.cnet.com/how-to/what-is-bitcoin/.

123.   Debt.com, "8 in 10 Americans use a budget – up 10 percent from the last two years," Retrieved July 23, 2020, https://www.debt.com/research/b est-way-to-budget-2019.

124.   Dave Ramsey, "80% of Americans Have This But Don't Want It," Retrieved April 8, 2020, https://www.daveramsey.com/blog/americans-have-debt.

125.   Jill Suttie, Jason Marsh, "5 Ways Giving is Good for You," December 13, 2010, https://greatergood.berkeley.edu/article/item/5_ways_giving_is_goo d_for_you.

126.   Jean Folger, "How to Manage Lifestyle Inflation," Published on July 19, 2019, https://www.investopedia.com/articles/personal-finance/092313/how-manage-lifestyle-inflation.asp.

127.   "2020 Medical Debt Statistics," April 11, 2020, https://www.singlecare.com/blog/medical-debt-statistics/.

128.   "When Little Geniuses Have Big Dreams," February 12, 2016, https://www.morganstanley.com/articles/little-geniuses-big-dreams/.

129.   Ibid.

130.   National Retail Federation, "Record Spending Expected for School and College Supplies," Published on July 15, 2019, https://nrf.com/media-center/press-releases/record-spending-expected-school-and-college-supplies.

131.   Brian O'Connell, "How to Lend Money to Family and Not Regret It," Updated October 26, 2019, https://www.investopedia.com/articles/personal-finance/121013/how-lend-money-family-and-not-regret-it.asp.

About the Author

KRISTIN SHERRY is a full-time author and creator of the YouMap® career profile, which helps individuals discover their Four Pillars of Career Fit™. In 2020, she was awarded a *Career Innovator Award* by Career Directors International for the YouMap® profile.

Kristin is an international speaker, trainer, and six-time author of Amazon international bestsellers, *YouMap* and *Your Team Loves Mondays ... Right?* She is the managing partner of YouMap, LLC, which certifies coaches, career services, and HR professionals as YouMap® coaches and facilitators.

Kristin has been a featured career expert on Wharton Business Radio and a DisruptHR speaker. She has contributed to *Entrepreneur Magazine* and Inc.com and was a contributor to the *2020 Career Industry Trends* white paper on the future of careers by global think tank Career Thought Leaders.

Her first children's book, *You've Got Gifts!*, released November 10, 2020. Kristin serves on two nonprofit boards, Parachute Bridge and Crossroads Career®. She lives in North Carolina with her husband Xander and their children.

Work with the Author

SPEAKING:

Kristin speaks on career topics such as:

The Four Pillars of Career Fit™
Career Management
People Management
Entrepreneurship
Relationships
Self-awareness
Fostering self-awareness in children

Contact service@myyoumap.com.

BECOME YOUMAP® CERTIFIED:

Visit **www.myyoumap.com** for information.

MEDIA:

Interview Kristin for your radio or TV show, podcast, or print media. She will deliver fresh insights with practical application for your audience.

Contact service@myyoumap.com.

Follow on Social Media

LinkedIn: linkedin.com/in/kristinsherry
LinkedIn Company Page: bit.ly/YouMapLLC
Company Website: myyoumap.com
Speaker/Author website: kristinsherry.info
Kristin Sherry Twitter: @YouMapCreator
YouTube Channel: youtube.com/c/kristinsherry

Other Books by Kristin Sherry

You've Got Values! *Coming March 11, 2021*

Katarina the woodland fairy teaches six-year-old Evelyn and her schoolmates about the importance of knowing their values.

You've Got Gifts!

Follow Katarina the woodland fairy as she guides six-year-old Evelyn to discover her special talents. Includes a simple exercise for children to create their TalentStory™.

Your Team Loves Mondays ... Right?

Only 1 in 10 people are naturally wired to manage others well. *Your Team Loves Mondays ... Right?* provides a proven six-step framework to earn your team's respect and get results.

bit.ly/YourTeamLovesMondays

YouMap: Find Yourself. Blaze Your Path. Show the World!

A step-by-step guide to discover and land a job you'll love. bit.ly/YouMapBook

"*YouMap* is such a life-changing book that it should be a required reading in all colleges and universities to provide the tools needed at an early age to Finding Yourself, Blazing Your Path, and Showing the World!! Not only does this book provide the roadmap to discovering YOU and your career best ... it also creates clarity, confidence, and empowerment to searching for the right job. Thanks to *YouMap*, I am now on the right career path, but OH how different my life would have been if I had discovered *YouMap* 25 years ago!! Don't just get one book ... buy several for your family and friends! It's one of the best investments you will make for your loved ones." – Amazon review

5 Surprising Steps to Land the Job NOW!

A quick and easy-to-read, value-packed interview prep and performance guide.

bit.ly/5SurprisingStepstoLandtheJobNOW

"I got the job I wanted! This guide is the perfect combination of comprehensive and concise—74 pages of everything you should think about and prepare for when job hunting. I've never felt so prepared or confident before an interview as I have after reading this book. I wrote down questions detailed in the book verbatim to ask during my interview. I applied to only one position, and I'll be starting my new job soon!" – Amazon review

Index

accomplishments, 253
accounts, review, 393
Adversity, 251
affairs, avoiding, 208
affairs, surviving, 209
affirmations, 4
aggression, passive, 197
aging, healthy, 63
agreement building, 167
alone time, 85
anger, 7
anxiety, social, 235
apologies, 181
apologizing, stop, 310
appreciation, 169
approachability, 227
approval seeking, 228
arguing, 185
asking, 305
assertiveness, 229
assumptions, 161
attitude, 91

attraction, opposites, 205
authority, question, 267
auto leasing, 350
awe, 117
bank accounts, 376
bankruptcy, 349
beauty, 118
community, 72
complaining, 95
compound interest, 353
compromise, 183
concentration, 307
confidence, 87
conflict, healthy, 176
conflict, parent/teen, 213
conflict, picking battles, 180
conflicts, personality, 177
consistency, 304
contentment, 86
control, 30
conversation, 172

courage, 106
creativity, 134
credit card interest, 336
credit card payoff, 335
credit reports, 337
credit scores, 338
credit unions, 326
critical thinking, 43
curiosity, 222
day tight living, 27
death, 153
debt collection, 346
debt, medical, 344
debt, revolving, 334
debt, student, 345
debt-to-income ratio, 340
decisions, making, 42
failure, career, 240
failure, learn from, 302
faith, 120
fasting, intermittent, 61
feedback, giving, 163
feedback, taking, 164
feeling, personal, 217
feelings, acknowledging, 162
fighting fair, 184
finance apps, 356
financial calendars, 323
finance IQ, 355
financial literacy, kids, 383

financial vision board, 357
finger pointing, 193
flexibility, 226
food and mood, 60
forest bathing, 16
forgiveness, 140
free, value of, 274
freedom, 114
friends, choosing, 70
frugality, 325
fun, 75
functional medicine, 62
generosity, 142
giving, 366
goal setting, 36
goals, missed, 264
God, waiting on, 129
God's character, 128
job applications, 288
job boards, 286
job loss, 283
job offers, 297-299
journaling, 83
joy killers, 94
judgment, self, 92
judgment, others, 144
justice, 143
justification, 37
kids, priority, 212
kindness, 138
laughter, 76

learning, lifelong, 306
legacy, 115
legalism, 135
lifestyle inflation, 368
LinkedIn, 258-261
listening, 160
loan forgiveness, 342
loan refinancing, 343
loans, consolidation, 347
loans, cosign, 341
loans, payday, 348
loneliness, 13
love, 137
love languages, 204
loving yourself, 3
loyalty, 232
loyalty, misplaced, 257
lying, 173
opportunity cost, 367
optimism, 47
organizing, 19
overpowering, 196
overspending, 333
patience, 89
paying yourself, 319
perfectionism, 48
persistence, 308
perspective, 49
power, managing, 263
prayer, 127
preferences, 219

presence, 312
prioritization, 265
problems, root cause, 178
procrastination, 35
promotions, 266
prospective clients, 275-276
protect yourself online, 391
prudence, 100
purpose, finding, 103
raises, getting, 379
real estate, 363
realistic thinking, 41
reassurance, 168
reconciliation, 150
regrets, 14
rejection, 233
relationship games, 179
relationship needs, 174
simplifying, 17
skills, discover, 245
skin health, 64
sleep, 65
social media, 73
social security, 374
space, giving, 171
speaking, public, 313
spending habits, couples, 377
spending, holidays, 329

spending, impulse, 320
spirit, fruit of the, 121
spiritual fatigue, 156
spiritual poverty, 122
spirituality and crisis, 157
stewardship, 155
stonewalling, 201
strength statements, 242
strengths, discover, 241
strengths, overuse, 243
stress management, 66
stuck, 51
beauty on a budget, 327
belief, 104, 119
belittling, 186
belonging, 71
betrayal, 210
bias, experience, 98
bitcoin, 362
bitterness, 151
blessings, 130
body image, 56
budget, household, 365
burnout, 67
C.R.A.P. Boards, 50
career fit, 238
career interests, discover, 246
career planning, 254
career success, 255
career transition, 248

cash system, 324
caving in, 187
cell phones, 23
changing people, 215
character traits, 88
childcare, costs, 381
children, cost, 380
college alternatives, 384
college savings, 385
comfort zone, 82
commitment, 211
decluttering, 18
defensiveness, 188
delegating, 22
dependability, 230
despair,107
difficulty, 32
disappointment, 8
discipline, 31
discontentment, 108
discouragement, 109
dismissing others, 189
diversity, 23
divorce, 149
divorce, finances, 371
drama, 190
email, 262
emergency fund, 318
emotional insecurity, 10
emotional intelligence, 220
emotional temperature, 11

emotions, monitoring, 6
entertaining, no cost, 328
entrepreneurship, 271
entrepreneurship, thrifty,
388
exaggerating, 191
exclusion, 192
excuses, 33
expectations, unmet, 216
experiences, 330
expertise, 268
failure/temporary defeat,
301
gossip, 194
grace, 141
gratitude, 26
greed, 96
growth mindset, 29
guilt, 152
gut health, 59
habit creation, 34
happiness, 113
help, asking for, 78
hope, 112
humility, 224
humor, 77
hypercriticism, 195
ideal day, 239
ideas, pitching, 277
identity theft, 392
imposter syndrome, 12

impressions, first, 309
income, extra, 361
income, passive, 278
indecisiveness, 38
inner harmony, 105
insurance, 370
intellectual wellness, 39
interviews, 289-295
intimacy, 206
introspection, 221
intuition, 123
investment ideas, 354
jealousy, 231
managers, bad, 252
marriage, success, 147
masterminds, 311
materialism, 101
meditation, 124
mental sharpness, 40
mentor, finding, 256
mentors, spiritual, 84
mercy, 139
mindful eating, 58
mindfulness, 125
miracles, 132
mistakes, admitting, 165
money arguments, 378
money buddies, 321
money mantras, 359
money mindset, 358
money, lending, 389

money, saving on rent, 331
mortgage, payoff, 339
mortgages, 369
motivation, 46
music, power of, 126
mystery, 133
needs vs. wants, 322
negative influences, 69
net worth calculation, 372
networking, 285
niches, 272
occupation research, 247
opinions, other people, 74
relationships, long
distance, 207
reputation, 234
resilience, 28
resolution seeking, 182
respect, 170
responsibility, taking, 218
resumes, 287
retirement plans,
employee, 360
retirement, borrowing, 386
returning to work, 284
revenge, 198
risk taking, 273
routine, 54
sabotage, 199
salary negotiation, 296
sarcasm, 200

saving money, ideas, 317
savings, 352
saying no, 79
school supply costs, 382
Seasonal Affective
Disorder, 24
second chances, 145
sedentary lifestyle, 55
self-absorption, 9
self-actualization, 93
self-care, 5
self-control, 45
self-reliance, 44
service, 154
sex and sexuality, 148
shame, 97
suffering, 110
tax refunds, 390
temptation, 99
thriving, in difficulty, 111
time management, 21
timing, 20
trust, 225
unity, 146
vacation, budget, 387
value statements, 249
values, discover, 244
vision boards, 52
volunteer work, 314
vulnerability, 166
weaknesses, 303

weight loss, 57
wills and estate planning, 373
wisdom, 90

withdrawing, 202
worship, 131
writing books, 279-281
zone of genius, 269

Note from the Author

Word-of-mouth is crucial for any author to succeed. If you enjoyed *Maximize 365*, please leave a review online—anywhere you are able. Even if it's just a sentence or two. It would make all the difference and would be very much appreciated.

Thanks!
Kristin

Thank you so much for
reading one of **Kristin A. Sherry's** books.
If you enjoyed our book, please check out our
recommendation for your next great read!

YouMap by Kristin A. Sherry

"YouMap is a terrific guide to all those who are struggling
in their 9-5 life and, beyond that, a terrific guide for
anyone interested in getting to know themselves better."
–IndieReader Approved

CPSIA information can be obtained
at www.ICGtesting.com
Printed in the USA
LVHW050312090221
678789LV00001B/9

9 781684 336364